访问北京

北京文化之旅·博物馆卷　　Cultural Tour in Beijing·Museum Volume　　北京文化之旅·

Visit Beijing

图书在版数目(CIP)数据

访问北京 / 马希桂等主编 – 北京:紫禁城出版社
2005
ISBN 7–80047–499–2 / J.231
Ⅰ紫…Ⅱ·马…Ⅲ·访问北京 – 通俗读物 Ⅳ K928.74
中国版本图书馆 CIP 数据核字(2005)第 8387 号

访 问 北 京

马希桂
　　　　主编
刘一达

紫 禁 城 出 版 社 出 版
(北京景山前街故宫博物院内)
北京市宝昌佳美图文设计有限公司印刷
新华书店首都发行所总经销
开本 120×205　字数 11.7 千　印张 8　图版 105 幅
2005 年 5 月第一版第一次印刷　印数 30000 册
ISBN7–80047–499–2 / J.231

定价:25.00 元

《访问北京》编辑委员会

指导顾问:（以姓氏笔划为序）

马希桂　　马法柱　　马　静　　刘一达

吕晓晶　　李文儒　　张驰平　　陈连营

郭洪新　　钟　昊　　章宏伟　　黄曼丽

编委会委员:

马希桂　　刘一达　　关　宏　　万镜明

康庆云　　何忠华　　李静茹

主　　编:马希桂　　刘一达

执行主编:万镜明

英文翻译:中国国家图书馆翻译中心

资料提供:北京博物馆学会

文稿核审:北京博物馆学会

责任编辑:张　楠

总 校 对:秦坚松

出 品 人:中国博物馆学会

北京博物馆学会

北京鼎春德房地产开发有限公司

北京德风华雨文化发展有限公司

给您的眼睛验验光

刘一达

著名京味作家、民俗学者

这个题目好像是上下句的歇后语：访问北京，给您的眼睛验验光。验什么光？视力。不过，这个"视力"前边得加上"文化"俩字。准确地说是给您的学问"验光"。

我曾经对一位来北京旅游的外地朋友说，来北京，只要您告诉我都去什么地儿了，我就知道您是什么眼光，或者说我就知道您是什么文化水平，您审美情趣、兴趣爱好是什么了。这是很肤浅的说法。说深点儿，北京城像是一个巨大的无形的视力表，您的眼神如何，您的视力怎么样？来一趟北京就能给验出来。

为啥这么说呢？同样是一块看上去破旧的城砖，眼神好的，看它是文物，是无价之宝。眼神差的，看它就是一块破砖头，砌墙不能用，盖房用不上，放在哪儿都占地方，百无一用。您瞧，视力好坏，就这么大的差距。

上个世纪70年代，著名的历史地理学家侯仁之老爷子访问美国匹兹堡大学，带去了两件礼物。您猜是什么？就是我说的城砖。这两块城砖，每块重14公斤，上面雕着"嘉靖三十六年"的字样。它一下把美国人给震了。您想嘉靖三十六年，就是公元1557年，它比美国独立还早219年。美国人能不拿它当宝贝吗？可是这样的老城砖，当年在北京到处都是。我住过的小院就扔着好几块，没人要。那是挖防空洞剩下的。您说眼光重要不重要吧？

我问过不少来北京旅游的朋友，都到哪儿参观了？他们颇感自豪地说，该去的地方都去了。我又问：哪些地方该去？他们掰着手指头数：天安门、故宫、颐和园、八达岭、长城、天坛。我耐着性儿让他们接着数。有的又数出了北海、景山、香山、紫竹院，有的还数出了动物园、雍和宫、什刹海。让我感到遗憾的是很少有人提到博物馆。当我问他们知不知道故宫是博物馆（院）时，这些人都愣了：不会吧，故宫就是故宫，怎么会是博物馆呢？可见访问北京的人对博物馆的认识不够，验光的话，眼睛得配镜子了。

当然，很多来北京旅游的朋友往往是来去匆匆，只能挑有代表性的旅游景点走一走。说走马观花，真是一点不假。所谓去过故宫了，不过是在故宫走一圈，照几张相留下纪念而已。至于故宫的文化内涵，似乎了解得很少。这是真事儿：我曾问一位游览过故宫的外地朋友，去没去过紫禁城。他摇头说紫禁城在哪儿，没去过。当然，我要问他去没去过储秀宫、翊坤宫、永寿宫（故宫内西路宫殿），他更得摇脑袋了。客观地说，目前国内旅游还留停在"玩"的层次上，要进入文化旅游，或者说旅游达到文化的层面，您还得耐心地等些年。所以我说北京城是给您眼睛验光的世界，因为北京有4000多年的建城史，850多年的建都史，北京的文化底蕴太厚实了，北京的历史名胜太多了。即便是走马观花，您把每一处景点都照顾到了，至少得半年，这还得说马不停蹄。

您会问了，一般人拿不出半年的工夫，去游览北京的每一处景点，您能不能说说，一个外地人或外国人来北京呆五天八天的，除了故宫长城颐和园,哪些地方最值得一看?您不是想让我们验验光吗?那么先给我们列出个"视力表"。

这话问得好!要让我说什么地方最值得看?我告诉你,博物馆。如果您访问北京,没去过博物馆,等于您白来一趟。为啥这么说?因为博物馆有历史、有文化。您说您大老远来一趟北京,没触摸一下北京的历史文化,是不是有点冤?

北京有一百多座博物馆,不论是数量,还是门类,不论是馆藏文物,还是馆的规模来说,在国内都居首位,在世界的大城市中也得排在前几位。这些博物馆,有一个算一个,哪个都值得您一去。去了,您就会觉得没白去,肯定能让您长见识,长学问。前几年,来北京旅游的朋友,在北京"玩"了几天以后,往往会得出:"白天看庙、晚上睡觉"的印象。实际上,有些旅游者忽略了博物馆,当然会留下许多遗憾。现在北京的旅游业已把参观博物馆作为旅游项目了,这应该说是把文化融入旅游内容的标志,它会大大提高旅游的文化品位。

十多年前,我曾写过一篇长篇报道《京城博物馆忧思录》,那会儿,北京的博物馆沉寂冷落,展览内容古板,陈列方式老旧,门可罗雀,门票几毛钱一张,仍没人来,博物馆也入不敷出,朝不保夕,让我为之扼腕长叹。时过境迁,现在北京的博物馆已今非昔比了,用句北京土话说,博物馆"变脸"了。一方面,国家非常重视博物馆的保护和开发利用,博物馆自身也在历史文化上进一步开掘其内涵,利用馆藏文物和馆内设施,开展丰富多彩的文化活动;另一方面,老百姓也认识到博物馆是文化生活的重要殿堂,人们要想获取历史知识,汲取文化营养,陶冶情操,必得到博物馆去养养眼,"熏陶"一下。北京博物馆的自身价值开始得到体现,老面孔的博物馆焕发了青春,同时,新的博物馆又不断涌现,每到双休日和节假日参观博物馆已成为北京市民的一项重要的生活内容。赶上博物馆有新的展出,人满为患。现在,可以说是北京博物馆的"黄金时代"。正是在这种大的文化背景下,《访问北京--北京文化之旅·博物馆卷》一书问世了。可以说,这本《访问北京》的出版,正是让人能解渴的时候。

有关北京博物馆的书,如果您留神的话,市面上能找到几本。但是像《访问北京》这样以"指南手册"方式出版的书,这得说是第一本。首先说,书中收集的博物馆比较全,内容比较新。由于有国内一流的博物馆专家和各博物馆的工作人员介入此书的编辑,所以各博物馆的介绍比较详尽。其次,此书带有"指南"性。各博物馆的地址方位、乘车路线以及门票价格、开馆闭馆时间等等,都有详细的介绍。所以,它的实用性很强,可谓一书在手,遍游京城博物馆。有了这本书,这回您在北京给眼睛"验光"就不用发愁了。

当然,您认不认这本书,或者说您拿到这本书,认不认北京的博物馆,那可就看您的"视力"如何了。要不我怎么会说访问北京,给您的眼睛验验光呢?

以上是为序。

2005 年 4 月 18 日於北京如一斋

Visit Beijing

Beijing, a millennial city, heart of the P.R.C., concurrently one of the seven ancient capitals in China, will greet the Olympic Games in 2008 which aims at fully demonstrating splendid culture and distinct ethnic characteristics of China.

Museum Volume of Visit Beijing Series is presented by Chinese Society of Museum, Beijing Administrative Bureau of Cultural Relics, Beijing Society of Museums and other relevant authorities. It gains great supports from Beijing Municipal Bureau of Press and Publication and Beijing Tourism Administration etc. Covering a wide range of museums and their nearby facilities, this small encyclopedia is an authoritative guide in the form of travelogue accompanied by exquisite iconographies of pen sketches and maps, integrating the introduction to the museum with tourist entertainment programs. In accordance with the division of Beijing administrative districts, and from the perspectives of history, architectures, cultural relics, transportations, nearby sightseeing, and restaurants etc, this book gives a general introduction to Beijing museums, bridging Beijing to the world and introducing the history and the current situation of Beijing to the people at home and abroad. On basis of this book, separate volumes on Beijing gardens, the world's cultural heritages, famous institutes of higher learning, Olympic building complex, places for folk-custom dramatic activities, theaters and showplaces will come out in sequence. They will present to the people a new image of Beijing that boasts profound cultural traditions and leads the way of modern development.

目 录

第一章 东城区

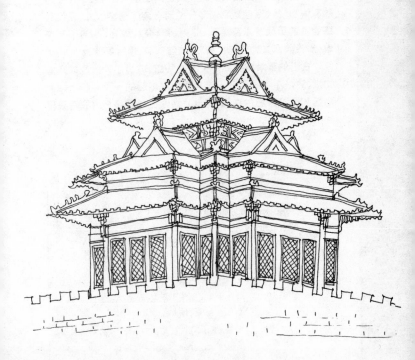

故宫博物院

青春,故宫博物院

人们常用"全国重点文物保护单位"和"世界人类文化遗产之一"来介绍故宫,可是在紫禁城建成585周年和故宫博物院80华诞的烛光里,你是否已见到它青春的笑靥?

故宫博物院原为明清两代的皇宫,坐落在北京城的南北中轴线上,从南面正中的午门向北,是故宫的外朝,建在三层汉白玉台基上的太和、中和、保和三大殿巍然耸立,封建帝王在这里行使权力,举行隆重典礼。继续向北,即为故宫的内廷。以乾清宫、交泰宫、坤宁宫为主体,是帝王办事和居住的地方。其两侧东西六宫为嫔妃的住所。此外尚有文华殿、武英殿和御花园等,是我国现存最大的古建筑群。整个建筑按中轴线对称布局,层次分明,主体突出,集中体现了中国古代建筑艺术的优秀传统和独特风格,反映了中国人民的高度智慧和创造才能。1925年,故宫博物院成立,这辉煌的古典建筑和百万件古代艺术品及明清历史文物归还于人民手中。现在的故宫博物院除保存复原一部分明清史迹陈列室以外,还设有综合性的历代艺术及绘画、铭刻、青铜器、陶瓷、明清工艺美术,清代典章文物,钟表、石鼓、清宫玩具、珍宝等专馆。

古老的紫禁城脱离了帝王的华盖,成为了人民的故宫博物院,这是中华民族五千年文明史最灿烂的一页。新中国的雨露和改革开放的春风,又让"携六百年雄姿"的故宫重现生机盎然。

啊!青春,故宫!青春,故宫博物院!

参观指南

地　　址:北京市东城区景山前街4号

开放时间:4月16日至10月15日 8:30-17:00(16:00停止售票),
　　　　　10月16日至翌年4月15日
　　　　　8:30-16:30(15:30停止售票)。

票　　价:4月1日至10月31日　　60元(学生20元);
　　　　　11月1日至翌年3月31日 40元(学生20元);
　　　　　珍宝馆10元;钟表馆10元。

周边景观:北海、景山公园、新文化运动纪念馆、中国国家
　　　　　博物馆、毛主席纪念堂、前门城楼。

咨询电话:010-65132255

The Palace Museum

The Palace Museum was built in 1420, covering an area of 720, 000m², among which the construction coverage is 160,000m² with 9, 000 buildings. It boasts China's even the World's largest and most integrated existing ancient palace complex. In 1961, it was listed among the first group of key cultural sites to be placed under state protection. In 1987, it was added to the UNESCO World Heritages. The Palace Museum was founded on the imperial palace and relevant collections of Qing and Ming Dynasties. It is a comprehensive national museum which mainly exhibits the history of Ming and Qing Dynasties, palaces and ancient art works etc. Millions of cultural relics are housed in the museum, and most of them are art treasures in past dynasties. The displays in the museum are composed of Palace Historical Sites Display and Art Works Display. The former includes the Taihe Hall, Zhonghe Hall, Baohe Hall, Qiangqing Palace, Imperial Garden, Yanxin Hall and Chuxiu Palace etc, and the latter include the halls and palaces along the axis of the museum, such as Porcelain Hall, Bronze Ware Hall, and Painting Hall etc, which reflect China's splendid ancient civilization.

Visitors Guide

Address: *North of the Tian'anmen Square, Beijing Opening Hours: April 16—October 15 8:30—17:00(16:00 stop selling tickets), October 16—next April 15 8:30—16:30 (15:30 stop selling tickets)*

Admission Fee: *April 1—October 30 RMB 60 Yuan,and 20 Yuan for students; November 1—Next March 31 RMB 40 Yuan, and 20 Yuan (students); 10 Yuan for Treasure Hall and 10 Yuan for Clock Hall*

Tel: *86—10—65132255*

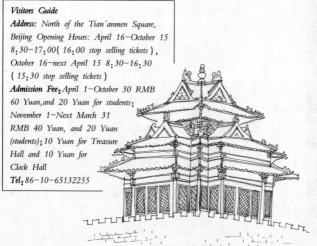

中国国家博物馆

一部伟大光辉的史册

　　黄河和长江两条母亲河从世界屋脊向东流去，浊清水流，承载着中国历史和中国革命的春风秋雨，蜿蜒在云卷云舒的天空下。中国历史博物馆和中国革命博物馆把从炎黄五帝到元明清五千年中华文明史和从鸦片战争到改革开放新时代的中国革命史合编为一部伟大的光辉史册，呈现给中华民族和世界人民。2003年2月28日，"中国国家博物馆"的铭牌悬挂在天安门广场东侧这座雄伟的建筑物上。

　　中国历史和中国革命的近8000件馆藏展品，如同黄河长江的滔滔浪潮，在中国人民的心头汹涌澎湃。苦涩的泪和殷红的血在这里奔流；愤怒的呐喊和豪迈的歌唱在这里激荡。中国国家博物馆里每件文物、每张图片、每个摹绘品和复制件，都是这块土地上屈辱和自豪的写照，无论是介绍说明的字里行间，还是解说员的语义话音，都满怀着爱这方土地，爱这些人民的感情。历史在告别与起步之际，革命也已迎来一个崭新的时代，这里将展现的是中华民族伟大复兴的足迹。

　　中国国家博物馆已经启程，中华民族厚重的历史给你宽阔的襟怀，中国人民艰辛的革命给你浩瀚的气魄。人们走进这里，静穆中有无限崇敬；人们走出这里，崇敬化作一种力量，这种力量在轰鸣。

参观指南

地　　址：北京市东长安街16号。

乘车路线：长安街沿线公交车都可到达，地铁于天安门站下。

自驾车线：沿长安街行驶到天安门广场，在广场东侧。

开放时间：9：00-16：30。

周边景观：故宫、天安门广场、人民大会堂、毛主席纪念堂。

票　　价：30元；学生、老人15元。

咨询电话：010-65128901

National Museum of China

The museum was set up on February 28, 2003 directly under the Cultural Ministry. Founded on the former History Museum of China and Revolutionary Museum of China, it is a comprehensive museum centering on history and arts with the purpose of displaying Chinese People's time-honored culture and history systemically.

The museum incorporates the discovery, collection, research and exhibition of cultural relics. It houses many valuable cultural relics reflecting China's ancient history, modern history and contemporary history. It has regular basic displays and many specialized displays, showing the audiences at home and abroad the great history and brilliant culture of the Chinese people, and also introducing the world's civilizations and excellent cultures into China. The advanced researches on history, archeology, cultural relics study and museum study constantly enrich and deepen the public's understanding on history and culture, thus further promoting the development of the museum cause. The National Museum of China will become an important location in the center of the capital for the people's enjoyment of great cultural atmosphere.

Visitors Guide
Address: East side of Tian'anmen Square, Beijing
Bus Route: Subway to Tian'anmen Station and buses along Chang'an Street
Self—drive Route: Along Chang'an Street to Tian'anmen Square, east of the Square
Opening Hours: 9:00—16:30
Nearby Sights: Palace Museum, Tian'anmen Square, the People's Grand Hall, Chairman Mao's Memorial Hall
Admission Fee: RMB 30 Yuan; 15 Yuan for students and seniors
Tel: 86-10-65128901

中国美术馆

美术之光

中国美术馆是国家级造型艺术博物馆，是建国十周年的十大建筑之一，1958年动工兴建，1962年落成，1963年正式向社会开放。主体建筑为仿古楼阁式现代建筑，总面积21000多平方米，现有10个展厅，6000平方米的展览场地及4000余平方米的现代化新型藏画库。

美术又称造型艺术，通常指绘画、雕塑、工艺美术、建筑艺术等，在东方还涉及书法和篆刻艺术。中国美术馆立足于严格选择藏品陈列，逐步扩大陈列范围，注重展览层次和品位的提高，积极开展收藏、研究和对外文化交流活动，把推动中国美术事业的发展，提高中国美术创作和研究在世界上的地位作为立馆宗旨。中国美术馆现收藏各类美术作品数万件，类别包括国画、油画、书法、版画、雕塑、年画、连环画以及民间美术品、还有许多国外美术作品。

德国著名收藏家彼得·路德维希夫妇向中国美术馆捐赠的117幅欧洲现代艺术品为我国美术界和广大观众了解20世纪70年代至90年代西方美术的发展状况提供了实证和素材，扩充了藏品的容量，特别是实现了收藏国际艺术大师作品零的突破。

美术里有人类灿烂明亮的目光。中国美术馆是中国美术的最高的艺术殿堂，这里折射出来的是历史之光，民族之光，时代之光，这就是我们中华民族的美术之光。

参观指南

地　　址：北京市东城区五四大街1号。

乘车路线：103、111、112、814、819路公交车于美术馆站下。

自驾车线：长安街-南河沿大街-北河沿大街东侧。

开馆时间：9:00-16:30。

周边景观：故宫、景山公园、北海公园、北京大学红楼、王府井。

周边餐饮：王府井大饭店、王府井小吃街、麻香婆、礼士便民小吃店、隆福寺小吃店、明华烧麦馆。

票　　价：20元；学生、残疾人、老人15元；美术家协会会员10元。

咨询电话：010-64017076

China Art Gallery

China Art Gallery is located on Wusi Street. It is a national-class art museum centering on display, collection and research of Chinese modern and contemporary art works. Its stele was inscribed by Chairman Mao. With a total coverage of 30,000m², the museum devotes 6,000m² to the exhibition halls. The construction of the museum was initiated in 1958 and completed in 1962. It is not only one of China's top ten architectures in 1959, but also the largest domestic art gallery. The main body of the museum is a modern building in the style of ancient pavilion with distinct ethnic characteristics, decorated with yellow glaze tiles and surrounded by corridors. Inside the museum, there are three floors with 13 exhibition halls illuminated by fluorescent lamps preventing ultraviolet radiation. The round hall is 480m² with large art works hung on the wall. The side halls on the first floor are 470m² respectively with huge glass arks for exhibition. Four corner halls each are 500m². The exhibition areas on the second and third floor are in response to the main hall. The new painting storing house covers an area of 5,000m². Services for exhibiting and selling art works can be found inside the gallery.

Visitors Guide
Address: No.1 Wusi Street, Dongcheng District, Beijing
Bus Route: Bus No. 103、111、112、814、819 to the stop of art gallery
Self-drive Route: Chang'an Street—Nanheyan Street—east of Beiheyan Street
Opening Hours: 9:00—16:30
Admission Fee: RMB 20 Yuan, 15 Yuan for the students, the disabled and the seniors, and 10 Yuan for members of Artist Association
Tel: 86—10—64017076

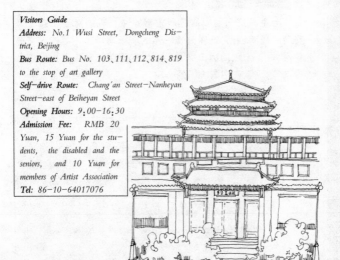

毛主席纪念堂

心中的毛主席纪念堂

人们每次来到毛主席纪念堂,都会放慢脚步,轻轻地在他的身旁走过。人们实在不愿打扰他的休息,不愿打断他甜蜜的睡梦。

纪念堂瞻仰厅正中间的水晶棺中,安放着毛泽东遗体,他身着灰色中山装,覆盖着中国共产党党旗。水晶棺基座用东岳泰山黑色花岗石制成,棺座四周分别镶嵌着金饰党徽、国徽、军徽和毛泽东的生卒年份。水晶棺周围是君子兰和玻璃栏杆。大厅正面的汉白玉墙面上,镶着17个镏金隶书大字"伟大领袖和导师毛泽东主席永垂不朽"。毛泽东60年革命生涯,为国家独立,为民族复兴,为人民幸福进行着不屈不挠的英勇奋斗,贡献了他毕生的精力。此刻虽然安睡在这里,但是他的心中永远铭刻着祖国和人民,祖国和人民也永远怀念这位伟人的音容笑貌。

毛泽东纪念堂里,分别设立毛泽东、周恩来、刘少奇、朱德、邓小平、陈云革命业绩纪念室。通过大批文物、文献、图片、书信,反映了六位伟大的无产阶级革命家创建中国共产党、缔造人民军队、成立中华人民共和国、领导社会主义建设的丰功伟绩。在陈列形式上,采用了先进的制作材料和制作工艺,每个纪念室都有等离子超薄电视和电子资料触摸屏,播放展现伟人风采的资料片,调阅反映伟人思想风范的格言。

毛主席纪念堂以其庄严肃穆雄伟壮观的身姿屹立于天安门广场南侧,为这座气魄宏伟的广场增添了无尽的人文神韵,扩展了无限的历史纵深。巍峨的建筑掩映在苍松翠柏之中,也永远装在中国人民的心中。

参观指南

地　　址:北京市天安门广场南侧。

乘车路线:长安街沿线公交车均可到达;一线地铁天安门西站、天安门东站或环线地铁前门站下。

开放时间:8:30—11:30,13:30—16:40;每周一、三、五下午及周日全天休息。

周边景观:故宫、天安门广场、国家博物馆、人民大会堂。

票　　价:免费

咨询电话:010-65131130

The Memorial Hall of Chairman Mao

The memorial hall is shaped like a square with coverage of 20, 000 square meters and a height of 33.6 meters. Currently there are 10 halls open to the public. The north hall to the main gate can accommodate over 700 people. It is the place where the memorial activities are held. In the center of the hall erects Chairman Mao's three-meter-high sitting statue made of white marbles. Chairman Mao wears smiles with grand manner. Behind the statue is a large-scale floss embroidery entitled Throughout China. Revolutionary achievements of Mao Zedong, Liu Shaoqi, Zhou Enlai and Zhu De are on display in the west and the east halls. Inside the halls, visitors can found many cultural relics, historical documents, letters and pictures.

The core of the memorial hall is the Respecting Hall, in the middle of which is the crystal coffin that contains the remains of Chairman Mao in grey sun yat sen's uniform and covered with the red banner of the Chinese Communist Party. Made of black granite, the coffin platform is surrounded by flowers. On the white-marble wall of the hall, gold-plating characters are beset: Eternal glory to our great leader and teacher Chairman Mao!

Visitors Guide
Address: *South side of Tian'anmen Square, Beijing*
Bus Route: *Buses along Chang'an Street. Subway I to the east or west station of Tian'anmen, Circular Subway to the station of Qianmen*
Opening Hours: *8:30 −11:30, 13:30 −16:40; Except Monday, Wednesday and Friday afternoons and Sunday*
Nearby Sights: *Palace Museum, Tian'anmen Square, National Museum and the People's Grand Hall*
Admission Fee: *Free*
Tel: *86−10−65131130*

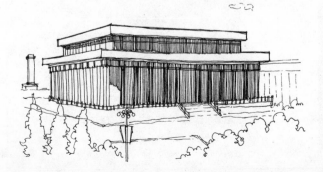

首都博物馆

首博,发掘历史,描绘未来

因为这里是元明清三代皇帝祭孔的场所,所以这里有祭孔礼乐器的原状陈列,令人想见当年鼓乐齐鸣、庄严肃穆的祭孔场面。这里还有闻名于世的元明清三代进士题名碑林、公车翰墨,是中国科举制的珍贵实证。这里的十三经碑林,金书玉雕,华章璀璨,堪称中国古代文化的钟秀集锦。这里就是位于东城区国子监街的孔庙。把首都博物馆设立在孔庙内,足可见它在北京人民心中的位置。

首都博物馆推出了全新的"北京历史文物陈列"。该展览分为"方国都邑"、"北方重镇"、"辽金京城"、"帝王都城"四个重点专题,以文物为主体,由800多件体现北京历史发展的稀世珍宝组成,如牛头纹伯矩鬲、西晋料钵、定窑白瓷童子诵经壶、元代琉璃镂空三彩龙凤纹熏炉、明嘉靖斗彩八卦纹炉和元代书法家鲜于枢的草书《劝学篇》长卷等,这些文物都是绝代佳品,反映了自史前至清代北京政治、经济、文化、艺术、宗教、社会风俗等各个方面的历史面貌。

丰富而珍贵的文物与红墙金瓦、雕栏玉砌的殿宇相映增辉,成为辉煌北京的一颗灿烂的明珠。同时,肩负发掘历史和描绘未来双重任务的新馆即将在不久的将来与观众见面,人们在那里重新欣赏唐代阎立本的《孔子弟子像》手卷和全国仅此一件的元代景德镇青白瓷观音像等镇馆之宝时,将会感叹历史与当今时代之间的时空隧道是多么迅捷,亘古的转换是多么倏然,由此,你可能想到该如何珍惜生命中的分分秒秒。

参观指南

地　　址:北京市东城区国子监街13号。

乘车路线:104、108路公交车方家胡同站下;或13、116、807路国子监站下。

开放时间:8:30-17:00

周边景观:国子监、柏林寺、地坛公园、青年湖公园、雍和宫。

周边餐饮:映月楼、阿里郎餐厅、悦杨陕西风味、居德林。

票　　价:10元;学生3元。

咨询电话:010-64012118

The Capital Museum

The Capital Museum is located in the Confucius Temple at Guozijian Street. After elaborate preparation, the museum has now presented a brand new exhibition which presents the Beijing's history in four sections: (1) the development of an organized community from ancient settlements; (2) gradual development as an important northern center; (3) the capital during the Liao and Jin dynasties; (4) the world renowned imperial city. The exhibition consists of over 800 pieces of treasure with rare cultural relics as its representatives. The treasures include a bronze wine vessel decorated with three rams; a Western Zhou bronze tripod; and a bronze ox cast during the Tang Dynasty. Other ancient pieces include an earthenware teapot of the Spring and Autumn Period; a gilded Buddha inlaid with turquoise of the Yuan Dynasty; a blue and white lotus plate of the Ming Dynasty (1368-1644); and a folding fan with an ivory handle inlaid with precious stones and a tiny watch. Besides that, many exquisite models and pictures will help you better understand the glorious civilization of Beijing. The precious historical and cultural relics fully demonstrate the time-honored history of Beijing from the aspects of politics, economy, culture, art, religion and folk customs.

Visitors Guide
Address: No.13, Guozijian Street, Dongcheng District, Beijing.
Opening Hours:
Bus route: Bus Nos. 13, 116, 807 to the stop of Guozijian; Bus Nos. 104, 108 to the stop of Fangjia Hutong
Nearby Sights: Guozijian, the Confucius Temple, Bailin Temple, Ditan Park, Qingnianhu Park, and Yonghe Lamasery
Nearby Restaurants: Yingyuelou Restaurant, Alilang Restaurant, Yueyang Shaanxi Style Restaurant, and Judelin restaurant
Admission Fee: RMB 10 Yuan; 3 Yuan for students
Telephone: 86-10-64012118

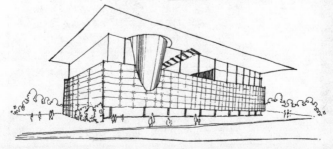

北京古观象台

让我们足下生风

　　"天有不测风云"的无奈,并没有禁锢人们探求天文气象奥秘的脚步。天文学家在这里夜以继日地辛勤工作,为人类积累了大量的天文观测史料,为中国和世界天文学的发展做出了巨大贡献。这里就是北京古观象台。

　　古观象台始建于明朝正统元年(公元1442年),比英国格林尼治天文台和法国天文台早200多年。明代初建时取名观星台,清代改名为观象台,辛亥革命后又称中央观象台。这里曾是明清两代的皇家天文观测中心,至今,透过树木和建筑的掩映,仍然可以看见台体上几架精美的天文仪器屹然挺立,仍然可以感受到古代天文学智慧带给你的自豪与自信。

　　中国古代天文学展览在这个城堞式青砖建筑里向人们介绍天象纪事、灵台仪象和时间历法。世界上最早的日食、太阳黑子、彗星、流星的记录,第一部天文学专著《五星占》和星图、星表,宋代天文学家苏颂制作的水运仪象台和称漏的复制品,古代记时的仪器圭表、漏壶和日晷,二十四节气钟等实物或复制品在催促你走进大厅,去体味那种探索未知领域的快乐。沿着台阶登上古老的天文台,300多年前制造的八台铜制天文观测仪器会让你震撼。先不要看它们各自奇妙的功能,仅仅是那巨大的形体,美观的造型,精湛的工艺,华美的雕饰就让你感到气势逼人。

　　中国是天文古国,也是天文大国。这里,会让我们足下生风,去遨游太空,去登上月球或其他星球,与天体中的生命对话。

参观指南

地　　址:北京市东城区裱褙胡同2号。

乘车路线:乘1、4、特1、特2、120、120支、20、37、420、728、744、802北京站口下车向西走200米;乘9、10、20、39支、52、122、403、420、729、744支、848、859、907、907支、908、908至938等在北京站或北京站东街下车;地铁建国门站下车,出西南口即到。

开放时间:9:00-16:30(周一休息)。

票　　价:10元;学生5元。

咨询电话:010-65128923、010-65242202

Beijing Ancient Observatory

Beijing Ancient Observatory was built in 1442 during China's Ming Dynasty, over 200 years earlier than British Greenwich Observatory and French Observatory. It was the royal astronomical observation center in both Ming and Qing Dynasty. "Notes of Astronomical Phenomena" in Ziwei Palace displays the earliest records about solar eclipse, macula, comet, meteor and new-discovered stars as well as star map, star chart and "Divination of Five Planets", the first monograph of astronomy. "Platform Phenomena" in the eastern room shows the development history of Beijing Ancient Observatory and its historical evolution. "Time and Calendar" in the western room introduces several major excellent calendars among China's hundreds of calendars. Climbing up the ancient observatory, you can see 8 imposing and delicate copper astronomical observation instruments made in the Qing Dynasty: Equatorial Armillary, Ecliptic Armillary, Observatory's Theodolite, Azimuth Theodolite, Quadrant, Sextant, Celestial Globe and Jihengfuchen Equipment.

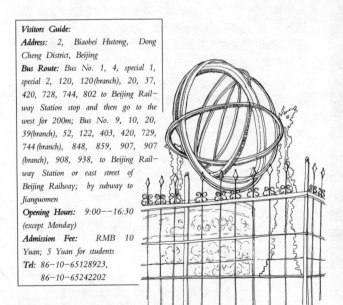

Visitors Guide:
Address: 2, Biaobei Hutong, Dong Cheng District, Beijing
Bus Route: Bus No. 1, 4, special 1, special 2, 120, 120(branch), 20, 37, 420, 728, 744, 802 to Beijing Railway Station stop and then go to the west for 200m; Bus No. 9, 10, 20, 39(branch), 52, 122, 403, 420, 729, 744(branch), 848, 859, 907, 907 (branch), 908, 938, to Beijing Railway Station or east street of Beijing Railway; by subway to Jianguomen
Opening Hours: 9:00--16:30 (except Monday)
Admission Fee: RMB 10 Yuan; 5 Yuan for students
Tel: 86-10-65128923, 86-10-65242202

雍和宫藏传佛教艺术博物馆

触摸历史　体味佛学文化

可能清世祖胤禛的在天之灵怎么也没有想到,他当雍亲王时的府第后来成了藏传佛教的寺院,也就是俗称的喇嘛庙。1994年,这里举行了纪念改庙250周年的法会和学术研讨会,僧人和学者站在雍和门前,身后的雍和宫大殿、法轮殿、万福阁、绥成殿在阳光的照耀下泛着深邃的光泽,使这座北京保存最完好的著名古建筑群更加巍峨壮观和肃穆神秘。

雍和宫各殿供奉着众多的佛像和大量的珍贵文物,其中有紫檀木雕刻的五百罗汉山,金丝楠木雕刻的佛龛和载入吉尼斯世界纪录的18米高的白檀香木大佛。在藏品中,许多都是16世纪以来西藏上层人士、高僧大德进献给皇室和本宫的珍贵礼品,至今保存完好,具有极高的历史与艺术价值。因此,雍和宫有权力说,自己是藏传佛教在京畿地区鼎盛佛事的写照。310年的雍和宫有一双饱含沧桑的眼睛,它的瞳孔中有清中叶的盛世荣昌和清末的颓败衰微,有中国近代史的屈辱与奋争以及新中国的生机与梦想。这里作为全国第一批重点文物保护单位,制定有十分严格的管理与保护措施,承蒙周恩来总理的关怀,它甚至能躲过十年动乱中的劫难,更使人倍加庆幸。1979年,政府拨巨款进行全面修整,十几年后,新僧舍、佛学院等工程相继竣工,雍和宫像巨人一样挺立在世人面前。它的底蕴和风姿赢得的不仅仅是赞誉的目光,而是对中国历史佛学文化的触摸和体味。

人们初踏宫门,从牌坊进去,穿过深长悠远的辇道来到天王殿,看见大肚弥勒佛坐在那里,佛主好像在笑容可掬地征询僧俗众人:你们能做到"笑世间可笑之人,容天下难容之事"吗?于是众人会心地笑了。

参观指南

地　　址:北京市东城区雍和宫大街12号。

乘车路线:乘13、62、116、117路公交车或地铁雍和宫站下车。

开放时间:9:00—16:30。

票　　价:25元;学生12元。

周边景观:首都博物馆(孔庙)、国子监、钟鼓楼。

咨询电话:010-64044499

Yonghegong Lama Temple

Historically, the Yonghegong Lama Temple was a residence for Emperors Yongzheng and Qianlong of the Qing Dynasty. It was built in the 33rd year of Kangxi's reign (1694) and was changed into a Emperor's palace in the 3rd year of Yongzheng's reign (1725). In the 9th year of Qianlong's reign (1744), it became a temple of the Lama Buddhist sect.

The Yonghegong Lama Temple was made up of three exquisite arches, the Yonghe Door, the Yonghegong Hall, Yongyou Hall, Falun Hall, Wanfu Hall, and the Neicheng Hall. It also has the East and West side halls, the "Four Halls of Scholarship (Medicine Hall, Mathematics Hall, Mizong Buddhist Sect Hall, and Scripture Recital Hall) as well as two display rooms for relics.

The halls of Yonghegong Lama Temple worshipped many Buddhist statues, Tangka (a kind of Tibetan painting) and precious relics. These include sandlewood sculpture of the Five Hundred Arhat (Luohan) Mountain, golden nanmu sculpture of the Buddha niche and the 18-m high sandlewood Buddha statue. The Buddha statue was listed in the Guinness Book of Records in 1910. Among the collection, many were precious gifts presented by the Tibetan elite and senior monks to the Emperor since the 16th century. They are well preserved and have very high historical and artistic value.

Visitors guide
Address: Inside Northeastern Andingmen, Beijing City
Bus routes: Take Buses 13, 62, 116, 117 or take the subway and alight at Lama Temple Station
Opening hours: 09:00 – 16:39
Admission fees: RMB 25 Yuan, 12 Yuan for students
Tel: 86–10–64044499

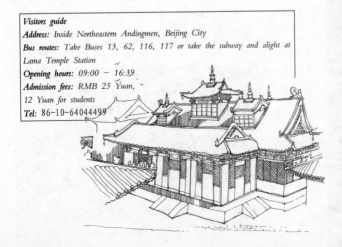

中央美术学院美术馆

感悟美术妙谛

中央美术学院美术馆原为该院的陈列馆，建于 20 世纪 60 年代初期，主要是服务于学院各类教学活动，每年定期举办在校生成绩展，本科生与研究生毕业作品展，教师作品展等系列展览。除教学展览之外还经常举办各类馆藏展、国内外美术交流展等，是北京地区重要的美术展馆。

美术的情味和审美价值是社会生活的反映，无论是色彩丰富的西洋画还是达情畅神的中国画，都展示着时代的风貌。北宋画家张择端的《清明上河图》描绘当年汴京近郊清明时节社会各阶层的生活景象，是一部具有重要历史价值的社会写真画卷。而荷兰画家凡高用灰暗的色彩画就《吃马铃薯的人》，反映工人和农村生活的艰辛困苦。在中央美术学院美术馆里，几十年来形成了丰富、系统的馆藏，包括中国古代书画、近现代中国书画、民间美术、中外油画、版画、雕塑以及部分古代壁画临本，从中可以窥见当时的社会历史变迁，观览人物或山川景色的状貌。

馆内还收藏建院以来历届学生的优秀作品，反映了中国美术教育的进程及特色。从 20 世纪初梁启超提倡开办国立北平美术学校至今，中央美术学院几经变迁，但是它的美术教育成就永远镌刻在中华民族的史册上。

在美术馆的展厅里，你可以和栩栩如生的人物交谈，你还可以在绮丽秀美的风景里漫游，一件件美术作品如同春风送来的点点雨丝，滴落在你的脸上，也浸润在你的心头，那种美好的感觉，让你一生受用。

参观指南

地　　址：北京市东城区校尉胡同 5 号。

乘车路线：103、104、803、814 路公交车百货大楼站下，路东。

开放时间：9：30-16：30（16：00 停止售票）。

周边景观：劳动人民文化宫、中山公园、故宫、天安门广场、王府井、北京工艺美术博物馆、王府井古人类文化遗址博物馆。

周边餐饮：明坊酒家、西北穆斯林奇志餐厅、王府井大饭店、麻香婆。

票　　价：5 元；本院学生凭证免票。

咨询电话：010-65282022。

The Art Gallery of Central Academy of Fine Arts

The art gallery used to be the display hall of Central Academy of Fine Arts. Built in early 1960s, it mainly holds various teaching activities of the academy. The students' works will be regularly exhibited every year, which include the works of the undergraduates, the postgraduates and the teachers.

Inside the art gallery, rich and systemic collections have been accumulated in the past decades. They fall into such categories as ancient Chinese paintings and handwritings, modern and contemporary Chinese paintings, folk arts, oil paintings, prints, sculptures and some ancient mural paintings. From these works, you could see the social vicissitudes, people's appearances and natural landscapes.

The gallery also houses many excellent works created by the students in Central Academy of Fine Arts, which reflects the process and features of China's fine art education. In early 20th century, Liang Qichao called for the establishment of State-run Beiping Fine Art School. Till nowadays, the academy has undergone dramatic changes, but its achievements in fine art education will be forever recorded in the annals of the Chinese people.

Visitors Guide
Address: No.5 Xiaowei Hutong, Dongcheng District, Beijing
Bus Route: Bus No.103、104、803、814 to the stop of Department Store, east of the road.
Opening Hours: 9:30—16:30(16:00 stop selling tickets)
Nearby Sights: Cultural Palace of the Working People、Zhongshan Park、the Forbidden City、Tian'amen Square and Wangfujing
Nearby Restaurants: Mingfang Restaurant、Northwest Muslim Qizhi Restaurant, Wangfujing Hotel and Mapoxiang Restaurant
Admission Fee: RMB 5 Yuan
Tel: 86—10—65282022

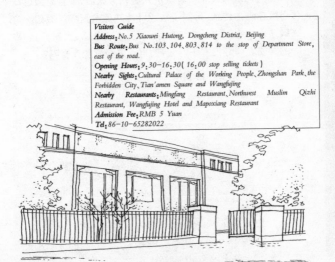

北京文博交流馆

古乐古寺

北京文博交流馆的前身为智化寺文物保管所。作为文博交流馆，这里有着北京地区博物馆之间的交流、博物馆与民间收藏组织之间的交流等项功能。这里经常举办个人收藏展览，展品范围广阔，内容丰富多彩，吸引了大量观众。从参观者那种专注的神态中，你还可以感悟智化古刹原有的那种凝神与睿智。

智化寺是北京市内现存唯一一座完整的明代古建筑群，它始建于明正统八年（1443年），由明中期大宦官王振的部分私宅改建。规模不大，但特色显著，虽经历500余年，其基本布局和原有格调未遭侵损。用料独特、庄重典雅的黑琉璃瓦顶，素雅清新、古朴精美的装饰彩绘，有中国音乐活化石美誉的"智化寺京音乐"，都是不可多得的瑰宝。智化寺虽身处闹市，但环境清幽静穆，四进院落中古树名木浓荫蔽日，装点一年四季景色，是北京城内难见的览胜佳境。智化寺内现有藏品200多件（套）。其中一批梨园牌匾是北京戏曲研究的重要史料，这里推出"梨园牌匾展"，出版了《梨园旧匾》画册，在各界引起强烈反响。

这里的京音乐演奏堪称历史绝唱。它既包含有唐宋佛教法乐的精髓，又吸收宋、元、明民间俗乐的调式，成为一种雅俗共赏的艺术形式。京音乐进入智化寺以后，一直是通过口传心授在寺内传承，可以说是原汁原味保留至今。假如你有兴致来智化寺听一听古老的京音乐，在智化殿、大智殿、如来殿的梁檩之间寻找古乐的余音，岂不是绝好的享受吗？

参观指南

地　　址：北京市东城区禄米仓5号。

乘车路线：特2、44、750、800路公交车雅宝路站下；24路禄米仓站下。

自驾车线：东二环金宝街出口向西100米至小牌坊胡同，向北100米，第二个胡同口即到。

开放时间：7：00-17：30

票　　价：20元；学生10元。

咨询电话：010-65286691

Beijing Museum for Cultural Relic Exchange

Beijing Museum for Cultural Relic Exchange is located in the Zhi-Hua Temple at 5 Lumicang, Dongcheng District. The purpose of this museum is to collect information and data about museums in the world and show the status quo of all the museums in Beijing region.

Zhi-Hua Temple has five courts, including Bell and Drum Tower, Zhi-Hua Gate, Zhi-Hua Hall, Buddha Hall and Dabei Hall. All the roofs are built with black glazed tiles, so the whole temple is solemn and magnificent, with unique style different from other temples in Beijing.

There are rich cultural relics preserved in the temple, with a number of over 1500. In the temple, the large fresco 4.8m's long and 3.1m's tall, which shows Dizang Buddha' preaching picture, is an extant elite of fresco in Ming Dynasty. The Tripitaka hall still preserves a "wheeling tripitaka", which is the extant oldest one. The music of Zhi-Hua Temple is one of the five kinds of ancient music in China. It has been passed down through 28 generations for over 540 years, so it is called a "living fossil" in the field of music.

Visitors Guide:
Address: 5 Lumicang, Dongcheng District, Beijing
Bus Route: by bus No. 2 (special), 44, 750, 800 to Yabaolu stop or 24 to Lumicang stop.
Self-drive Route: from Jinbao Street of the east second round to the west for 100m until Xiaopaiifang lane, then to the north for 100m until the second lane entrance.
Opening Hours: 7:00-17:30
Admission Fee: RMB 20 Yuan; 10 Yuan for students.
Tel: 86-10-65286691

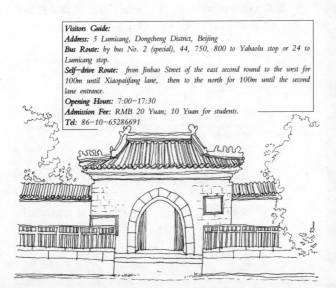

正阳门

正阳风光

人们习惯于把正阳门称作前门，正阳门是北京保存最为完好的一座城门，由于它具有得天独厚的地理位置和历史资源，所以受到社会各界的普遍关注。

正阳门多舛的命运承载了中国历史上的风风雨雨，自明初始建以来，正阳门已经几次遭毁，又几次重修，人们现在看到的正阳门是1906年修建的。城楼和箭楼两座建筑屹立在天安门广场南侧，犹如两把利剑刺向青天，形成对共和国中心的拱卫。人们漫步在广场上，遥望南天，巍峨如高山，浩荡似春风，就在不经意间，作一个中国人的自豪感袭上你的脑际。

其实正阳门更多的是凝聚着中国普通老百姓的人气。大栅栏、珠市口、天桥，曾经发生和正在发生着多少个激昂悲壮、缠绵悱恻、乐天乐地的故事。如今，你可以登上正阳门，看崇文烟霞中的日出，望宣武雾霭中的日落，无论是大笑或者长叹，都证明你懂得了人生的意义。另外，登上城楼或者箭楼，还可以在这里欣赏诸多展览，书画、摄影、奇石，让你在感慨人生之际松弛一下疲惫的心弦，注入清新的甘泉。也许你未曾登上城楼，未曾领略过正阳门天地景色，但是当你步行或驱车从城楼箭楼脚下过往时，肯定会抬起头，看看灰砖碧瓦，看看飞檐画栋，看看城楼上的云朵与彩霞，看看城楼下车水马龙万家灯火，其实，这就是你久已盼望的正阳风光。

参观指南

地　　址：北京前门大街。

乘车路线：长安街沿线各路公交车或地铁于天安门站下。

自驾车线：北依毛主席纪念堂，南邻繁华的前门大街。

开放时间：8：30-16：30。

周边景观：天安门广场、毛主席纪念堂、故宫、国家博物馆。

周边餐饮：中侨潮州酒楼、鑫香妃烤鸡、全聚德烧鸭店、老正兴饭庄。

票　　价：10元；学生5元。

咨询电话：010-65229384

Zhengyang Gate

Zhengyang Gate is located on the south-north axis of Beijing, south of the Tian'anmen Square and north of Qianmen Street. Now only the city tower and the embrasure watchtower are in existence.

The city tower sitting on a brick platform takes up 3,047. 1.2-meter-high eave walls are respectively on the north and south. The city tower is trimmed with grey pantiles and green glazed tiles in the double-eave and Xieshan style. Doors can be found in four directions upstairs and downstairs. The tower is 36.7-meter wide, 16.5-meter deep and 27.3-meter high. The whole building is 42 meters in height, which makes the gate the highest among all the gates in Beijing. The brick embrasure watchtower covers 2,147.The roof is also trimmed with grey pantiles and glazed tiles in the double-eave and Xieshan style. The tower has four storeys. Seven rooms on the south are 62 meters wide,12 meters deep and 26 meters high. The total height of the watchtower with its platform is 38 meters, which makes the watchtower the highest one among those in Beijing. On the first floor, an exhibition named Beijing in history introduces the folk customs of Beijing.

Visitors Guide
Address: Qianmen Street, Beijing
Bus Route: Buses along Chang'an Street or subway to the Tian'anmen station
Self-drive Route: North to the Memorial Hall of Chairman Mao, and south to the busy Qianmen Street
Opening Hours: 8:30–16:30。
Nearby Sights: Tian'anmen Square、Memorial Hall of Chairman Mao、Palace Museum、and National Museum
Nearby Restaurants: Zhongqiao Chaozhou Tavern、Xinxiangfei Roast Chicken、Quanjude Roast Duck Restaurant、Laozhengxing Restaurant
Admission Fee: RMB 10 Yuan；5 Yuan for students
Tel: 86-10-65229384

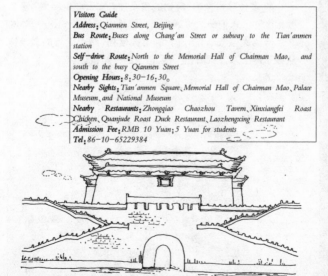

文天祥祠

他从零丁洋走来

　　北京文天祥祠是明清两代祭祀文天祥的祠堂,其旧址为文天祥被囚于元大都(今北京)时的土牢,几经迁徙、重建和修葺,祠堂于1984年10月向社会开放。祠堂坐北朝南,占地面积600平方米,布局紧凑、庄严肃穆。院内一株苍劲的古枣树,相传为文天祥亲手种植,树干倾斜指向南方,与地面成45度夹角,似乎表达着他"臣心一片磁针石,不指南方誓不休"的精神。前院整个东墙镶嵌着明代大书法家文徵明所书《正气歌》刻石,全文300个字,气势恢弘凝重,从另一个角度折射出文天祥的英雄气概。祠堂的大门、过厅、堂屋殿柱檐下,当代书法家以文天祥诗句为内容手书木刻匾额、楹联,用浓郁的文化气息告慰这位文学家和抗元英雄的英灵。

　　文天祥1236年生于江西吉州庐陵,南宋德佑二年(1276年),临危受命任右丞相。两年后元军大举进犯南宋,文天祥起兵抗元,不幸在广东海丰兵败被俘,他坚拒投降,并作千古名篇《过零丁洋》,以"人生自古谁无死,留取丹心照汗青"来明志。1279年被解至元大都,关在兵马司的土牢里,面对威逼利诱,文天祥终无所动,以一腔忠贞和不屈写下了永垂不朽的《正气歌》,其凛然正气让元统治者无计可施,于元至十九年(1283年)将他杀害。

　　20多件珍贵文物、遗物的展示使"文天祥生平展"更加翔实生动。人们一边吟诵文天祥掷地有声的诗句,一边体味文天祥的民族气节,仿佛看到身披桎梏、昂首挺胸的文天祥从零丁洋走来,还看到他身后留下的一路豪迈。

> **参观指南**
>
> 地　　址:北京市东城区府学胡同63号。
>
> 乘车路线:104、108路公交车北兵马司下;2、13、115、
> 　　　　　734、834路宽街下。
>
> 开放时间:9:00-17:00。
>
> 周边景观:和敬公主府、茅盾故居、孙中山逝世纪念地、
> 　　　　　欧阳予倩故居。
>
> 票　　价:5元;学生3元。
>
> 咨询电话:010-64014968

Ancestral Temple for Wen Tianxiang

The ancestral temple is located at No.63 Fuxue Hutong, Dongchen District,Beijing.It was built in memory of Wen Tianxiang, a hero in South Song Dynasty who fought bravely against the enemies of Yuan Empire. Based on the place where Wen Tianxiang was imprisoned, the temple has preserved the architectural style of Ming Dynasty.

The ancestral temple is composed of the main gate, the corridor and the hall, covering an area of 600 square meters. Some precious cultural relics have been preserved in the hall, such as the stone tablets about Wen Tianxiang. Besides that, Wen Tianxiang life experience exhibition gives a detailed introduction to his major heroic deeds, such as studying when young, being an officer when in his prime, gathering the soldiers to fight against the invasion of Yuan Empire, being captured and killed by the enemies etc. Inside the hall, there is a folding screen, on which Mao Zedong wrote the famous poem which goes to such an extent: No one will be spared by death, but brave heart remains to serve the country. On the back of the screen, there is the full version of Wen Tianxiang's poem entitled Laud to Moral Spirit.

Visitors Guide
Address:*No.63 Fuxue Hutong, Dongchen District, Beijing*
Bus Route:*Bus No.104、108 to the stop of Beibinmasi;*
Bus No. 2、13、115、734、834 to the stop of Kuanjie
Opening Hours:*9:00−17:00*
Admission Fee:*RMB 5 Yuan;3 Yuan for students*
Tel:*86−10−64014968*

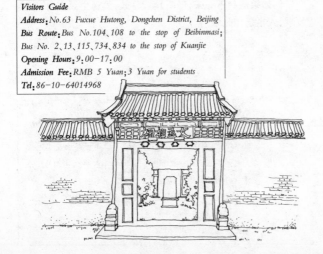

北京钟鼓楼文物保管所

倾听晨钟暮鼓

当红日从东方升起的时候,耳畔响起晨钟的呼唤;当夕阳落入西山的时候,踏着暮鼓的音符走向归程。这就是你的人生,无论甜蜜还是苦涩,无论富贵还是贫穷,无论苍老还是年轻。

北京钟鼓楼旅游景点具有着不可抗拒的魅力。近年来,到钟鼓楼参观的游客逐渐增多,雄伟的建筑,传统的司时方式,精彩的更鼓表演,民俗文化的氛围,深深地吸引着世界各地的人们。作为元、明、清三代的司时中心,钟鼓楼是人类认识时间、掌握时间的里程碑,从这里传出的每个声响,都与日出而作,日落而息的人们构成一幅画卷,一幅讴歌生命的画卷,一幅追求希望的画卷,一幅代代相连的画卷。

现在人们来到这里,登上钟鼓楼,总揽古都风貌;观赏"中国古钟之最"的报时铜钟和传统更鼓的表演;参与击鼓、撞响报时铜钟;体味舞狮、舞龙、耍幡、鼓词等民俗风情的清风雅韵,会使你对钟鼓楼浓郁的人文情调产生深切的依恋。不仅如此,还有一种以水作为动力,具有传统计时功能和机械报时功能的"铜壶滴漏"随箭尺浮升,铙神击铙报时。其实它只是古人探求掌控时间的一个足迹,但从中你已经看到中华民族掌握自己命运的聪明才智和创造能力。难怪众多的外国朋友对这里情有独钟,子夜的钟声和正午的鼓声在心中奏响,这是生命的节奏。

你如果能静下心来,倾听晨钟暮鼓,重温生活岁月,你会发现,人生是如此多情。

参观指南

地　　址:北京市东城区钟楼湾临字9号。

乘车路线:乘5、60、107、124、815、819、834路公交车或地铁在鼓楼大街站下车,沿旧鼓楼大街南行。

开放时间:9:00-17:00。

周边景观:什刹海风景区、国子监、孔庙、雍和宫、南锣鼓巷四合院保护区。

咨询电话:010-84036706

Beijing Bell and Drum Towers

Beijing Bell and Drum Towers are a group of ancient buildings with grand and magnificent sights in the north of Beijing. As the telling time center during the Yuan, Ming and Qing Dynasties (1271-1911), the towers boast a time-honored history.

The Drum Tower was made of wood with a height of 46.7meters. The telling time instrument in the Bell Tower was made during the Ming Dynasty. It is as tall as 5.5 meters and as heavy as 63 tons. The big bell is famous in the world for its royal position, first-class technique, and unique style of hanging and telling time function. It is the heaviest and biggest copper bell in China. It can produce long and heavy sound. In the three dynasties, it was beaten 108 times every two hours from 19:00 to 3:00 at night.

Visitors Guide:
Dress: Drum Tower Street, Beijing
Bus Route: Bus No. 5, 60, 107, 124, 815, 819, 843 or subway to Drum Tower Street, and then walk southwards
Opening Hours: 9:00—17:00
Nearby Sights: ShiChaHai Scenic Area, Guozijian, Confucius Temple, Palace of Harmony, Luogu South Lane Siheyuan under protection
Tel: 86—10—84036706

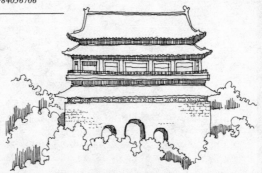

茅盾故居

难忘茅盾

电影《林家铺子》和《子夜》是令人难忘的,其原因主要是对原著社会意义的深刻理解。于是,人们永远记住了茅盾。

坐落于东城区后圆恩寺的茅盾故居,是一座普通民居式的两进四合院,茅盾1974年至1981年逝世前曾在这里居住。茅盾故居的藏品主要有他的数千册藏书和照片,他曾经使用过的文具、生活用品,家居陈设以及证件、印章、面模、手模等。起居室和会客室以茅盾生前原貌向观众开放,人们从这里可以看到茅盾亲历的中国现代史上那一个个跌宕起伏的岁月,自1916年从北京大学预科班毕业,一直到建国后他担任新中国的文化部长,半个世纪中他用笔描绘着社会的世态炎凉,万象风景。

在故居的前院,设置"伟大的革命文学家茅盾"的展览,全面系统地展示了这位中国现代进步文化的先驱,卓越的无产阶级文化战士的一生:积极参加五四运动和早期共产主义运动;参加中国左翼作家联盟并担任领导工作;抗日战争中积极投身抗日救亡工作,到新疆任教并从事文化交流活动,到延安参观和讲学,在香港、桂林、重庆等地从事革命文化工作,应邀去苏联访问以及建国后他担任重要领导职务,为建设社会主义文化、团结壮大革命文艺队伍、促进中外文化交流所做出的卓越贡献……

茅盾以他众多的现实主义杰出作品矗立于中国社会,影响了几代中国人。参观者从茅盾故居走出来,都不约而同地认定,这位文坛巨匠的身姿还将永远映现在人们心头,永远难以忘怀。

参观指南

地　　址:北京市东城区交道口后圆恩寺13号。

乘车路线:104、107、108、113、124路公交车交道口站下;5路鼓楼站下。

开放时间:9:00~16:00,周二、周四、周六开放。

周边景观:和敬公主府、文天祥祠、孙中山逝世纪念地、欧阳予倩故居、孔庙、国子监。

周边餐饮:侣松园宾馆、仁和酒楼、金景圣、阿迪力大食府。

票　　价:5元;学生3元。

咨询电话:010-64040520、010-64044089

The Former Residence of Mao Dun

The residence is a traditional Beijing quadrangle located in the Yuan'ensi Hutong behind the South Street of Jiaodaokou.

Facing the south, the residence is divided into the front and the back courtyards with 22 rooms in total. The studies, the bedrooms and the parlor are kept their original looks. The west wing-room of the front courtyard is the parlor. The sofa, the vase and the couplets are in their old places. In the north room, an introduction to Mao Dun's life and his literature achievements are displayed. In the east wing-room, pictures and old practicalities demonstrate his achievements in China's cultural construction and his efforts in pursuit of the world's peace since 1949. The exhibits include his warrants, representative cards, manuscripts, letters as well as the pens, recorders and seals he once used. Mao Dun's study and bedroom are in the back courtyard. Inside the rooms, books, ancient and modern, home and abroad are found everywhere. His collections of book and his literatures have been gathered in the Library of Mao Dun.

Visitors Guide
Address: No.13 the Yuan'ensi Hutong behind the South Street of Jiaodaokou.
Bus Route: Bus No. 104、107、108、113、124 to the Jiaodaokou stop and Bus No. 5 to the Gulou stop.
Opening Hours: 9:00-16:00 on Tuesday, Thursday and Saturday
Nearby Sights: Hejinggong Mansion, Wen Tianxiang Ancestral Temple, Sun Yat Sun's Memorial Place, and the Former Residence of Ouyang Yuqian
Nearby Restaurants: Lvsongyuan Hotel, Enhe Restaurant, Jinpiaosheng Restaurant and Adili Restaurant
Admission Fee: RMB 5 Yuan; 3 Yuan for students.
Tel: 86-10-64040520、86-10-64044089

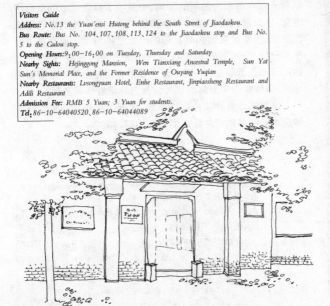

老舍纪念馆

解读老舍

北京市东城区灯市口西街丰富胡同 19 号，是一所普通的四合小院。老舍 1950 年初自美回国后购置，在这里生活了 16 年。1999 年春天，正值老舍先生诞辰 100 周年的时候，老舍纪念馆建成并正式对外开放。

从在这里创作的第一部剧本《龙须沟》获"人民艺术家"称号开始，作家创作了大量作品，其中话剧《茶馆》曾为新中国杰出话剧作品之一；然而，洗劫的波涛冲垮了作家心里的堤坝，于是，他告别了这座小院，走进碧绿的湖水中。

1924 年，25 岁的老舍登上赴英的轮船。多年的寒窗苦读和潜心研究，东方文学已在心中愈加熟稔，他在伦敦大学东方学院向西方世界展示东方文学的魅力；6 年后回国，在齐鲁大学、山东大学执教，其后主持文协工作；抗战前夕发表小说《骆驼祥子》，把当时中国社会被侮辱被损害者的奋斗与挣扎写得淋漓尽致；抗战胜利后，老舍去美国讲学，而新中国热气腾腾的景象吸引他回到祖国，回到生他养他的北京，也就来到了这座小院，亲手栽下柿树，曾经绿叶丹柿，今亦诗情画意。

小院的西耳房是老舍的卧室兼书房。写作的写字台上，放着一枚齐白石为他刻的印章，一只冯玉祥送给他的玉石印泥盒，一方清代戏曲理论家李渔的书画砚台。他的眼镜还放在那里，但眼镜后面那双忧郁的眼睛已不见了。墨水瓶里的墨水已经枯干，收音机里狂热的喧嚣已经远去，只有台历上的日子却永远凝固在那里。老舍曾说这里是全院中最安静的地方，但作家心中澎湃的热血曾是怎样地壮怀激烈啊？

这里已恢复作家生前的原貌，大量的手稿和遗物以及各种版本的图书和照片让人们不断地解读老舍。

参观指南

地　　址：北京市东城区灯市口西街丰富胡同 19 号。

乘车路线：2、8、60 路公交车妇产医院下车；103、104、108、
　　　　　111 等在灯市西口下车。

票　　价：5 元；中小学生免票。

周边景观：中国美术馆、王府井天主堂、北京工艺美术馆、
　　　　　王府井古人类文化遗址博物馆。

咨询电话：010-65599218、010-65224469

Lao She Memorial Hall

The memorial hall is a small courtyard with two rooms facing the south. In the west, there is a compound with houses on three sides, which constitutes the major part of Lao She's former residence. Three east and west wing-rooms are opened as exhibition rooms. From "The Tinkler", Lao She's first novel to "Under the Red Banner", his last unfinished autobiographic novel, Lao She's works that represent his lifetime literary achievements are all housed here. In the north, there are three rooms with a penthouse respectively on the left and right. The penthouses are kept in original state and the living scenes of Lao She are on display. The bright room and the second west room make up the small living room where many cultural celebrities used to gather. Premier Zhou Enlai paid three visits to Lao She and also met him here. The second east room is the bedroom. The west penthouse is Lao She's study and workroom which is small and unadorned. On the hardwood desk embedded with marble are several antiques: a seal made by Qibaishi, a jade inkpad box given by General Feng Yuxiang, and an inkslab once owned by Li Yu in Qing Dynasty.

Visitors Guide

Address: No. 19 Fengfu Hutong, West Street of Dengshikou, Dongcheng District, Beijing

Bus Route: Bus No.2、8、60 to the stop of Hospital for Gynecology and Obstetics; Bus No.103、104、108、111 to the stop of West Dengshikou

Admission Fee: RMB 5 Yuan; Primary and middle school students are free from charge.

Tel: 86-10-65599218、86-10-65224469

保利艺术博物馆

从火烧圆明园谈起

1860 年,英法联军侵入北京,在洗劫京城的同时,又闯入被誉为"万园之园"的圆明园大肆抢掠珍宝,并纵火将这个驰名中外的皇家园林烧个精光。140 年后,保利艺术博物馆在香港抢救保护了即将再次流失的三件圆明园国宝 — 牛首铜像、虎首铜像和猴首铜像。当由博物馆举办的"圆明园国宝全国巡展"先后在国内 20 多个中心城市和宝岛台湾进行展出时,无数人的心潮掀起一阵阵热浪。

耻辱莫大于国耻。圆明园的那场大火,至今烧灼着中国人的心。然而,保利艺术博物馆的"中国古代青铜艺术精品陈列"和"中国古代石刻佛教造像艺术精品陈列"却让国人获得了前所未有的自豪感。在这里,许多稀品和孤品都是首次与你见面:商代的三牛首兽面纹尊、史尊、西周神面卣、王作左守鼎、遂公盨、凤首扁盉、戎生编钟等,展现中国古代青铜文明的发展历程和独特魅力;40 多件北朝至唐代(公元 5 世纪至 8 世纪)的石刻佛像勾勒出巅峰时期中国佛教艺术的风采。其中北朝时期(公元 6 世纪至 7 世纪)山东青州地区雕造的一批佛像,工艺之精,保存之好世所罕见。

1999 年 12 月,当保利艺术博物馆建成并正式对公众开放的时候,吸引人们目光的不仅仅是几百件馆藏珍品,还有那"不求多而全,只求精、珍、稀"的收藏宗旨。这座博物馆是中国首家由大型国有企业兴办的,而这里的绝大多数藏品来自于海外,我们可以想象得出,每件珍品回归的背后都会有一个动人的故事。

参观指南

地　　址:北京市东城区东直门南大街 14 号保利大厦二层。

乘车路线:115、118 路公交车于东四十条站下车。

自驾车线:到东四十条东北角。

开放时间:周一至周六 9:30—16:30;
　　　　　国家法定假日闭馆。

周边景观:保利大厦、保利剧院、港澳中心、亚洲大中心。

票　　价:50 元;学生、离休老人持有效证件半票。

咨询电话:010-65001188 转 3250

Poly Art Museum

This is the first museum operated by a state-owned enterprise on China mainland. Most of its collections are retrieved from abroad. You will see many treasures on China Ancient Bronze Art Exhibition and China Ancient Stone Carvings Exhibition, such as three-ox-head goblets of Shang Dynasty, cooking vessels and bells produced in ancient times. They reflect the development and the unique charm of China ancient bronze civilization. 40 carved figures of Buddha give an outline of the prosperity of Buddhism in China from 5th century to 8th century. The carved figures of Buddha found in Qingzhou, Shandong Province are well preserved and exquisite in techniques.

In December 1999 when Poly Art Museum was officially opened to the public, what attracted the audience was not only hundreds of treasures housed here, but also its purpose that is seeking delicate, precious and rare collections instead of large numbers and wide ranges.

Visitors Guide

Address**:** No. 14 Dongzhimen South Street, 2nd floor of Poly Building, Dongcheng District, Beijing.

Bus Route**:** Bus No.115、118 to the stop of Dongsishitiao

Self-drive Route**:** Northeastern corner of Dongsishitiao

Opening Hours**:** Monday—Saturday 9：30--16：30；close on state holidays

Nearby Sights**:** Poly Building、Poly Theater、Hong Kong and Macao Center、Asia Center.

Admission Fee**:** RMB 50 Yuan；25 Yuan for students and the retired people with relevant proofs.

Tel**:** 86-10-65001188-3250

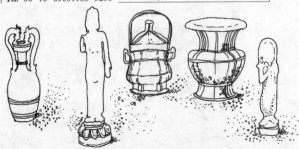

北京工艺美术馆

瞧啊，这些精雕细琢的工艺品

那日，我怀着一颗玩心和约略的方向感，边走边唱来到了北京工艺美术博物馆。国际奥委会的海伯格先生将这里的藏品称为："中华瑰宝，世界奇观！"我则感叹：绝啦，中华民族的智慧及巧夺天工的巨匠！

这里有享誉京城的传统工艺美术四大名旦：玉器、牙雕、景泰蓝、漆雕，有众多艺术大师呕心沥血的绝世佳作：国画、瓷器、青铜、刺绣、木雕……传奇的翡翠象垒，独特的白玉济公，巨型牙雕"新旧北京"将新北京的十大建筑与老北京的风土人情融为一体，简直就是一幅当代的"清明上河图"。

呆呆立定在栩栩如生的黄杨木雕"梁山伯与祝英台"前，这惊天动地的爱情故事啊，让我黯然："问世间，情为何物？直教人生死相许……"看迷了眼，旁边有人惊呼："嘿，够艺术！"是啊是啊，够艺术！任何人、任何事、任何技能，达到最高境界时都被冠以"够艺术"的赞许。老北京常有蹬三轮的，能翘起一只轮子，离地飞跑，还大呼小叫着，得其意忘其形，往来观者也伸起拇指："艺术！"这就是人类，以其极致精微的活计对自身局限的超越，这是一种精神，一种境界！

有空不妨来这里看看，这是一个让人心灵相遇的地方。

参观指南

地　　址：北京东城区王府井大街南口工美大厦四层。

乘车路线：103、104、803路东长安街站下车；地铁或1、4、
　　　　　10、52等长安街沿线车王府井站下车。

开放时间：9：00—17：00。

票　　价：成人10元，学生5元；老人、儿童、教师、军人持
　　　　　证半价。

周边景观：王府井古人类文化遗址博物馆、老舍故居、王府
　　　　　井天主堂、中国美术馆。

咨询电话：010-65288866 转 4031 或 4033

Beijing Arts and Crafts Gallery

This is an art palace full of fantasies. The renowned four treasures of arts and crafts in the capital (jade articles, ivory carvings, cloisonee enamels, and carved lacquerwares) and traditional Chinese paintings, filigrees, porcelains, bronzes, embroideries, golden lacquers and wooden carvings are the great masters' excellent works rarely found on earth. Here you could appreciate the exquisite works of Beijing traditional arts and crafts. The emerald elephant is legendary; the delicate white jade "Monk Jigong" is uniquely designed; the coral craft named hundreds of birds worship the phoenix and the marvelous agate dragon are attractive. The large-scale ivory carvings entitled Old Beijing and New Beijing incorporates the top ten architectures of the new Beijing with the traditional social customs of the old Beijing, which is honored as the contemporary scroll of painting "The Festival of Pure Brightness on the River". The boxwood carving entitled Liang Shangbo and Zhu Yingtai created in 1950s vividly retells people the beautiful love story of Liang and Zhu, a Chinese version of Romeo and Juliet.

Visitors Guide

Address: On the fourth floor of Gongmei Building, Wangfujing Street, Beijing

Bus Route: Bus No.103、104、803 to the stop of East Chang'an Street; Subway or Bus No.1、4、10、52 to the stop of Wangfujin

Opening Hours: 9:00--17:00

Admission Fee: RMB 10 Yuan, 5 Yuan for students, seniors, children, teachers and PLA men with relevant cards

Tel: 86-10-65288866-4031 or 4033

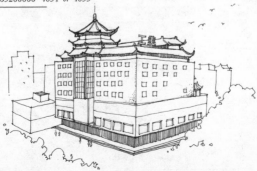

北京警察博物馆

抚今追昔的启示

抚今追昔，是人类的重要品德。无论是对远去的历史，还是面对近在咫尺的现实，都在向每一个人征询这个词汇的含意：那就是责任。有这样一群人，把责任重于泰山当作人生的坐标，用青春铸就，用热血浇洒，这就是新时代的中国警察。

迄今为止，中国的警政建设已经整整一个世纪了。殷红的血，苦涩的泪，蒸腾的汗幻化成一个记忆，一个中国近代史、现代史的记忆。博物馆里，京城近百年的警察史料文物，是中国近代警察史的千钧之重的缩写。中国第一个专职警察机构巡警部是哪年建立的？"京城飞贼"如何折断了翅膀？"红色间谍"是怎样的英雄？毛泽东入住香山双清别墅的第一个夜晚发生了什么？建国后北京第一宗特务潜伏案如何破获？故宫珍宝馆被盗案怎样侦破？是谁冒充周恩来笔迹诈骗银行提走大量现金？……那许许多多尘封经年的往事在这里褪去了神秘的外衣，让你进入这个由历史碎片构成的天地。重数那一个个风流人物，重忆那一个个惊天大案，重读那一个个有着时代烙印的非常名词。

掌控京师九门内外守卫巡警之职的提督和军士们已成为小说家茶余饭后的谈资，但是在这里，照片和文物上没有一丝浮尘，因为它记录的是一个时代的开端。末代皇帝溥仪走出派出所，手上那户口本印证了他已成为共和国的一个普通公民。也许当你走出北京警察博物馆时，会感到里面的每一件藏品的份量是那样掷地有声。

参观指南：

地　　址：北京市东城区东交民巷36号。

乘车路线：9、729、744、819、859路公交车正义路站下车；2、5、20、22、120、120支、726路前门站下车。

模拟射击：固定靶2元/10发；移动靶4元/10发；全真场景10元/12个场景，子弹不限。

票　　价：门票5元；套票20元（包括门票，全套模拟射击1次，警察博物馆馆徽1枚，卡通钥匙1个）；学生、军人、警察、老人、残疾人、儿童免票。

周边景观：中国国家博物馆、天安门、毛主席纪念堂、前门城楼、人民英雄纪念碑。

咨询电话：010-85225018

Beijing Police Museum

Beijing Police Museum, under the jurisdiction of the public security bureau of Beijing, lies in the old site of former Citibank NA. It was built in 2001 and was the first police museum in China. It shows from many angles the hard course of safeguarding capital public security and the great contribution and achievement made by capital police in maintaining stability, protecting people and cracking down on crimes since the reform and opening-up.

The museum is divided into four exhibition rooms: Beijing public security history exhibition room on the ground floor, criminal investigation exhibition room on the 2nd floor, police functions exhibition room on the 3rd floor and police culture and equipment exhibition room on the 4th floor. Each exhibition room is distinctive. Visitors can experience such hi-tech detective means as "getting and comparing fingerprints" and "drawing suspect's appearance through the witness' description" by operating computer. In front of martyrs' wall on the 3rd floor, visitors can pay a tribute to 60 martyrs of Beijing public security bureau since the urban construction; in real laser simulation shooting training on the 4th floor, visitors can experience such critical and thrilling moment of opening fire to criminals…

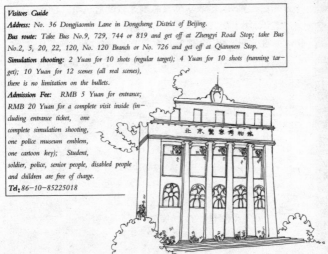

Visitors Guide

Address: No. 36 Dongjiaomin Lane in Dongcheng District of Beijing.

Bus route: Take Bus No.9, 729, 744 or 819 and get off at Zhengyi Road Stop; take Bus No.2, 5, 20, 22, 120, No. 120 Branch or No. 726 and get off at Qianmen Stop.

Simulation shooting: 2 Yuan for 10 shots (regular target); 4 Yuan for 10 shots (running target); 10 Yuan for 12 scenes (all real scenes), there is no limitation on the bullets.

Admission Fee: RMB 5 Yuan for entrance; RMB 20 Yuan for a complete visit inside (including entrance ticket, one complete simulation shooting, one police museum emblem, one cartoon key); Student, soldier, police, senior people, disabled people and children are free of charge.

Tel: 86−10−85225018

北京自来水博物馆

对水资源说一个"爱"字

随手拧开阀门,清亮的自来水从管道中流出来,你知道自来水的来历和历史变迁吗? 如果你走进北京自来水博物馆,或许会对你身体中血液的组成部分产生无限的亲切之情。

自来水博物馆是在北京城历史上第一座水厂——东直门水厂原蒸汽机房旧址上修建的。馆内陈列着各种与水有关的实物 130 件,图片 110 幅,模型及沙盘近 40 件,全方位地反映北京自来水 90 多年的发展历史。第一部分反映了从 1908 年京师自来水股份公司始创,到 1949 年建国以前,历经晚清、北洋、日伪和国民党统治时期,北京自来水事业苦难艰辛的发展历程。第二、三部分集中展示新中国成立后到 70 年代末以及改革开放 20 多年以来北京自来水事业的突飞猛进。同时,还运用现代科技手段,展示自来水复杂的生产工艺、地下自来水管网的分布状况以及严格的水质监测手段,使参观者真正理解自来水不是"自来"和"自来水来之不易"的道理。

水是生命之源。无论是地下水还是地表水,都承载着科学和时代所赋予的内涵流进管道,又从管道的若干个出口流出的时候,这汩汩的水声不正是时代前进的脚步声吗? 一进一出也许是那么平平常常,司空见惯,可是你曾想过:地下水开采已近枯竭,地表水储量急剧递减的危机吗? 今天可以南水北调,明天南方缺水又从何方调集呢?

在这里,人们会想到对水资源说一个"爱"字。从这个时刻起,你再拧动自来水开关的时候,一定十分认真与庄重。

参观指南

地　　址:北京市东城区东直门外北大街甲6号院清水苑内。

乘车路线:44、106、117、123、800路或地铁东直门站下车,从东直站桥沿二环路向北500米路东。

自驾车线:东直门桥往北500米,沿二环辅路行驶,清水苑社区内。

开放时间:9:00-16:00,周三至周日开放。

票　　价:成人5元,学生2元。

咨询电话:010-64650787

Beijing Museum of Tap Water

The museum is built on the original place of the first water plant in Beijing- Zhongzhimen Water Plant. Inside the museum, 130 real objects, 110 pictures, 40 models and sand tables on display reflect the 90-year-old history of Beijing tap water. The first part is about the difficult development of Beijing tap water cause from the establishment of Jingshi Tap Water Co.Ltd in 1908 to the foundation of the People's Republic of China in 1949. The second and the third parts center on the rapid progress in developing tap water cause from 1949 to late 1970s and since reform and opening up. Meantime, by modern technological means, complicated tap water manufacturing techniques, the distribution of underground tap water tunnels and strict monitoring measures on the water quality are presented in front of the visitors who will truly understand that tap water is hard-earned.

Visitors Gudie

Address: No.6 Courtyard (Qingshuiyuan Neighborhood), north street outside Dongzhimen, Beijing

Bus Route: Bus No. 44、106、117、123、800 or subway to the station of Dongzhimen, walk north along the second ring road, 500 meters east of the road.

Self-drive Route: 500 meters north of Dongzhimen Bridge, along the assistant way of second ring road, and inside the Qing-shuiyuan Neighborhood.

Opening Hours: 9:00-16:00, open from Wednesday to Sunday

Admission Fee: RMB 5 Yuan for adu, lts, 2 Yuan for students

Tel: 86-10-64650787

王府井古人类文化遗址博物馆

遥想篝火

北京自金代以来，建都历史已达八百多年，在这样有着悠久历史、又是国际大都市的中心地区发现古人类文化遗存，在世界范围内是绝无仅有的。1996年12月，正在北京大学攻读研究生的岳升阳来到王府井南口东方广场的施工现场，地层中一条黑色炭迹引起他的注意。随后在其周围，他挖掘到了动物碎骨和被人类击打过的碎片。经考古专家鉴定，该地为旧石器时代晚期遗址，距今约2.5万年。

遗址发现5周年后，北京市东城区人民政府和李嘉诚先生共同投资兴建的王府井古人类文化遗址博物馆正式对公众开放。馆中遗址块为距地面12米的土层，上面保留了远古人类点燃篝火的遗留物——炭灰坑、炭屑岩等，还有远古人类宰杀和肢解动物的地点——富含骨片的遗址探方。这里的石制品、骨制品以及用火遗迹都保持出土时的原貌，2000余件文物不仅填补了平原地区没有旧石器时代遗址的空白，也是研究古人类工具制作、生活方式、生存能力的珍贵资料。通过它，我们看到当时北京地区的生态环境，也能遥想出篝火旁边许许多多的人物和故事。

一个秋风初起的傍晚，一条汩汩流淌的河水旁，燃起一堆堆熊熊的篝火。人们聚集在火堆旁，享受着白天捕获的猎物。火光与晚霞相映，孩子们围绕着篝火嬉戏玩耍，那灿烂的笑脸被火映得通红……这是2万5千年前发生在北京王府井的场景。人们驻足在展厅的大型壁画前，与这个古老故事中的人们对话；这里是我们共同的家园，她会越来越美好！

参观指南

地　　址：北京市东城区东长安街1号，东方广场W1P3。
乘车路线：地铁王府井站A出口往东方广场方向；乘1、4、10、37、52、57、103、104、337、867、813、814路公交车王府井站或东单站下车，由王府井南口东方新天地第一街进入，在通往地铁站的通道内。
开放时间：周一至五10：00-16：30；周六至日10：00-18：30。
景　　价：10元；学生5元。
周边景观：北京工艺美术馆、王府井天主堂、中国美术馆、老舍故居。
咨询电话：010-85186306

Wangfujing Palaeoanthropology Cultural Relic Museum

In December, 1996, Yue Shengyang, the postgraduate of Peking University, came to the construction site of the Oriental Plaza situated at the south mouth of Wangfujing. A black charcoal mark drew his attention and then around the spot, he dug out the broken bones of animals and fragments beaten by humans. After the appraisal of the experts who come from Chinese Academy of Sciences, the site is the relic of late Old Stone Age, 24,000 or 25, 000 years ago. Distance between the site and the surface of the ground is 12 meters.

The discovery of palaeoanthropology relic in Wangfujing is the first time around the world discovering palaeoanthropology in the downtown of an international metropolis. On December, 28th, 2001, Wangfujing Palaeoanthropology Cultural Relic Museum was open to the public officially. The relic piece is a layer of earth 12 from the ground, in which there are needfire remains the human beings meters in remote antiquity left, such as charcoal ash pits, layer of charcoal bits and the spot where human beings in remote antiquity slew and dismembered animals. The stone products, bone products and the needfire remains are kept in their original look when they were unearthed.

Visitors Guide
Address: Oriental Plaza W1P3, No. 1, East Changan street in Dongcheng district of Beijing
Bus Route: from Exit A of the subway stop of Wangfujing to the direction of Oriental Plaza; Take No. 1, 4, 10, 37, 52, 57, 103, 104, 337, 867, 813, 814 bus to the stop of Wang—fujing or Dongdan, then enter the First Street of the Oriental Plaza and the museum is in the passage to the subway station.
Opening Hours: 10:00—16:30 (Monday to Friday); 10:00—18:30 (Saturday to Sun—day)
Admission Fee: RMB 10 Yuan, 5 Yuan (student)
Tel: 86—10—85186306

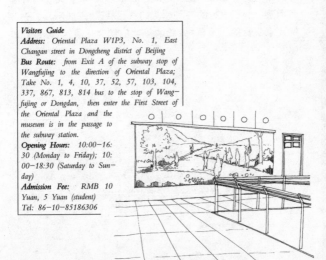

北京皇城艺术馆

皇城幽思

　　无论站在北京皇城艺术馆的哪个位置,或眺望紫禁城的琼楼玉宇,感受曾经的肃穆与威严;或背靠红墙,做一个飞天姿态,欲生翅翱翔万里长空,你都会别有一番悟味。

　　北京皇城始建于明代初叶,是四座城垣的第二重,内贴皇宫,外辐内外两城,内设衙署、宫殿、坛庙、御库、园囿等,拱卫和服务功能发挥极佳。天安门城楼、北海、景山、太庙(今劳动人民文化宫)、社稷坛(今中山公园)、普度寺等都位于皇城之内。这样的地域和空间,这样独特而又鲜明的历史文化和社会风情,说它是中华民族和全人类的共同遗产,也许找不到异议。

　　在将明清北京皇城整体申报世界文化遗产的同时,北京皇城艺术馆于 2003 年 6 月开馆。北京传统民居建筑,青砖灰瓦,朱漆大门;馆内小径曲幽,草碧竹清,古朴怡然之风拂面而来:前面是反映康乾盛世的铜雕,后面是八旗绿营护卫的盔甲;这里悬挂着精美的官服补子,那边是承载三百年历史的明皇城城砖;还有皇家气派的御用蜡烛、帘子、灯笼,展示宫廷戏曲文化悠久历史的钦点戏单,记载历史皇帝成长的玉牒圣训……也许只有在这个时候,你才理解了目不暇接的含义,但站在《光绪大婚档》画卷前,你是否已融入光绪皇帝大婚的空前盛况之中?至于那展示各地官员、商贾为了讨好皇帝而费尽心机进献的各种珍宝的贡品展区,那展示几近失传的北京观赏鸽以及鸽挎、鸽哨等物的鸽文化展区,你会放过吗?

参观指南

地　　址:北京市东城区菖蒲河公园内。

乘车路线:1、2、4、10、20、37、52、59、120、120 支、728、
　　　　　820、特 1 在天安门站下车;地铁在天安门东站
　　　　　下车。

开馆时间:9:00-16:30。

票　　价:成人 20 元;学生 10 元。

咨询电话:010-85115104

The Imperial City Art Museum

The imperial city of Beijing was initially built in early Ming Dynasty. It is the second of the four city walls. Adjacent to the imperial palace, it connects the exterior and interior cities. Inside the imperial city, there are departments, palaces, temples, warehouses and gardens. The defense and service functions are perfect in the city. The Tian An Men gate tower, Beihai park, Jingshan Hill, Imperial Ancestral Temple (now the Working People's Cultural Palace), Altar to the god of the land and grain (now the Zhongshan Park) and Pudu Temple are all situated inside the imperial city.

When the imperial city of Beijing on the whole applied for the World Cultural Heritages, Beijing imperial city art museum was open on June, 2003. Ahead are the copper sculptures and behind are the armors of the guards. Here hangs the exquisite official costume, and there displays the city brick recording the 300-year-old history of Ming Dynasty. The imperial candles, shades, lanterns, and play-bills, and jade inscriptions···treasures as tributes to the emperor and those pigeon whistles and other rare cultural items concerning pigeon culture, will you let them pass without giving a second glimpse?

Visitors Guide

Address: Inside the Puchanghe Park, Dongcheng District, Beijing

Bus Route: Bus No. 1、2、4、10、20、37、52、59、120、120 (branch)、728、8201 (special) to the bus stop of Tian'anmen, Underground Railway to the station of East Tian'anmen.

Opening Hours: 9:00–16:30

Admission Fee: RMB 20 Yuan (Adults), 10 Yuan (Students)

Tel: 86–10–85115104

北京新文化运动纪念馆

北京新文化运动纪念馆之魂魄 — 红楼

作为历史的见证,红楼理所当然承载了北京新文化运动纪念馆的重任。

民国年间,北京大学有三院,其中之一的文学院即是有名的红楼。民国初年建造的红楼,本想用作宿舍,但建成之后即改为文科教室,终于,红楼就与许多与文有关的知名人士比如蔡元培,比如陈独秀、毛泽东,比如胡适等结下了不解之缘。

作为中国新文化运动的滥觞之地,红楼的重要性数也数不清:民主与科学诞生在此,《新青年》北迁落刊在此,"外抗强权,内惩国贼"、"废除21条"等口号由此及彼,遍及中国,马克思主义与中国工人运动相结合,中国革命的"星星之火"由此点燃,燎遍了中华大地……

纪念馆正是以红楼深厚的文化底蕴和得天独厚的地理位置为依托,常年辟有专题陈列:蔡元培与北大红楼、新文化运动主将 — 陈独秀、新文化运动陈列等。

"逝者如斯","物是人非",挥之不去的"红楼",藏匿着太多的这座古城的一些叫人魂系梦萦的东西,一些让人不断回首的细节。

虽然这个城市日新月异,但不了解红楼,北京对你将始终是"雾里看花"。所以无论何时,你都可以到这儿来。历史在这里驻足等候你 — 听听它的声音,看看它的足印!

参观指南

地　　址:北京市东城区五四大街29号。

乘车路线:乘101、103、109、111、810、812、814、819、846等公交车于沙滩路站下车。

开放时间:8:30—16:30(周一休息)。

周边景观:东临中国美术馆,西接景山公园和故宫博物院,南行不远是王府井、东安市场,北行几步就是地安门、鼓楼。

票　　价:成人5元;团体(10人以上)4元;学生3元;老年人、残疾人、现役军人及中、小学生集体参观提前预约登记者均免票。

咨询电话:010-64024929

Beijing Memorial Hall of New Cultural Movement

The memorial hall is located on Wusi Street, Dongcheng District. Its original location is the red building of Peking University. The red building is the battalion for China's New Cultural Movement, and also the cradle for May 4th Movement in 1919.

Beijing Memorial Hall of New Cultural Movement is founded on the red building. Through displays, recovered scenes, journals, videos, it exhibits the history of New Cultural Movement in an all-round way. 90 pictures and 60 practicalities vividly tell the stories of the emergency of New Cultural Movement and the establishment of the Chinese Communist Party. On the first floor, office of Li Dazhao who acted as the director of Peking University Library at that time keeps its original look. The reading room in which Chairman Mao once worked and the big classroom where the students of Peking University studied are well reserved. In the display hall of journals, 20 kinds of journals and magazines belonging to National Museum of China published in that period are on display. Two special films made by the memorial hall respectively entitled May 4th Movement and The Former Residences of Celebrities in New Cultural Movement are put on in the video room.

Visitors Guide

Address: No.29 Wusi Street, Dongcheng District, Beijing

Bus Route: Bus No.101、103、109、111、810、812、814、819、846 to the stop of Shatanlu

Opening Hours: 8:30--16:30(Except Monday)

Admission Fee: RMB 5 Yuan for adults; 4 Yuan for groups(over 10 people); 3 Yuan for students.

Tel: 86-10-64024929

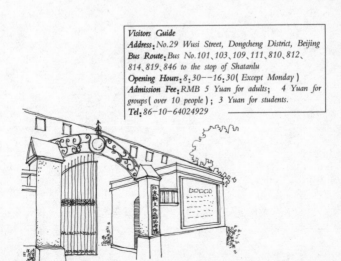

第二章 西城区

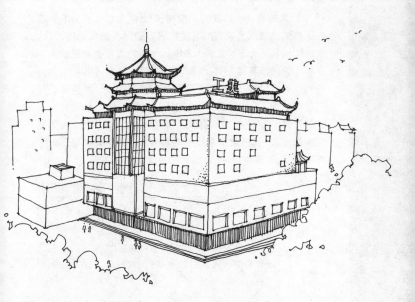

北京鲁迅博物馆

鲁迅，在这里伟大而平凡

　　有这样一位文学家，他的著作真实而深刻地反映中国人民近现代革命斗争的历史，也记录他的思想发展历程；有这样一位思想家，他用笔创造性地、深刻地分析各种社会问题，表现出高瞻远瞩的政治远见和坚韧不拔的战斗精神；有这样一位革命家，他积极参加革命文化活动，介绍马克思主义文艺理论，同反动文人反动文学进行不懈地斗争，成为中国文学革命的伟人，这就是鲁迅。

　　北京鲁迅博物馆是在鲁迅故居东侧建设的一座现代仿古建筑，1956 年 10 月 19 日在鲁迅逝世 20 周年纪念日正式开馆。后又增设鲁迅研究室，兴建新展厅、文物库房及其他配套设施，1996 年 10 月，在鲁迅逝世 60 周年、鲁迅博物馆成立 40 周年的日子里，鲁迅博物馆重新开放，以崭新的面貌迎接各界观众。

　　鲁迅博物馆里有一个长年陈列不动的文物 — 鲁迅故居。他于 1924 年买定并亲自设计改造，建成一座带有"老虎尾巴"和后院的独具特色的小四合院。这是鲁迅在北京居住 14 年之久的最后一处住所。与故居相互配合相互映衬的鲁迅生平陈列是鲁迅博物馆的基本内容。通过大量文物图片，这个陈列既表现鲁迅这位"代表中华民族的大多数向着敌人冲锋陷阵的民族英雄"（毛泽东语）的风采，又表现他甘愿做人民大众的牛，甘愿做培植鲜花的"腐草"的风范。真实再现鲁迅与同时代人（如胡适、林语堂等）的关系，同时也客观地反映其亲属、家人（如其弟周作人、其原配夫人朱安等）在他生活中的位置，通过全面系统的内容介绍，使参观者看到一个真实丰满、有爱有恨、伟大而平凡的鲁迅。

参观指南

地　　址：北京市西城区阜内大街宫门口二条 19 号。

乘车路线：13、42、102、103、409、603、709、814、823、846、
　　　　　850 路公交车或环线地铁阜成门站下。

自驾车线：沿长安街到复兴门桥往北到阜成门桥东北角。

开放时间：9:00-15:30。

票　　价：5 元；学生 3 元。

周边景观：白塔寺、历代帝王庙、中国地质博物馆、广济寺。

咨询电话：010-66156548

Lu Xun Museum

Lu Xun (1881 — 1936), born in Shaoxing, Zhejiang Province, is China's great modern litterateur, ideologist, and revolutionist. The museum houses nearly 30,000 items of cultural collections, among which 21,000 items belong to Mr. Lu Xun, including manuscripts, letters, diaries and his collect books, portrait bricks in Han Dynasty, and rubbings etc. The basic display in the museum is entitled Lu Xun's Life, which vividly displays the glorious achievements of Lu Xun, the general in generals in China's revolution on culture. Inside the museum, there is an exhibition reflecting the old scenes of Lu Xun's former residence, which is an exquisite quadrangle, with three rooms respectively in the west and in the east, and one room in the east and in the north. They are all kept their original looks. The south room is the parlor. The east and west rooms were respectively occupied by Lu Xun's mother and Madame Zhu An. The middle room is for dining. A small room facing the north with only 8 square meters was Lu Xun's bedroom and study, namely "The Tiger's Tail". Mr. Lu Xun called it "Greenwood Study" in which the furnishings are very simple.

Visitors Guide
Address: No.19 Gongmenkou Er-tiao, Funei Street, Beijing
Bus Route: 101、102、103、109、309、603(Branch)
Self-drive Route: Along Chang'an Street to Fuxingmen Bridge, then go North to Fuchenmen Bridge, the museum is northwest of the bridge.
Opening Hours: 9:00-15:30。
Admission Fee: RMB 5 Yuan; 3 Yuan for students
Tel: 86-10-66156548

民族文化宫博物馆

锦绣大地上的珍珠

民族文化宫博物馆坚持"为少数民族服务,为民族文化工作服务,为民族团结进步事业服务"的方针,在民族文物的搜集、整理、陈列、研究以及利用民族文物进行民族文化宣传等方面,作了大量有实效的工作,取得卓越成绩。民族文化宫博物馆于1959年9月建成并开放,拥有3800平方米的五个展览大厅, 一大批优秀的少数民族传统文化展览在这里举办,吸引着国内外广大观众的目光。

民族文化宫博物馆经过多年的调查、征集和整理,在世界妇女大会在北京召开之际,隆重推出"中国少数民族面具文化展览"。这次展览共展出各少数民族面具300余件,分为跳神面具、节祭面具、生命礼仪面具、镇宅面具和戏剧面具五部分,系统地展示了面具伴随各民族的宗教祭典、节令时序、生产居住、婚丧嫁娶及日常生活,传递了诸多历史、文化的信息。这一展览被学术界誉为中国面具文化研究的里程碑。

为了宣传藏传佛教文化,反映自古以来西藏与中央政府的关系,民族文化宫博物馆举办了"历世达赖班禅敬献中央政府礼品展"。展览分为达赖、班禅封号由来和与中央政府的关系,十四世班禅敬献的礼品和十一世班禅敬献的礼品三部分,近百件礼品及相关展品既有反映藏传佛教文化艺术博大精深的宗教器物,也有反映雪域高原丰富物产和人民勤劳智慧的生活用品。该展览先后在十多个城市巡回展示,在全国引起巨大反响。

民族文化宫博物馆的5万件馆藏文物,是中国56个民族镶嵌在祖国锦绣大地上的珍珠,在每个参观者的心头熠熠发光。

参观指南

地　　址:北京市西城区复兴门内大街49号。

乘车路线:长安街沿线公交车都能到达。

自驾车线:沿长安街到西单以西100米。

周边景观:西单商场、北京图书大厦、西单文化广场、首都时代广场。

周边餐饮:民族饭店、微山湖渔村、东方萨拉伯乐。

咨询电话:010-66024433,010-66019375

The Exhibition Hall of Ethnic Cultural Palace

The exhibition hall is located on West Chang'an Street of Beijing. It has unique constructions with distinct ethnic characteristics. Rated as one of the top ten architectures in 1950s, the exhibition hall houses over 40,000 cultural items and 5 display rooms with a coverage of 3,000m². In September 1994, the serial exhibition on China's minorities' traditional cultures-costumes, musical instruments, arts and crafts was launched. The exhibition is divided into three parts. The first part is about the ethnic costumes, differentiated by the long costumes and short costumes. The second part is about ethnic musical instruments. Ethnic minorities are usually good at singing and dancing. They have time-honored music history. Here you could see the deer whistles and flying dragon whistles used by the hunters of Ewenki nationality and Oroqen nationality and copper drums used by southern nationalities as well as the musical treasure of Uygur nationality-the whole set of musical instruments for the performance of "Shi Er Mu Ka Mu". The third part is about arts and crafts. Chinese ethnic minorities are clever and deft. Their art crafts are colorful and exquisite.

Visitors Guide

Address: No.49 Fuxingmennei Street, Beijing

Bus Route: Buses along Chang'an Street

Self-drive Route: along Chang'an Street to 100m west of Xidan

Nearby Sights: Xidan Marketplace、Beijing Book Building、Xidan Cultural Square、Capital Times Square

Nearby Restaurants:
Ethnic Restaurant、Weishanhu Fishing Village、East Salabole

Tel: 86-10-66024433、
86-10-66019375

中国地质博物馆

感谢地壳，感谢地球

地质学是研究地壳组织物质、各种地质作用以及地球的形成和发展的历史及其在人类社会生活中的应用等内容的一门科学。在地质学研究领域，中国人值得为此骄傲，因为我们有地质博物馆。

始建于 1916 年的中国地质博物馆在世界上享有盛名。其馆藏的 20 万件标本以历史悠久、典籍量大、真品率高、陈列精美、科研成果丰富称雄于亚洲。地球厅、矿物岩石厅、宝石厅、史前生物厅和国土资源厅五个基本陈列展厅数以万计的标本，昭示地球奥秘、阐释地学神奇。在这里，重达 3.5 吨的全球最大水晶单晶晶体、翡与翠完美结合的雕件、"中华龙鸟"等原始鸟类系列化石和世界上最高大的鸭嘴龙类化石——举行山东龙以及"北京人"、"山顶洞人"、"元谋人"等相关化石都是世界绝无仅有的藏品，更是这里的"镇馆之宝"。

中国地质博物馆的大厅里，从地面铺设的斑状花岗岩到立柱中间镶嵌的三叶虫化石，科普知识渗透在细微之处、点滴之中。声光电、多媒体、仿生、虚拟等技术使实景模拟更加科学生动，三维立体更加栩栩如生，数字地图更加大气磅礴，你可以通过亲身参与、亲手操作，轻松地步入精彩纷呈的地质学殿堂。

地球尽管很神奇，但平均厚度 35000 米的地球地壳已不堪重负，人类无休止地向地壳索取煤炭、石油、天然气、矿藏，还有水。所以，请你到中国地质博物馆来，看一看地壳为人类所做的贡献，也表达感谢地球、感谢地壳的心情，好吗？

参观指南

地　址：北京市西城区西四羊肉胡同 15 号。

乘车路线：乘 13、22、38、47、68、101、102、103、105、109、124、409、603、709、726、806、808、812、814、823、826、846、850 路公交车在西四站下车。

自驾车线：西四大街南北向禁止左转，由西单向北提前从西安门大街绕行西四东大街。

开放时间：9:00-16:30（周一休息）。

票　价：30 元；学生、军人、老年人半价。

周边景观：广济寺、历代帝王庙、白塔寺、鲁迅纪念馆、北海公园。

咨询电话：010-66557858

The Geological Museum of China

The Geological Museum of China, built in 1916, is world-renowned geological museum, boasting 200 thousand specimens. It has been the leading light among the same kind of Asian museums for its time-honored history, large number of ancient records, high percent of curiosities, delicate display and rich achievements in scientific research.

After more than 3 years of large-scale renovation, on July 14, 2004, the Geological Museum of China was reopened with a new look. Granite spreads on the floor of the hall and trilobite fossils are inlayed in the pillars. In the five major displaying halls (earth hall, mineral rock hall, gem hall, hall of life before history and hall of land and resources), displaying tens of thousands of precious specimens. Furthermore, the museum provides such service as specimen appraisal and consultation, specimen mending and experiment display. All the above activities show that the Geological Museum publicizes scientific knowledge from small points to explain the mystery of the earth and geology.

Visitors Guide
Address: Fujing Culture Street, Beijing
Bus Route: Bus No. 13, 22, 38, 47, 68, 101, 102, 103, 105, 109, 124, 409, 603, 709, 726, 806, 808, 812, 814, 823, 826, 846, 850 to Xisi Stop.
Self-drive Route: Start from Xidan to the north and then turn to the east Xisi Street from Xi'anmen Street.
Opening Hours: 9:00---16:30 (except Monday)
Admission Fee: RMB 30 Yuan; 15 Yuan for students, armymen and senior citizens
Tel: 86-10-66557858

中国古动物馆

触摸科学脉搏

这里有距今 5 亿多年前的古鱼类化石,也有在几万年前寒冷的冰河时代才灭绝的黄河古象等哺乳动物化石;这里有身长 22 米的庞然大物马门溪龙化石,也有小到在放大镜下才能看清的人类的祖先 — 祖先曙猿的下颌骨和牙齿化石;这里不乏曾为新闻热点的恐龙蛋化石,更有近年来最为世人瞩目的中生代鸟类化石……。如此类型齐全、量质具佳的国宝级自然遗产荟萃一堂,使得中国古动物馆在同类博物馆中雄居中国之先,亚洲之最。

中国古动物馆是中国科学院古脊椎动物与古人类研究所于 1994 年创建的国内唯一以动物化石为载体,系统普及地学、古生物学知识和生物进化知识的专题博物馆。馆藏展品近 20 万件,精品化石 600 余件,是我国四代科学家经过 70 多年的时间用心血和汗水采集而来的。为了使这些珍品发挥其科普功能,中国古动物馆相继在本馆内及其他城市举办"中国之最恐龙特展"、"中国恐龙巡回展"、"飞翔之歌 — 中国首届古鸟类化石展"、"香港 4 亿年前古鱼类展"、"南水北调中线工程丹江口水库淹没区古脊椎动物化石地点与古人类文化遗址调查成果展"等高水平展览,同时还聘请古脊椎动物与古人类研究所的科学家担任科学顾问,一方面为观众进行交流式的讲解,一方面到中小学去送科学知识上门。

也许你认为亿万年前的化石离当代生活是那么遥远,也许你感觉神秘的科学殿堂是那么不可企及,当你来到中国古动物馆,其实你已触摸到了科学的脉搏。

参观指南

地　　址:北京市西城区西直门大街 142 号。

乘车路线:27、105、107、714、特 4 路公交车。

开放时间:9:00-16:30(16:00 停止售票);周一闭馆;春节初一、初二、初三闭馆。

票　　价:20 元;学生、军人、离休人员 10 元。

周边餐饮:西苑饭店、德宝饭店。

周边景观:北京天文馆、北京动物园、北京展览馆、北京石刻艺术博物馆、国家图书馆、首都体育馆。

咨询电话:010-68935280

China Palaeozoological Hall

China Palaeozoological Hall is located on Xizhimenwai Street. It is a specialized national museum of natural science which gives a systemic introduction to the origin and development of vertebrates. The hall houses more than 200,000 fossil samples of vertebrates of various kinds in different regions. The basic displays are composed of four parts: Dinosaur World (electric mechanical simulation), Ancient Fish Hall, Ancient Reptile Hall, and Mammal Hall. The fossils and other means of display show the audience the origin and evolution of pre-historic vertebrates. Academic findings in the field and the fossils inlayed in the oceanic and land stratums formed in different periods are also on display. From the primitive jawless fish to the hard-bone and soft-bone fish, from amphibians to reptiles, from the past glorious dinosaur kingdom to the dominant mammal world, from ancient apes to Homo sapiens, various fossils will come into your eyes and tell you a clear outline of the development of vertebrates.

Visitors Guide

Address：*No.142 Xizhimen Street, Beijing*

Bus Route：*Bus No.27、105、107、714、4(special)*

Opening Hours：*9：00—16：30 （16：00 stop selling tickets）；close on Monday；Close on the first, the second and the third days of Lunar Calendar. Nearby Sights*：*Xiyuan Restaurant、Debao Restaurant*

Admission Fee：*RMB 20 Yuan；10 Yuan for students, army men, and retired people*

Tel：*86—10—68935280*

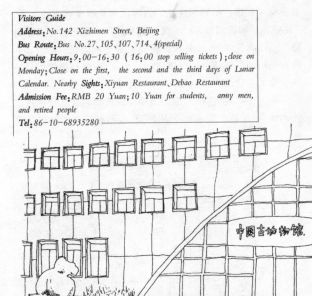

中国科学技术馆

科技教育的殿堂

中国是科学技术的文明古国，但是在近现代，中国的科学技术同世界先进国家拉开了距离。新中国的建立为科学技术的发展鼓起了浩荡的东风，尤其是改革开放以来，科学技术插上腾飞的翅膀，向着精尖领域，向着国际先进水平奋起直追。

中国科学技术馆的建设凝聚了周恩来、邓小平等国家领导人以及周培源、钱学森等驰名科学家的夙愿。1988年建设完成的一期工程只实现了科技馆功能的很小部分，无论在功能还是规模上，尚未形成真正意义上的国家科技馆。建筑面积达4万平方米的二期工程为中国科技馆更好地为首都和全国人民服务，不断地充实馆存藏品，提高展览水平提供了一个广阔的舞台，为中国科技馆走向世界奠定了坚实的基础。

在科学技术方面，中国古代曾经创造过辉煌的成就，四大发明对世界文明的进步起了伟大作用。但是祖先的成就只能用来坚定中国人赶超世界先进水平的信心，而不能用来抚慰现实的落后。中国科技馆把展览内容与世界科学发展中的前沿领域和热点问题相结合，以推动国家科技事业的发展。"环境保护科普展览"、"克隆科普展览"、"南极科学考察展览"、"飞向天空－火星探测展览"等一系列展览把中国和世界最新的科学研究成果展现给广大观众，使科技馆的社会科学教育为建设科技强国发挥推动作用。

今天，中国科学技术馆肩负中华民族科学普及和科技创新的使命，正以无限的聪明和智慧，在科技强国的大道上迅跑。

参观指南

地　　址：北京市西城区北三环中路1号。

乘车路线：乘21、300、302、361、367、387、407、422、702、
　　　　　718、725、730、731、734、735、801、825、830、831、
　　　　　835、967、运通101、运通104等路公交车于中
　　　　　国科技馆下。

开放时间：9：00-16：00，周一闭馆。

票　　价：30元；学生20元；周二至周五（寒暑假除外）
　　　　　儿童由家长陪同免票。

咨询电话：010-62371177

China Science and Technology Museum

China Science and Technology Museum on northern section of the 3rd Ring Road is China's first state-class comprehensive science and technology museum. The audience can view China's glorious scientific and technological achievements in the hall of China's traditional ancient technology. In the hall of modern science and technology, the audience can operate some instruments by themselves. The displays of modern science and technology-electromagnetism, mechanics, heat, acoustics, optics, nuclear technology and information technology-are organized to encourage participation.

The sphere screen cinema inside the museum is China's first OMNOMAX cinema, where the audience can enjoy the high-tech movies. The screen is double spherical surfaces with a diameter of 27 m. Six four-track acoustics and scenes beyond visions make the audience fail to locate the brim of the screen as if they themselves were in the scenes. The museum exhibits China's ancient achievements and modern science and technology. It reveals the secrets of nature and records the explorations of the Chinese people on the track of civilization.

Visitors Guide

Address： No.1 middle section of North Third Ring Road, Beijing

Bus Route： Bus No. 380、409、8(special)

Opening Hours： 9：00—16：00, close on Monday

Admission Fee： RMB 30 Yuan；20 Yuan for students；From Tuesday to Friday (except summer and winter vacations), children with their parents' company are ticket-free.

Tel： 86-10-62371177

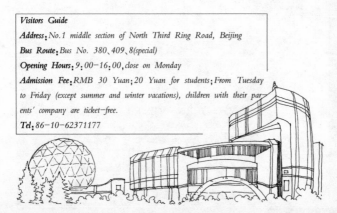

宋庆龄故居

让你入梦

先生从这里启程,走向自己心中的天堂,走向那云霓绚烂的西天,她的脚步是那样从容稳健,她的神情是那样安详仁慈,让为她送行的人都泪水涟涟、依依不舍;先生从这里启程,离开了自己生活工作近 20 年的庭院,离开了她无限眷恋的人民。

宋庆龄故居坐落在北京风景秀丽的什刹海后海北沿。门前水天相映,波光潋滟;院内楼堂亭榭,曲径回廊,山石嶙峋。绿树为湖面系上翡翠绿带;花香引来鸟儿呢喃,好一处雍容典雅、幽静别致的庭院。但是,这里居住的主人比优美景色更出神入化。《宋庆龄生平展》向人们展示了她一生的丰功伟绩;"鲜花代门票"活动让人民的爱戴之情得以尽情抒发。她和孙中山先生的合影,她和毛泽东主席的合影是她前半生的伟大和后半生的伟大的生动写照,她结婚时母亲送的"百子图"被面寄托着青春的梦想,她曾佩戴过的小手枪真实地记录着生命的历程,也曾美丽,也曾艰辛,也曾雄壮,也曾幸福。把"濠梁乐趣"那曾有的笑声记录下来;把"畅襟斋"里那坚定的语音记录下来;在"听鹂轩",先生思考的大脑仍在运转;在"恩波亭",先生炯炯的双目仍在眺望。来这里参观的人无限缅怀她的光辉业绩和崇高精神,每移动一次脚步都似乎能感到她的足迹中那种无形的力量。先生的身躯虽然离开了这里,但是她的人格仍在闪耀光辉。

参观归来,故居的王府历史让你入梦;先生的照片文物让你入梦;先生的音容笑貌让你入梦;先生给你的美丽和幸福让你入梦。

参观指南

地　　址:北京市西城区后海北沿 46 号。

乘车路线:乘 5、27、44、55、345 路公交车德胜门站,地铁积水潭站下车。

开放时间:5 月 1 日-10 月 31 日　9:00-17:30;
　　　　　11 月 1 日-4 月 30 日　9:00-16:30。

票　　价:20 元;大学生 10 元;中小学生 5 元;老年人 10元(70 岁以上免票)。

周边景观:徐悲鸿纪念馆、郭沫若纪念馆、广化寺、什刹海、恭王府。

咨询电话:010-64073653

The Former Residence of Mme Soong Ching Ling

The Former Residence of Mme Soong Ching Ling is situated at the northern side of the Houhai Lake characterized by lovely scenery. Originally it was the family garden of Prince Chun, and the main buildings include the antehall named "Haoliang Lequ", the rear hall "Changjinzhai" (Mind-Broadening Hall), the side hall "Tinglixu-an"(the Hall for Listening to the Orioles),   the east chamber "Guan-huawu" (the Place for Enjoying Followers).   The west chamber is connected with the main building which was newly-built and a cov-ered corridor linking them to the Southern Building across a lake. The antehall named "Haoliang Lequ" fully displays Soong's contri-butions in democratic revolution before the establishment of the PRC in 1949.   The hall named "Changjinzhai" displays her great achievements in socialist construction since 1949.   400 pictures and 300 materials concerning Soong's life are on display in these tow halls,   including her photos with Sun Zhongshan,   photos with Mao Zedong in Chongqing, her wedding quilt embroidered "100 sons and daughters" given by her mother, and her pistol etc. All these precious photos and materials record Soong Ching Ling's glorious life with hardships.

Visitors Guide

Address: *No.46 North Side of the Houhai Lake, Xicheng District, Beijing*

Bus Route: *Bus No.5、27、44、55、345 to the Deshengmen Stop, subway to Jishuitan Station*

Opening Hours: *May 1−Oct 31   9:00−17:30;*

Nov.1−April 30   9:00−16:30

Admission Fee: *RMB 20 Yuan;10 Yuan for college students;5 Yuan for primary and middle school students;10 Yuan for seniors（Free for seniors over 70）*

Tel: *86−10−64073653*

北京天文馆

天体在人类心中

北京天文馆是中国内地唯一一座以向公众普及和宣传天文学知识为主的大型专业化科普场馆。开馆40多年来,创编上演了近百部天象节目,举办了80多个不同规模的天文展览,每年都吸引着大量观众和青少年天文爱好者前来参观学习。"恐龙灭绝及天体碰撞"从天文因素讲述及岩石恐龙灭绝的原因;"一个外星人的宇航笔记"讲述一个"外星人"走访太阳系,由远到近认识太阳系内九大行星,最后到达地球,告诫人类要珍惜和爱护赖以生存的地球。"地球外面有生命吗?"反映人类探寻地外生命所付出的不懈努力和目前进展,告知人们探寻地外生命是人类永远的课题。

北京天文馆现有两座天文观测台,既可以对外开放,让观众直接用望远镜观测天体,还承担着观测太阳黑子的科研任务。东侧太阳色球观测台上的色球望远镜对公众开放,参观者可以通过望远镜直接观测到太阳色球层和日珥喷发等现象。西侧天文台承担科研任务,40多年来积累了相当丰富的有价值的太阳黑子资料。此外,北京天文馆还收藏有国内外各种陨石和宇宙尘,是中国国内收藏陨石品种最多的地方。

中国是天文学发达最早的国家之一,日食、月食、太阳黑子、彗星、流星雨、新星、超新星等天文现象都是中国予以最早和最丰富的记载。如果你去过北京天文馆,你就会感觉到,整个天体都应该是在人类心中。

参观指南
地　　　址:北京市西城区西直门外大街138号。
乘车路线:公交车动物园站下。
开放时间:周三至周五　9:00-16:30;周二"数字宇宙"
　　　　　专场10:00-16:30;周六至周日　8:30-16:30。
周边景观:紫竹院公园、动物园等。
周边餐饮:奥林匹克饭店、滨海大排档、西苑饭店、金爵大
　　　　　酒家等。
票　　　价:10元;学生5元;学生团体(50人以上)免费;
　　　　　周二"数字宇宙"专场50元。
咨询电话:010-68312570

Beijing Planetarium

Beijing Planetarium is located on the Xizhimenwai Street. Specialized in natural science, it is Asia's first planetarium open to the public since September, 1957. The uniquely designed white building and the hemisphere copper roof will leave you a wonderful impression. The planetarium is composed of the Celestial Phenomena Hall, the Video Room and the Observatory. The Celestial Phenomena Hall's diameter is 23.5 meters. On the hemisphere screen inside the hall, you could watch various mysterious celestial phenomena, such as meteors, meteor showers, auroras, Halley's Comet and other rarely seen astronomical phenomena···besides that, you could see the star skies of various times and on different locations. It will be a truly wonderful star journey. If you still feel reluctant to leave, you could go to the small observatory to observe macula, Ring Mountains and red spots of the Jupiter and the halo of the Saturn through the advanced refractor. The planetarium records the glorious journey of China's astronomical development as well as the relentless efforts and explorations of people in the circle of astronomy.

Visitors Guide
Address: No. 138 Xizhimenwai Street, Beijing
Bus Route: Buses to Beijing Zoo
Opening Hours: Wednesday to Friday 9:00−16:30; Tuesday 10:00−16:30
Digital Universe: Saturday and Sunday 8:30−16:30
Nearby Sights: Zizhuyuan Park and Beijing Zoo
Nearby Restaurants: Olympic Restaurant、Binhai Restaurant、Xiyuan Restaurant、Jinjue Restaurant
Admission Fee: RMB 10 Yuan; 5 Yuan for students; Free for student group with over 50 students; 50 Yuan for Digital Universe on Tuesday
Tel: 86−10−68312570

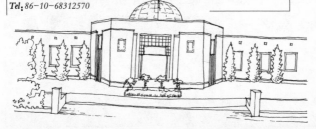

徐悲鸿纪念馆

人民景仰的艺术大师

徐悲鸿先生是中国卓越的绘画艺术大师、杰出的美术教育家。新中国成立以后,曾任中央美术学院院长、中华全国美术工作者协会主席。坐落在北京市新街口北大街的徐悲鸿纪念馆让无数美术爱好者痴迷。

徐悲鸿纪念馆建筑面积 3250 平方米,馆内藏品 2400 余件,徐悲鸿先生的画作及其他文物为馆藏珍品的主体。1995年是徐悲鸿先生诞辰 100 周年,纪念馆举办的"纪念徐悲鸿诞辰 100 周年艺术大展"在中国美术馆隆重开幕,之后又相继在上海、南京、泉州及徐悲鸿先生的故乡江苏宜兴开展,徐悲鸿博大精深的艺术成就和为推动中国美术事业健康发展所做出的贡献感动了无数观众。

徐悲鸿先生少年刻苦学画,后又留学法国。在绘画创作上提倡"尽精微,致广大",对中国画画风的变化起了倡导作用。他擅长油画、中国画,尤其精于素描,又融合中西画技,自成特征面貌,所画花鸟、风景、走兽,简洁明快,富有生气,以画马驰誉中外,赢得了中外人士的高度赞誉。来自法国、韩国、日本、新加坡、马来西亚、越南、美国等十余个国家的访问团来参观徐悲鸿纪念馆。前印度总理拉·甘地的夫人索尼亚参观时盛赞徐悲鸿"用绘画把我们两个古老国家联系起来"。欧洲国家捷克也在徐悲鸿诞辰 100 周年的时候举办"徐悲鸿艺术大展"。徐悲鸿是中国人民的画家,但是他的作品已走出国门,走向世界,成为许多国家人民景仰的艺术大师。

在徐悲鸿诞辰 110 周年来临之际,将会有更多的人来到这里,缅怀大师的成就,瞻仰大师的风采。

参观指南

地　　址:北京市西城区新街口北大街53号。

乘车路线:乘 22、38、47、626、726、409、709、810、826 路公
　　　　　交车在新街口豁口站下或地铁积水潭站下。

自驾车线:二环豁口往南或积水潭往东;西四平安里往北;
　　　　　西直门到新街口丁字路口往北。

开放时间:9:00-16:00,周一休息。

票　　价:5元;大学生3元;中小学生免费。

周边景观:宋庆龄故居、郭守敬纪念馆。

咨询电话:010-62252042

Xu Beihong Memorial Hall

Xu Beihong (1895-1953) is China's famous painter and an out-standing art educationist. When appreciating the immortal master-pieces of Mr. in the exhibition hall, we will be moved by his noble ethos penetrating through his works. The large-scale traditional Chinese painting entitled "A Man Named Jiufanggao" is a reflection of Xu Beihong's deep concern with the nation's destiny and his longing for bright future. The painting "Yvgong Moves the Mountain" created in 1940 aimed to encourage the Chinese people to strive for the final victory of the Anti-Japanese War. "Tianheng 500 Soldiers" sings high praises for the determination of the Chinese people. Horse paintings created by Xu Beihong embody his own feelings. Along with the lions and the roasters in his paintings, horses are symbols of a fighting spirit. Besides that, we could see the great artistic strengths of Xu Beihong from his 100 line drawings. The collections of the memorial hall include a masterpiece entitled "87 Immortals" and other excellent works.

Visitors Guide

Address: No.53 Xinjiekou North Street, Xicheng District, Beijing

Bus Route: Bus No.22、103、409、709 or subway to the Jishuitan station

Self-drive Route: Drive south from the exit of 2rd Ring Road or east from Jishuitan; Drive north from Xisi or Ping'anli; drive north at the crossing linking Xizhimen and Xinjiekou

Opening Hours: 9,00-16,00, close on Monday

Admission Fee: RMB 5 Yuan; 3 Yuan for college students; free for primary and middle school students

Tel: 86-10-62252042

郭沫若纪念馆

永远的郭沫若

1954 年的一天，郭沫若为祝福患病的夫人于立群早日康复，与孩子们共同种下一棵银杏树，并把它命名为"妈妈树"。当 9 年后郭沫若全家迁入这里时，"妈妈树"也移植过来，成为庭院里深情意浓的一景。

石头狮子本是摆在大门外驱鬼避邪的，难免给人一种凶煞的感觉。然而这位现代鸿儒把一对石狮子放进了草坪，仿佛在与人嬉戏玩耍，园中还有石洗、古钟相匹，不经意间映衬出主人的洒脱。

郭沫若在这里走完了他风雨人生的最后 15 年，庭院处处浸染着他诗人的浪漫情怀，也饱含着十年动乱中祖国遭劫、儿子罹难的切肤之痛。庭院的静谧中，一代文豪把放歌天上街市的思绪隐藏，把祈祷凤凰涅槃的心扉关闭，把后皇嘉树、桔徕服兮的兴致掩饰，把胡笳十八拍的情趣埋葬，主人只有默默低泣，汩汩泪水。虽然如此，但诗人仍在垂暮之年用心血写出"大快人心事"的诗句，因为诗人自有诗人的情怀。

百年的过往烟云，留下现在的清幽故园。这里曾是蒙古人民共和国的大使馆，这里曾是国母宋庆龄先生的寓所。作为这里最后的主人，郭沫若把自己的身心连同柔黄的连翘、含羞似雪的海棠、娇艳华贵的牡丹、淡雅的紫藤、如火的凌霄一同铺就在这个庭院。虽然主人辞别这里已经 27 年，但这里依然郁郁葱葱、群花烂漫。《郭沫若的文学世界》、《郭沫若与中国史学》、《郭沫若的人生历程》的展览向世人讲述他在文史领域的成就贡献以及追求理想、以身报国、与时代同息共命的人生之路。

这里有永远的郭沫若。

参观指南

地　　址：北京市西城区前海西街 18 号。

乘车路线：13、107、111、118、701、810、823、850、850 支路公交车北海后门站下。

开放时间：9：00-16：30（周一闭馆）；每周二、五，预约免费接待未成年人团体观众；每年最后一个周二至次年农历初三为冬季修整期，预约接待团体观众。

票　　价：8 元；学生 4 元。

周边景观：恭王府、什刹海、北海公园、广化寺。

咨询电话：010-66125392、010-66125984

Guo Moruo Memorial Hall

On the Qianhai West Street inside Shichahai Scenic Spot, there is a quadrangle in good preservation. It was here that Guo Moruo, a great writer of his time, spent the last 15 years of his life full of ups and downs. The living room, the office, the bedroom used by Guo Moruo when he was alive and the scriptorium used by his wife Yu Liqun are kept in the original state. The east and the west wing-rooms and the backroom are opened as exhibition rooms. The exhibition in the east wing-room is entitled "the Literary World of Guo Moruo", which includes three subjects: "Prose and Poems", "Historical Plays" and "Translation Works"; the exhibition in the west room is entitled "Guo Moruo and Chinese History", which includes four subjects: "China's Ancient Society Study", "Exploration of Chinese Ancient Languages", "Criticism on the Men of Great Learning in Pre-Qin Period" and "A Review of Historical Figures". Seeing the two exhibitions, visitors can catch a glimpse of Guo Moruo's literary and historical achievements and contributions. "Life's Journey of Guo Moruo" in the backroom tell the visitors his 86-year life story during which he aspires after his lofty ideal, devotes his life to our country and keeps apace with the times.

Visitors Guide:
Address: No. 18, Qianhai West Street, Beijing
Bus Route: Bus No.13, 107, 111, 118, 701, 810, 823, 850 to the stop of the North Door of Beihai Lake
Opening Hours: 9:00−16:30(close on Monday); pupil groups can visit on Tuesday and Friday free from charge by reservation; the period from the last Tuesday of the year to the 3rd of the first month of the lunar calendar in the next year is the winter renovation period and group visitors should visit by appointment.
Admission Fee: RMB 8 Yuan, 4 Yuan (student)
Tel: 86−10−66125392, 66125984

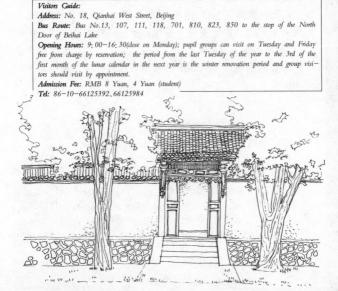

梅兰芳纪念馆

儒香四溢的院落

京剧《洛神》中的宓妃，《宇宙锋》中的赵艳蓉，《贵妃醉酒》中的杨玉环，《霸王别姬》中的虞姬，众多生动优美的艺术形象永远铭刻在中国人的记忆中。塑造这些艺术形象的大师就曾经在这里居住11年之久。

梅兰芳纪念馆是一座典型的北京四合院，每年接待着许多国内外参观者，是中国戏曲文化的一个窗口。纪念馆陈列的内容主要是梅兰芳先生家属捐赠的物品中精选出具有代表意义的图片、资料、纪念品和实物。多层次、多角度地展示他舞台艺术以及对中国戏剧所做的贡献。为适应当代人们的审美需求，每年都要将部分陈列内容进行调整，使陈列展览更好地展示京剧艺术的瑰丽。

梅兰芳8岁学戏，11岁登台，善演青衣、花旦、刀马旦等角色的人物。在长期的舞台实践中，对京剧旦角的唱腔、念白、舞蹈、音乐、服饰、化妆等方面都有创造发展，形成独特的艺术风格，世称"梅"派。梅兰芳在20世纪30年代至50年代，曾多次赴日、美、苏等国进行文化交流。抗日战争时期，留居香港、上海等地，蓄须明志，拒绝演出，具有坚强的民族气节。纪念馆通过大量图片、照片、史料、实物，全面系统地将梅兰芳的传奇经历、思想精神及生活情趣展现给参观者。

在这座具有古朴、典雅、恬静风格的老北京四合院里，参观者全神贯注地看着每一件馆藏珍品。梅兰芳那优美的扮相，圆润的嗓音，流畅大方的唱腔把人们的思绪带出这个儒香四溢的院落，带入享受中国传统戏曲艺术之美的那个空间。

参观指南

地　　址：北京西城区护国寺街9号。

乘车路线：22、38、47、409、626、709、726、826、826支路公交车护国寺站下车，进护国寺；13、42、55、68、107、111、118、204、701、810、823、850、850支路公交车于厂桥站下车，向北进护国寺。

开放时间：9:00-16:00(周一闭馆)。

周边景观：宋庆龄故居、新街口商业区、恭王府花园、郭沫若故居。

票　　价：6元；学生3元。

咨询电话：010-66183598、010-66180351

The Memorial Hall of Mei Lanfang

The hall is located on the Huguosi Street, Xicheng District, Beijing. It is a typical quadrangle with double courtyards where Mei Lanfang spent his last ten years.

The front courtyard is for exhibition. Photos and practicalities on display retell the art career of Mei Langfang who started to learn Peking Opera at the age of eight and made his debut at eleven. Mei performed the female roles and gained enormous popularity. He became chairman of China Federation of Literary and Art Circles and China Federation of Drama Societies as well as president of China Drama Academe since 1949, and he made great contributions to the prosperity and development of China's art cause.

Inside the parlor, visitors can find the hardwood furniture Mr. Mei once used and his mirror and pigeon whistles. On the wall is a painting entitled 13 Treasures in Tongguang created by Shen Rongpu in the Qing Dynasty. The living room is behind the parlor. The east penthouse is the bedroom and the west penthouse is the study. The west wing-room is opened for exhibition on Mr. Mei's cultural achievements. The east wing-room is the video room for showing the performances of Mei Lanfang.

Visitors Guide

Address: No.9, Huguosi Street, Xicheng District, Beijing

Bus Route: Bus No. 22,38,47,409,709,726,806,810,826 to the Huguosi stop and Bus No. 13,42,55,107,111,118,701, 823,850 to the Changqiao stop

Opening Hours: 9:00−16:00, close on Monday

Nearby Sights: the former residence of Song Qingling, Xinjiekou commercial zone, Gongwangfu Garden and the former residence of Guo Moruo

Admission Fee: RMB 6Yuan; 3 Yuan for students

Tel: 86−10−66183598,66180351

北京市古代钱币展览馆

从"贝币"到"通宝"的故事

　　现代人的功利思想和行为无不浸透在社会生活的方方面面。在大大小小的城市,不同的钱币市场中,淘金者熙熙攘攘,热闹非凡,他们热衷于对古钱币的收藏、研究和交易。然而,有谁会意识到古钱币也是中华民族文化的一部分呢?

　　北京市古钱币展览馆内的藏品把中华民族历史的悠久和文化的浩瀚昭示得那么真切。黄帝、秦汉、隋唐、金宋、明清,一枚枚古钱币把古老民族的岁月映得如此辉煌,说奇,说妙,说深,说厚,都显得词不达意。古钱币文化源远流长,光芒万丈,不正是中华民族文化的海纳百川的写照吗?那些展品,诸如贝币、秦半两、汉五铢、唐开元、宋通宝以及历代的钱币,无不诠释着时代的兴废。林林总总的近代纸币,在图案、文字、品相之间凝刻着时代的铅华与艰涩。小小的形貌与版面,如云卷云舒,如海纳百川,一种独有的艺术张力,给观者以美的享受。

　　也许是古钱币展览馆设在古老的德胜门箭楼的缘故,使这天圆地方的小小钱币把明太祖朱元璋"兴仁义之师"推翻元朝的丰功伟业也蕴含其中,参观者有意无意之间履行了一次与先人的对话,一次续写故事的循流溯源,把亘古与现实都穿透在自己心中。古钱币的历史足迹中,德胜门箭楼仍然顶天立地般的伟岸,箭楼垛口的浩荡春风中,古钱币的文化艺术把中华民族的精神浓缩与沉积。

　　这就是从"贝币"到"通宝"的故事。

参观指南

地　　址:北京市西城区北二环路德胜门箭楼。

乘车路线:乘5、27、44、55、315、345、380、409、815、819、820、919路公交车德胜门站下车。

开放时间:9:00-16:00(周一闭馆)。

参观购物:德胜门钱币市场、德泉斋钱币商店。

周边景观:什刹海景区、郭守敬纪念馆、徐悲鸿纪念馆、钟鼓楼、宋庆龄故居。

票　　价:10元;北京市中小学生免票。

咨询电话:010-62018073

Beijing Ancient Currency Exhibition Hall

The Chinese cultures are great and brilliant. In particular, the culture of currency is resplendent of long standing. It is the witness to the history, reflecting the economic blending among nations, countries and regions. Through the development of the currencies, the vicissitudes in the history and the grandness of the culture have been detected. The ancient currency exhibition puts on the show of Chinese 5000-year-old civilization and gives full play to the charms of ancient currencies. The glories of Qin, Han, Sui, Tang, Jin, Song, Ming, Qing Dynasties have been retrieved. Shell currency, Banliang in Qing Dynasty, Wuzhu in Han Dynasty, Kaiyuan in Tang Dynasy, Zhenglong in Jin Dynasty, Hongwu in Ming Dynasty, Tongbao in Qing Dynasties are the names of currency, all reflecting the changes of the times. The contemporary bank note, its design and characters represent the revolutionary optimism featuring constantly striving to be stronger and believing in the bright future of the revolution. On a small piece of note contains many bearings. The currencies are of great artistic charms that give the audience great pleasures.

Visitors Guide

Address: Deshengmen, North Second Ring Road, Beijing

Bus Route: Bus No.5、27、44、55、315、345、380、409、815、819、820、919 to Deshengmen

Opening Hours: 9:00—16:00, Close on Monday

Shopping: Deshengmen currency market、Dequanzhai currency store

Nearby Sights: Shichahai Scenic Spot

Admission Fee: RMB 10Yuan; Primary and middle school students in Beijing are free from change.

Tel: 86-10-62018073

北京白塔寺管理处

回望白塔寺

走进白塔寺文物保管所，"藏传万佛造像艺术展"中6000多件套展品，让参观者目不暇接。元明清三代近万尊藏传佛教遗像，囊括了藏传佛教各种风格的造像精品，从一个方面折射出中华文化的浩博与精深。

白塔寺即为妙应寺，妙应寺白塔是中国著名的喇嘛塔，始建于元代至元八年（1271年）。塔高50多米，通体皆白，故称作白塔。塔下有三层台基，台基上覆莲托位平面圆形塔身，再往上为塔脖、十三天、青铜宝盖和宝顶。白塔比例匀称，气势磅礴，是藏传佛教喇嘛塔的代表作。1980年，白塔寺文物保管所对外开放，尤其是近几年来，白塔寺的修缮、保护与利用进入了一个全新的历史发展时期。

"白塔寺珍藏文物展"是为复建后的白塔寺正式对社会开放而举办的展览，主要展示了乾隆十八年（1753年）敬装塔顶的数十件文物，其中的赤金舍利长寿佛、五佛冠等均为国家一级文物，价值无法衡量。人们站在展柜前，一座座栩栩如生的佛像，一件件世间罕见的文物吸引着参观者的目光。透过这些展品，藏传佛教的妙谛也潜移默化地浸润着人们的心灵。正因如此，它在广阔的地域上生根开花，中国的西藏、内蒙地区及不丹、锡金、尼泊尔、蒙古等国家是主要传播地域。值得一提的是，妙应寺的白塔还是尼泊人阿尔尼格设计的呢！

走出白塔寺的山门，回望寺内钟鼓楼的配殿，参观者心中自然生成楹联一幅：

古树白塔蓝天成一帧佛家绝响，

葱郁巍然清彻藏无限世间妙景。

参观指南

地　　址：北京市西城区阜成门内大街171号。

乘车路线：13、42、101、102、103、409、603、709、812、814、823、846、850路公交车白塔寺站下或环线地铁阜成门站下。

开放时间：9：00-17：00（16：30停止售票）。

门　　票：成人10元，学生5元。

咨询电话：010-66133317、66176164

White Dagoba Temple

Miaoying Temple, also named White Dagoba Temple, got its name because there is a white dagoba in the temple. The temple is composed of Tianwang Hall, Yizhu Xinjing Hall, Qifo Hall, Jvliu Shentong Hall and the temple courtyard. Jvliu Shentong Hall retains its original pattern, inside which there are wooden carvings of Sakyamuni, Amitabha, and Medicine Buddha. On the east and west walls, there are eight portraits of Buddha dharma protectors in Tibetan Buddhism. The white dagoba is 50.9 meters high, exquisite and spectacular. At present, the gate of the temple has been renovated and there is an exhibition on precious cultural relics housed in the temple. Many precious cultural relics found at the top of the dagoba, such as sutras written by Emperor Qianlong, an exquisite golden Buddha statue, a Buddha coronet and a cassock decorated with over a thousand of jewelries and a colorful hada etc. All the cultural relics are of best quality and extraordinary techniques. The art exhibition on Tibetan Buddha statues displays nearly ten thousand of bronze, gilded statues made in Yuan, Ming and Qing dynasties.

Visitors Guide

Address: No.171 Fuchengmennei Street, Xicheng District, Beijing

Bus Route: Bus No. 13、42、101、102、103、409、603、709、812、814、823、846、850 to the stop of White Pagoda Temple or subway to Fuchengmen Station

Opening Hours: 9:00—17:00 (16:30 stop selling tickets)

Tel: 86—10—66133317、66176164

郭守敬纪念馆

他为北京留下一个美丽的地方

　　融新建与古建于一体的汇通祠,造型古朴素雅,是北京什刹海风景区内的一座仿古建筑,郭守敬纪念馆就建在祠内。正是由于郭守敬一生对水利事业的成就与贡献,他的纪念馆建在俗称镇水观音庵的汇通祠里,才别有一番意义。

　　纪念馆分三个展厅向游人展示我国元代水利专家郭守敬的功绩和生平,详细地介绍他一生大部分时间从事水利事业,足迹踏遍半个中国,尤其对大都(今北京)水利建设的贡献最为突出,他总结了前人的经验教训,提出重开金口河,为元大都的建设提供了一条十分经济的水路运输线。他领导开发了元大都水源白浮堰,开凿由通州到大都积水潭的大运河最北端码头通汇河工程(今北京什刹海)。并且根据地型地貌变化和水位落差,在运河中设闸坝、斗门,解决了运河的水量问题,便于船舶返航,促进了元大都的经济发展。纪念馆展厅里,布置着元大都水利设施的模型,并用灯光显示通汇河、坝河及白浮堰的丰姿。

　　郭守敬不仅是水利专家,还是中国古代著名的天文学家、数学家。他编制《授时历》,创造和改进十余件观测天象的仪器,在当时引起轰动。纪念馆用图片资料及其他文物向观众展示这位元代科学家影响中国700年所走过的道路。

　　人们走进这座二进四合院里,看着郭守敬的画像,遥想当年他带领众人顶烈日冒严寒,测量勘察栉风沐雨的场景。其实700年后,人们仍在感谢郭守敬,感谢他为北京留下了一个如此美好的地方。

参观指南

地　　址:北京市西城区德胜门西大街甲60号。

乘车路线:55、305、315、815、946路公交车德胜门站下。

开放时间:8:30-17:00。

周边景观:后海公园、人定湖公园、什刹海、宋庆龄同志故居。

周边餐饮:华天小吃、德义居、旺火居麻辣烫、紫金城酒家。

票　　价:5角。

咨询电话:010-66183083

Memorial Museum of Guo Shoujing

Memorial Museum of Guo Shoujing, located in the Huitong Temple north of Xihai, is a theme person memorial of social science.

The memorial museum has three halls, displaying the achievements of Guo Shoujing, the astronomer and scientist on water conservancy of Yuan Dynasty in China. Guo Shoujing formulated Shoushi Calendar that inferred there are 365.3425days a year, and took charge of the making of more than ten astronomical instruments, such as the abridged armilla, yangyi, gaobiao, etc. These achievements are made 300 years earlier than that of Europe. Guo Shoujing's major achievements are in water conservancy, which can be seen from the exhibit of "Guo Shoujing and Dadu water resources". He spent most of his time conducting water conservancy. He went around half of China and harnessed over a hundred rivers and lakes. He played a leading role in Dadu water conservance, taking charge of the development of Baifuyan and Huihe River as the water resource of Dadu, which promoted the economic development of Yuan Dadu. Besides, there are models of water pass in Yuan Dynasty, iron anchors of foodstuff ships and some books concerned. Guo Shoujing's water harnessing achievements in Hebei are also introduced.

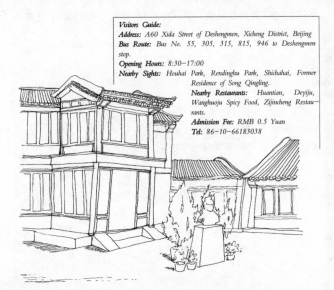

Visitors Guide:
Address: A60 Xida Street of Deshengmen, Xicheng District, Beijing
Bus Route: Bus No. 55, 305, 315, 815, 946 to Deshengmen stop.
Opening Hours: 8:30−17:00
Nearby Sights: Houhai Park, Rendinghu Park, Shichahai, Former Residence of Song Qingling.
Nearby Restaurants: Huantian, Deyiju, Wanghuoju Spicy Food, Zijincheng Restaurants.
Admission Fee: RMB 0.5 Yuan
Tel: 86−10−66183038

中国工艺美术馆

羡慕的眼神深处

无论任何人面对这四件翡翠珍品都会产生一种说不出的惊诧之感：山子《岱岳奇观》，花薰《含香聚瑞》，插屏《四海腾欢》，提梁花篮《群芳揽胜》，它们的价值用"超级国宝"四字来衡定，那是再准确不过了。除上述珍品外，这里还陈列着从全国各地征集来的工艺精品700多件（套），主要种类有玉器、象牙雕刻、木石雕刻、陶瓷器、漆器、织绣、抽纱、景泰蓝、金银摆件、花丝镶嵌、锡器、斑铜等，堪称中华民族珍宝的艺术品都在这里汇聚，这里就是中国工艺美术馆珍宝馆。

中国工艺美术馆是我国第一座国家级工艺美术博物馆。它荟萃了中国当代最优秀的工艺美术珍品，是展示中华民族工艺美术瑰宝的最高殿堂，正是由于其建筑具有浓郁的民族特色，它还被评为"群众最喜爱的具有民族风格的新建筑"。无论是外貌还是里面的展陈，中国工艺美术馆都是外交旅游部门的一个热门参观点。开馆以来，接待了许多来访的国家元首、政府首脑和国际知名人士。这里的国际交流活动也开展得如火如荼，先后在日本、马来西亚、澳门等国家和地区举办中国工艺美术精品展。在中国工艺美术馆五楼珍宝馆1800平方米的展厅里，众多的参观者中白皮肤黄头发的外国人居多。他们瞪着圆溜溜的蓝眼珠忙不迭地四处观望，一边伸出拇指，一边耸着肩膀。你仔细看，在他们眼神的深处，流露的是对中国和中华民族的羡慕！

参观指南

地　　址：北京市复兴门内大街101号。

乘车路线：1、4、15、37、52路公交车或地铁复兴门站下。

自驾车线：长安街复兴门立交桥东北角。

开放时间：9:30-16:30（周一闭馆）。

周边景观：民族文化宫、南礼士路公园、西单文化广场、西单商场。

周边餐饮：民族饭店、真味屋、微山湖渔村。

票　　价：8元；学生4元。

咨询电话：010-66053476

China National Arts & Crafts Museum

China National Arts and Crafts Museum, located near the overpass of Fuxingmen on Chang'an Street in Beijing, is the first arts & crafts museum of state level in China.

The museum comprises three parts: halls of preface, display and treasure. Under the hall of preface, there is a large copper relief on the wall, which shows the long history and excellent tradition of 5000 years in China's arts & crafts. In the hall of display assemble the elites of China's contemporary arts & crafts, including jade articles, ivory sculptures, wood and stone sculptures, potteries, porcelains, lacquer works, knitgoods, fancyworks, fagotted works, cloisonné, golden and silver wares, inlaid wares, tin wares, bornitic wares, etc. Among them, there are many treasures of state level such as the enduring works of last-generation arts & crafts masters, experts and professors, as well as the excellent works that have gained international or national golden prizes. There are also four rare national treasures of emerald: Wonder of Shanzidaiyue, Flowers inferring auspiciousness, Table Screen symbolizing happiness and Sightseeing with Flower Baskets.

Visitors Guide:
Address: 101 Inner Fuxingmen Street, Beijing
Bus Route: by bus No. 1, 4, 15, 37, 52 or subway to Fuxingmen.
Self-drive Route: Northeast to the Fuxingmen overpass on Chang'an Street
Opening Hours: 9:30−16:30 (except Monday)
Nearby Sights: Museum of the National Cultural Palace, South Lishi Road Park, Xidan Cultural Plaza, Xidan Shopping Mall.
Nearby Restaurants: Minzu Hotel, Zhenweiwu and Weishanhu Fishing Village restaurants.
Admission Fee: RMB 8 Yuan; 4 Yuan for students
Tel: 86-10-66053476.

中国钱币博物馆

中华钱币的光芒

中国钱币博物馆主要从事钱币的收藏、陈列展览和研究工作，肩负有指导推动钱币收藏、研究及宣传的任务。北京西交民巷的原北洋保商银行和原大陆银行经过加固改造，成为现在的中国钱币博物馆的陈列展览楼。

中国钱币博物馆钱币展览大楼共三层，首层的特展厅曾展出过 "中国银锭"、"黎巴嫩钱币展"、"奥地利钱币展"、"梁贻斌将军藏奥林匹克钱币展"、"山西民间票帖展"、"世界纸币文化展" 等多种题材的展览；第二层为 "中国古代钱币" 陈列，展现了中国钱币产生初期的铲形币、刀币、青铜贝等先秦钱币、秦始皇统一钱币、汉代制定五铢钱制、唐朝开元通宝、宋代的铜铁钱币、元明纸币、明清制币、贵金属货币等中国钱币的发展演变历程，其中不少是难得一见的珍品；第三层为 "中国近代钱币" 陈列，陈列分为 "晚清钱币"、"民国钱币" 和 "人民货币" 三部分。"晚清钱币" 表现了中国从古代货币体系走向近代，向世界靠拢的尝试；"民国钱币" 表现近代中国战乱频仍中货币的混乱现象；"人民货币" 记录了中国人民在中国共产党领导下，在建立人民政权的同时，建立自己的人民货币体系的奋斗历程。陈列中还用触摸屏、电影片等一些先进的展示手段介绍相关的钱币知识，得到国内外参观者的一致好评。

在这里，钱币不是充当一切商品的等价物，而成了展示文化韵味、体现审美意识、探究学术价值、进行科普教育的艺术品。参观者说：在这里目睹的每一件展品，都会让你获得别人羡慕的眼光。信不信由你。

参观指南

地　　址：北京市西城区西交民巷22号。

乘车路线：乘特2、特7、5、20、22、44、48、101、102、120、

　　　　　337、819、820、826、922公交车于前门站下车；

　　　　　地铁前门下车。

自驾车线：天安门广场西南侧，人民大会堂南侧。

开放时间：9：00-16：00，周一休息。

票　　价：20元；学生10元。

咨询电话：010-66081385（办公室）、

　　　　　010-66024178（社教部）、66071393（传真）

China Currency Museum

China Currency Museum is a special national museum affiliated to the central bank of People's Bank of China. It focuses on the collection, exhibition and study of currencies.

The museum has basic displays and special exhibitions. The former is placed in the currency showroom inside the headquarters of People's Bank of China. Because the basic displays are inside the office building of the bank, the audience should reserve the time for visit. The basic displays temporarily are not open to the public. The special exhibitions are inside the Special Exhibition Department of China Currency Museum, west of Tian'anmen Square. It has been opened to the public since August, 1999.

The museum houses nearly 300,000 items of currency or relevant cultural relics. They are divided into six categories: ancient currencies, gold and silver currencies, paper currencies, currencies of minorities, foreign currencies, and cultural relics relevant to currencies. They are well preserved and stored in the museum. Golden and silver currencies, contemporary currencies, RMB and foreign currencies are the representatives of the collections.

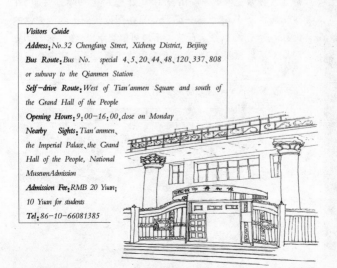

Visitors Guide

Address: No.32 Chengfang Street, Xicheng District, Beijing

Bus Route: Bus No. special 4、5、20、44、48、120、337、808 or subway to the Qianmen Station

Self-drive Route: West of Tian'anmen Square and south of the Grand Hall of the People

Opening Hours: 9:00–16:00, close on Monday

Nearby Sights: Tian'anmen、the Imperial Palace、the Grand Hall of the People, National MuseumAdmission

Admission Fee: RMB 20 Yuan; 10 Yuan for students

Tel: 86-10-66081385

恭王府及花园
又想起奕䜣

恭王府坐落在风景秀丽的什刹海畔,是北京保存最为完整的一座清代王府。其前身是清代乾隆年间大学士和坤的私宅,建于约 1777 年。后来和坤因罪赐死,府邸被赐给庆王永,称为庆王府。1851 年咸丰皇帝将其改赐给弟弟奕䜣,始称恭王府。1937 年,奕䜣之孙溥伟将它卖给辅仁大学作校舍及宿舍。新中国成立后,由几家单位使用。后经修复,恭王府花园于 1988 年 6 月对公众开放。

早在 150 多年前,这里就因建筑华丽,装修精美而名噪京城。恭王府总占地 6 万平方米,其中府邸占地 3.2 万平方米,三路四进的建筑格局;王府花园占地 2.8 万平方米,环山衔水,曲廊亭榭,融北方建筑造型与南方园林艺术为一体,营造了古朴、幽雅、华丽的环境氛围。恭王府花园开放以后,先后接待数十位外国领导人和大量的中外游客。为了更好地展示清代王府建筑和中国园林艺术,弘扬民族传统文化,恭王府以具有传统民族建筑特色的大戏楼为中心,为参观者举办京剧演出,还推出喝盖碗茶、品尝北京小吃、看民俗表演的系列活动,受到热烈的欢迎。

今日的恭王府已经是中华民族建筑园林艺苑中的一朵奇葩。人们在这里参观游览,会不由自主地想起这座府邸的原主人恭亲王奕䜣。奕䜣自 1851 年迁入至 1898 年去世,在这里居住了 47 年。这一阶段正是中国近代史上剧烈变化的时期。时光消逝,斯人已去。不过可以想象出,作为这一历史时期的清廷重要人物,奕䜣在这里肯定有过不少寝食难安的日夜。

在恭王府,人们又想起奕䜣。

参观指南
地　址:北京市前海西街。
乘车路线:13、107、111、118、701、810、823、850、850 支路公交车北海北门站下。
开放时间:8:30-16:30。
周边景观:后海公园、北海公园。
周边餐饮:塞外饺子店、西北香驴城、平安苑美食城、仿膳饭庄、福满楼等。
票　价:20 元;学生、老人、残疾人凭证半价。
咨询电话:010-66185005

Mansion of Prince Gong and Its Garden

Mansion of Prince Gong and its Garden are located at Qianhai Xijie, Xicheng district, on the western shore of Shichahai Lake, and to the northwest of the Forbidden City. It is one of China's major historical and cultural sites under state protection, the quintessence of landscape art of extant prince mansions in Beijing and also an important national cultural heritage in China's modern history and in the history of Qing Dynasty. The construction of the mansion is divided into residence and garden. The residence takes up an area of 31,000m². It is an exquisite combination of classical Chinese architecture and tasteful landscape. Princes Gong' mansion is composed of three complexes of buildings: central, eastern and western. The rear hall is a two-storey structure more than 160 meters wide. Behind the hall is the garden covering an area of 25,700m². It is also composed of three complexes of buildings: central, eastern and western. It is ingeniously constructed with complementary buildings and terraces, well spaced vegetation and hill paths that wind their way around pool and tranquil grottos. Built when Yixi was alive, the main gate of the garden is a white-marble archway in western architectural style.

Visitors Guide
Address: *Qianhai Xijie, Xicheng district, Beijing*
Bus Route: *Bus No.13,107,111 to the back door of the Beihai Park*
Opening Hours: *8:30—16:30*
Nearby Sights: *the Houhai Park and Beihai Park*
Nearby Restaurants: *Saiwai Dumpling Restaurant, Northwest Donkey City, Ping'anyuan Restaurant, Fangshang Restaurant and Fumanlou Restaurant.*
Admission Fee: *RMB 20 Yuan, 10 Yuan for students, the seniors and the disabled with relevant proofs.*
Tel: *86-10-66185005*

第三章 崇文区

北京自然博物馆

大自然将会更加美好

北京自然博物馆的古生物陈列、植物陈列、动物陈列和人类陈列等四个基本陈列以及"人体真奇妙"、"恐龙世界"、"水生生物"等三个专题陈列，吸引着大量的参观者的目光。

古动物陈列以大量化石标本、模型及图表展示出地球生命的起源，各个历史阶段各类生物的发生、发展和消亡的过程，整个生物界进化历史。展厅中间矗立的巨大恐龙和古哺乳动物的骨架化石以及大唇犀、山西兽、板齿象等大型化石骨架都是北京自然博物馆收藏的珍品。以"绿色的家园"为题的植物陈列，介绍了绿色植物在生态系统中的重要作用。另外，近百平方米的大型热带雨林景观可使观众亲身体验其氛围。动物陈列用栩栩如生的标本配合图片、照片展示现生动物多样性以及动物进化的总体趋势。动物一厅以动物谱系树为先导，介绍了现生动物各主要类群间的系统演化关系。动物二厅展示了脊椎动物中的鸟类和哺乳动物。近几年又增加巨大鲸鱼骨架、成年长颈鹿标本等重要展品。人类陈列以"人之由来"为主题，主要从系统发育和个性发育两方面介绍了人类的演化历程。"人体真奇妙"、"恐龙世界"和"水生生物"三个专题陈列引入全息照片、感应自动讲解耳机等现代科技手段，增加了展览的观赏性和趣味性。

随着人类文明不断进步，人们越来越热爱大自然，渴望与自然界其他生物和谐共处。从观众留恋的目光和脚步中，人们有理由相信，大自然将会更加美好。

参观指南

地　　址：北京市崇文区天桥南大街126号。

乘车路线：2、6、7、15、17、20、34、35、36、59、105、106、110、120、707、729、742、743、744支、803、819、822、859、百利宝101路公交车在天桥站下。

开放时间：8:30-17:00（16:00停止售票）。

票　　价：30元；学生15元；家庭票55元（两个成人带一个未成年人）；30元（一个成人带一个未成年人）；四馆通票60元（每馆一人次，含中国科技馆、中国地质博物馆、北京天文馆、北京自然博物馆）。

周边景观：天坛、先农坛（北京古代建筑博物馆）、永定门城楼发、前门城楼。

咨询电话：010-67024431（总机）、010-67023096（办公室）、010-67051158（热线）

Southeastern Corner Tower of Beijing

The Tower is China's only and biggest corner tower within city walls. Built in 1436 during the Ming Dynasty, it is located on the rectangular platform jutting out from the exterior of the city wall with 30 meters in height. The tower is built from the corner of the exterior city platform and has a curved-ruler shape. It is filled with tiled walls on all four sides and its roof rests on the mountain top. Its two ridges intersect at the corner. It has grey arched tiles and green sides. Green glaze line the ridges and decorate the beast's head. It has 144 openings for shooting arrows and is an ancient military defense facility. It gets its name from its location at the southeastern corner of the inner Beijing city.

The "Chongwen District Historical Relics" Exhibition displays the political, economic and cultural development within Chongwen District through rich historical materials, which revitalizes the rich cultural heritages in Chongwen District. In the internationally renowned and influential 'Hongmen Art Gallery", you could enjoy the modernist artworks and sculptures by many young artists from different schools.

Visitors Guide

Address: Inside Beijing Ming City Walls Relics Park

Bus Route: Take Buses Special 2, 39, 39−branch, 41−branch, 43, 44, 54, 63, 713, 820 to Dongbianmen Stop

Opening Hours: 9:00−17:00 (ticket sales stop at 16:30)

Admission Fee: RMB 10 Yuan (Adult), 5 Yuan (Student)

Tel: 86−10−65226008

北京睦明唐古瓷标本博物馆
文明碎片中的文化基因

　　茶和古瓷都是中华文化的精髓,在北京睦明唐古瓷标本博物馆,两者得以殊途同归,品一盏香茗,赏一款古瓷,听一曲琵琶古乐,仿佛时光倒流,在历史的闪回中,与古代文明不期相遇,进而相知相许,不能不令人怦然心动。

　　"睦明唐"本是北京东花市附近的一处茶艺社,由于这里藏品的丰富,布局的合理,被专家慧眼相识,于是,逐渐变成了古瓷爱好者的"天堂"。"睦明唐"的三位主人姜宇、白明、陈浩瑞虽然经历各殊,职业迥异,但是对古瓷片的共同爱好使他们乐此不疲并付出大量的时间、精力和钱财。走窑址、访工地、逛市场,呕心沥血收集到30类约5万余件古瓷片,这些瓷片虽称不上件件精品,但布置在350多米的展廊里,已显现出恢宏的气势。元清花的清晰厚重,明成化斗彩的精致优雅以及如冰似玉的越州青瓷,类雪赛银的邢窑白瓷,色彩缤纷的钧瓷,全部有类可寻。尽管这些展品只是一块块古瓷残片,但专家认定它们"残而不失其美,残而不失其珍,残而不失其值,残而不失为师"。参观者可以轻轻抚摸它们,好像在触摸一段历史,每一件瓷片上的色彩、画风、釉质似乎都在诉说一段往事。

　　睦明唐古瓷标本博物馆有着执著的信念,这就是"拼对文明碎片,追寻文化基因"。这里的每一块瓷片标本都凝固着千百年来中国古文化的印迹,甚至还存留着历史老人的体热余温。只要你善于发掘,很小很小的一块古瓷片,却有很大很大的历史空间。

参观指南

地　　址:北京市崇文区东花市北里东区1号,北京市房地产交易中心一层。

乘车路线:乘610、723路公交车白桥下车;43、44、48东便门下车。

自驾车线:广渠门桥西第一个红绿灯向北,白桥大街。

票　　价:10元。

咨询电话:010-67187266、67186940

Mu Mingtang Ancient Porcelain Sample Museum in Beijing

This is a museum specializing in performance of China's tea ceremony, studies and touches of ancient Chinese porcelain samples. Covering an area of 428 square meters, the museum is divided into exhibition are, touch area, network area, tea area, study area, and reading area. The museum now houses over 50,000 samples of ancient porcelain. There are about 1200 samples on regular display. The exhibits will be changed in accordance with the exhibition theme. The touch area is a platform to touch the history, where people can touch the samples since Tang Dynasty.

In the network area, the homepage of Mu Mingtang displays a wide collection range. In the database of the network, thousands of photos about those cultural relics lost abroad are displayed. In the tea area, girls perform China's tea ceremony accompanied by the ancient music. The light serves as a folio to the porcelain and the ancient music are accompanied by fragrant tea smells.

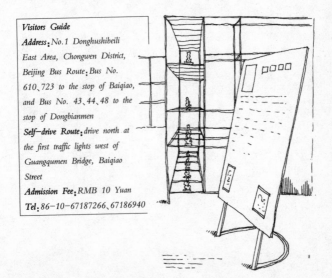

Visitors Guide

Address: No.1 Donghushibeili East Area, Chongwen District, Beijing Bus Route: Bus No. 610、723 to the stop of Baiqiao, and Bus No. 43、44、48 to the stop of Dongbianmen

Self−drive Route: drive north at the first traffic lights west of Guangqumen Bridge, Baiqiao Street

Admission Fee: RMB 10 Yuan
Tel: 86−10−67187266、67186940

第四章 宣武区

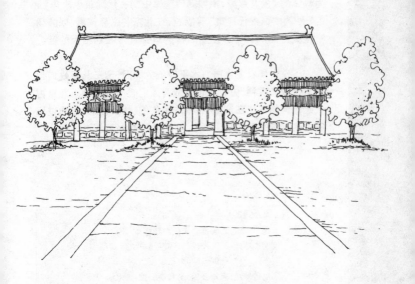

北京古代建筑博物馆

古建筑文化的展示

先农坛建于明代嘉靖年间,清乾隆十九年(1754年)重修,是明清两朝帝王祭祀先农神的地方。1991年9月,北京古代建筑博物馆在这里落成,正式对外开放。此后经过几年的修缮和复建,一座完整的明代皇家坛庙建筑群已恢复雄伟宏大的英姿。太岁殿、神仓、神厨、具服殿、观耕台、先农神坛、庆成宫等建筑成为北京市难得的历史遗存。

作为全国首座建筑类专题性博物馆,北京古代建筑博物馆已成为向社会传播建筑文化的科普窗口,得到社会各界人士,青少年学生和国内外游客的关注和热爱。这里举办"中国古代建筑发展简史"的基本陈列,以丰富多彩的文物、图片、照片、模型等反映中国建筑的灿烂成就;以独树一帜、雅俗共赏的展览体例、编制来展示中国古代建筑的风采神韵;以古代坛庙氛围和现代展览形式相结合来展示建筑文化的深邃蕴含。当你走进太岁殿、拜殿、西配殿等2000多平方米的展区时,中国古代建筑构架的恢弘,建筑材料的复杂多样使你不得不为前人的聪慧头脑和非凡创造能力而叫绝。以古建筑为载体的"爱北京城,捐城墙砖"、"中国古代建筑小广角"、"奇妙的中国古代建筑"等展览,在北京各区县巡展,以弘扬中国优秀建筑文化为主要内容的科普宣传收到巨大的社会反响。

正是古代农业生产力水平较低的原因,帝王及百姓们都非常崇敬先农神,先农坛也就成为人们心中的圣地。北京古代建筑博物馆建在这里,将中华民族的优秀传统文化通过坛庙古建筑群的形式展现出来,参观者无不为之心动。

参观指南

地　　址:北京市宣武区东经路21号。

乘车路线:2、7、15、20、110、120路天桥商场下。

开放时间:9:00-16:00。

周边景观:天坛公园、陶然亭公园、万寿公园。

周边餐饮:鸿运楼、肯德基、麦当劳。

票　　价:15元;中小学生、60岁以上老人免票。

咨询电话:010-63045608

Beijing Ancient Architecture Museum

Beijing ancient Architecture Museum is located in Beijing Xiannong Altar, which is the first special museum of China centering on collecting, researching and displaying of China ancient architecture technologies, art and its development history.

Xiannong Altar built in 1420 was the site visited by Ming and Qing Emperors to offer sacrifices to gods and to hold tilling ceremonies. It includes The Hall of Taisui, the Divine Kitchen, the Divine Warehouse and the Hall of Clothes and Tools etc. The Taisui Hall is the most grandeur complex in the Xiannong Altar. Facing the south, it has seven rooms decorated with black glazed pantiles and green brims in Xieshan style. There are 11 wing rooms respectively on the east and the west sides of the hall. The Prayer Hall in the south also has seven rooms, opposite to the Taisui Hall.

The museum's major exhibitions include Ancient Altar-Picture Exhibition on Xiannong Altar and China's Ancient Architectural Technology Development. China's ancient architectures occupy a very important place in the world architectural history. Lots of pictures, photos, material objects and elaborate models on display record Chinese labor people's marvelous creativity and Chinese ancient architecture's long history and brilliant achievement.

Visitors Guide

Address: No.21 Dongjing Road, Xuanwu District, Beijing

Bus Route: Bus No. 2、7、15、20、110、120 to Tianqiao Marketplace

Opening Hours: 9:00—16:00

Nearby Sights: Temple of Heaven、Taoranting Park、Longevity Park、Taoran Pavilion.

Nearby Restaurants: Hongyunlou Restaurant、KFC、MacDonald.

Admission Fee: RMB 15 Yuan; free for primary and middle school students and people over 60 years old.

Tel: 86—10—63045608

中国佛教图书文物馆

佛学经典藏古刹

红色的山门，左右两座石狮。门额的大理石上雕镌着金色的"法源寺"三字，显示出一座古老庙宇的雄伟气象。迎面的天王殿供奉着弥勒菩萨的化身布袋和尚像，笑面迎人。背后韦驮坐像与左右两壁四大天王，均为青铜鎏金"矢蜡法"铸造，勇猛威严，气势袭人。古老的法源寺如今已是中国佛教图书文物馆的所在地。

大雄宝殿里，乾隆皇帝御书的"法海真源"匾额悬于梁间，人们可以看到僧人上殿诵经以及50多件套明清各类法器。"法源寺古代石刻展"陈列着历代相传法源寺原藏的一批石质文物；毗卢殿内供奉着一座巨大的毗卢遮那佛，通体铜制，高齐屋顶，具有"千佛绕毗卢"之势。"历代佛教造像展"精选自东汉、三国、北魏、北齐一直到清代的不同材质的佛造像数十尊。殿后的大悲坛现称观音殿，奉有明代观音菩萨像七尊，种类包括毗卢观音、送子观音、准提观音、骑吼观音、绿度母、十一面千手观音立像等。

最后一进为藏经阁，阁前有数百年古银杏一株，枝干婆娑，荫覆半院。阶前两株名贵的"西府海棠"为乾隆年间栽植。阁内供有明代景泰年间的大型木雕释迦牟尼涅槃像，是北京地区最大的木雕卧佛。"清代佛龛艺术展"中，七组清代硬木佛龛精巧别致，是研究古代建筑艺术的宝贵资料。文物馆藏有《房山石经》的全部拓本，15000余块经版上刻佛经1000余部，3400余卷，堪与敦煌石窟相媲美，人称"北方敦煌"。

这里的佛教文物，件件珍品，卷卷珠玑。佛学经典的广阔与深邃，法源古刹的肃穆庄重使参观者得到一次空前的心灵净化。

参观指南
地　　址:北京市宣武区法源寺前街7号。
乘车路线:10、102、105、109路公交车或第四号地铁。
开放时间:8:00-15:00,周三闭馆。
周边景观:牛街伊斯兰教礼拜寺、报国寺、湖广会馆。
票　　价:5元。
咨询电话:010--63533772

China Museum of Buddhist Books and Cultural Relics

The museum is located inside the Fayuan Temple. Subject to China Buddhist Association, the museum focuses on collection, exhibition, research of Buddhist books and cultural relics. Fayuan Temple faces the south with six courtyards. Inside the Tianwang Hall, there is a sculpture of Hop-Pocket Monk. On its sides, there are four celestial emperors. The stele of the Daxiong Hall: True Source of Fahai" was inscribed by Emperor Qianglong. The sculptures of Sakyamuni, Samantabhadra, Manjusgri and eighteen arhats are in the hall. In the Kwan-yin Hall, there are many stone inscriptions on display. The Jingye Hall displays the bronze statue of Wufang Buddha cast in Ming Dynasty. The Dabei Hall is now opened as an exhibition hall to display the sutras in past dynasties. Sutras written in Tang, Song, Yuan, Ming and Qing Dynasties and in the languages of West Xia, Hui nationality, Dai nationality, Tibetan nationality and Mongolia nationality are exhibited. The last courtyard is the Cangjing Building, which is now the room for exhibiting Buddha statues in past dynasties. There are scores of exquisite statues cast from East Han Dynasty to Ming and Qing Dynasties on display.

Visitors Guide
Address: No.7 Fayuansi Qianjie, Xuanwu District, Beijing
Bus Route: Bus No.10、102、105、109 or Subway No.4
Opening Hours: 8:00−15:00, close on Wednesday
Nearby Sights: Mosque on Niujie Street、Baoguo Temple、Huguang Assembly Hall
Admission Fee: RMB 5 Yuan
Tel: 86−10−63533772

北京红楼文化艺术博物馆

重悟红楼文化

北京红楼文化艺术博物馆是一座具有古典园林外观、红楼文化内涵、博物馆功能的旅游场所，也是集红学、古建、园林、清史、民俗、文博等各方面专家集体智慧的结晶。从整体格局到景观规划，从建筑尺度到景物设置，都立足于忠实原著的描述和时代的风貌。近万平方米的建筑，近2万平方米的水面及40余处景点，重新画就了一个红楼故地。

众所周知，《红楼梦》标志着中国古典小说中现实主义的最高峰，而作为以大观园、红楼为主题的博物馆，注重在红楼文化的精髓和内涵方面下功夫：第一部分"元妃省亲馆"，展出了"省亲"活动时的红木宝座、屏风及红楼人物服饰，满布全壁的"贵妃册封"、"秀女名册"等。第二部分"红楼文物精品展"，展出《红楼梦》所处年代的家具、古玩、器皿，其中有一紫檀镶银对联为曹家文物。第三部分"红楼艺术馆"，展出近一个世纪以来以《红楼梦》为题材所演出的各种影视戏剧。第四部分"大观园馆"，展示了大观园十几年来的发展变化，集声、光、电于一体的沙盘模型演示着大观园从梦幻到现实的仙境。第五部分"曹雪芹家世与生平"，展示了这位伟大的文学家坎坷的一生。第六部分"红学学术研究馆"，介绍红学研究领域的几大流派。

贾史王薛四个家族早已灰飞烟灭，宝黛爱情悲剧已成过眼烟云。但是所有这些都无法让人淡忘《红楼梦》卓越的艺术成就。来到这里，可以感悟它的内涵，重温它的魅力，也许你会得到全新的感受。

参观指南

地　　址：北京市宣武区南菜园街。

乘车路线：特3、19、56、59、61、122、423、819路公交车直达。

开放时间：8：30—16：30。

票　　价：15元；学生8元。

咨询电话：010—63544994、010—63542299 转 534

Beijing Red Mansion Culture and Art Museum

Located in Xuanwu District southwest of Beijing, the museum(also called Daguanyuan (Grand View Garden) is a replica of the magnificent garden of an imperial family described in the well-known Chinese novel "A Dream of Red Mansions" by Cao Xueqin (1715-1763).

The Grand View Garden covers 13 hectares with a construction area of 10,000m². The architectures are in the style of Qing Dynasty. The environment there is very beautiful. Currently, there are 12 exhibition rooms in the garden. The garden boasts a collection of nearly 10,000 pieces of cultural relics and replicas such as craftworks, furniture, bronze wares, potteries etc. The large-scale permanent exhibition entitled Cultural and Artistic Exhibition on Red Mansion include homecoming by an imperial concubine, Red Mansions' precious cultural relics, Red Mansion culture and art, red mansion research, life of Cao Xueqin and the past and the current Grand View Garden. Many practicalities and data give a systemic and vivid introduction to the profound culture of Red Mansions.

When the festivals or holidays come, many interesting activities are held there. The famous ancient costume show called Homecoming by an Imperial Concubine is particularly attractive.

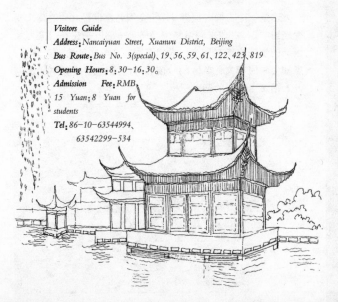

Visitors Guide

Address: Nancaiyuan Street, Xuanwu District, Beijing

Bus Route: Bus No. 3(special)、19、56、59、61、122、423、819

Opening Hours: 8:30-16:30。

Admission Fee: RMB 15 Yuan; 8 Yuan for students

Tel: 86-10-63544994、
63542299-534

古陶文明博物馆

一个寓言说陶器

　　有一个寓言说，坚硬的铁器嘲笑陶器："你如此易碎，在世界上能存活多久呢？"陶器笑了："那就等千百年以后再见吧！"若干年后，人们把陶器从地下挖出来，洗净擦干，仍是光彩照人；再去寻找铁器时，见到的却只是锈迹斑斑的泥土。这就是关于陶器的传说，它衍生了一个民族的文明。

　　古陶文明博物的展厅里，展示了四个系列近 600 件展品。"彩陶渊薮"系列展出了出土于甘肃、青海、宁夏境内距今约 5000 年 -3000 年的马家窑文化、半山类型、马厂类型、齐家文化等不同文化类型的彩陶近百件，其中有许多保存完好至今仍惊艳完美的珍稀之品。"瓦当大观"系列展出了从战国至东汉数百年间不同地域、不同品类的瓦当 137 件，其中不乏珍品孤品。"封泥绝响"系列展出秦汉封泥近 200 品，尤其是秦封泥部分被称为 "秦文化史上又一次重大发现"，涵盖了秦始皇三公九卿政治体制的各类属员，展示了许多与秦始皇及秦代文明相关的政治、经济、文化、军事内容。"古陶序列" 展出周秦汉唐 2000 年间不同器型和品类的陶质文物 130 件，从中可以看出古陶文明的演进与发展脉络。除鬲、鼎、罐、壶等基本品类外，还有画像砖、浮雕砖、陶箱棺、陶乐器等十分罕见的陶类文物。

　　这是一个古陶的世界。作为全国乃至世界唯一的陶文明专题博物馆，古陶文明博物馆演绎了一部近乎完整而又形象生动的中国古陶文明史，人们可以充分感知她的恒久魅力，感知中华民族文化艺术的价值和尊严，这也许就是博物馆创办人路东之先生的初衷吧！

参观指南

地　　址: 北京市宣武区南菜园西街 12 号。

乘车路线: 特 3、10、19、59、122、410、603、626、716、937 路公交车。

自驾车线: 大观园酒店北侧路口向东 100 米。

开放时间: 10:00-17:00, 周一休息。

周边餐饮: 大观园酒店、荣国府中餐厅、铜雀台餐厅。

周边景观: 大观园、辽金城垣博物馆。

景　　价: 20 元; 学生 10 元。

咨询电话: 010-63538884、63538811

Museum of Ancient Pottery Civilization

Near the Beijing Da-Guan Garden with antique flavor, there is a tranquil and original museum---the Museum of Ancient Pottery Civilization, one of the first batch of privately-run museums.

Museum of Ancient Pottery Civilization is one specialized in pottery culture. The culture relics it preserves are conformed of three series, including over 600 ancient painted potteries of Neolithic Age and potteries of Zhou, Qin and Han Dynasties, over 300 tiles with a circular facade of Warring States period and Qin and Han Dynasties, and over 1000 lutes of Qin and Han Dynasties, as well as about 3000 ancient potteries of other fields concerned. All these relics form a nearly complete and vivid history of pottery civilization. Many of the relics belong to 4R grade, among which the lutes of Qin Dynasty can be seen as the first collection of government official names and geography records of China's united feudal kingdoms, and the source and files of China's generations of government systems. The museum displays nearly 600 relics in a fixed way and the relics are divided into four parts: "painted pottery nest", "tiles panorama" "rare lutes" and "series of ancient potteries". Displayed together with these relics, there is the series of multi artistic languages of Lu Dongzhi.

Visitors Guide:
Address: 12 West Nancaiyuan Street, Xuanwu District, Beijing
Bus Route: by bus No. 3 (special), 10, 19, 59, 122, 410, 603, 626, 716 and 937.
Self-drive Route: Turn to east at the crossing north to the Da-Guan Garden Hotel and drive for 100m.
Opening Hours: 10:00-17:00 (except Monday)
Nearby Restaurants: Da-Guan Garden Hotel, Rongguofu and Tongquetai restaurants.
Admission Fee: RMB 20 Yuan; 10 Yuan for students.
Tel: 86-10-63538884, 63538811

北京戏曲博物馆

在这里倾听戏曲艺术的脉搏

不能否认现代的文艺形式令人眼花缭乱,对我国传统艺术构成强大的冲击,但是,从北京戏曲博物馆络绎不绝的参观者的脚步声中,我们却听到了戏曲艺术铿锵有力的脉搏。

坐落在宣武区虎坊桥的湖广会馆建于 1807 年,在这清代达官名流的宅地上,楼阁高阔,戏台畅耸,廊院曲折,厅堂幽蔽,山石亭林点缀生花,镏金匾额煊赫泛光,家具屏帘精美典雅,把北京戏曲博物馆建立在这里,那策划者的精辟构思就可以让人感慨一番了。孙中山曾五次莅临这里,发表政治演说,主持召开了国民党成立大会,都让来这里的人望之生敬;而湖北人谭鑫培、余叔岩在这里演出,不正是为北京戏曲博物馆做了绝好的奠基吗?

那些翔实的戏曲文献,那珍贵的文物、图片和音像资料无不向人们展示着以京剧艺术为主的北京戏曲发展史:曾有的辉煌,曾有的多舛,曾有的醇厚,曾有的恬淡。京剧名家王瑶卿、梅兰芳的拜师图,武生泰斗杨小楼演出用的戏装等珍贵藏品向人们讲述着一个个动人的故事。你如果驻足倾听,或许能听到京剧大师们在这里进行精彩演出的余音,或深厚饱满,或清脆婉转,或高亢嘹亮,或细腻圆润,艺术的魅力不会因时间推移而衰减,我们有许多理由越来越自信。

湖广会馆创建初衷是湘鄂两省学子赴京赶考居所及同乡联谊聚居之地,历史背景、政治内涵、文化韵味都使这里成为人文荟萃之地。时至今天,这样的认识与日弥坚。坐在优雅恬静、儒香浓郁的古戏楼里,欣赏京昆名家的精彩演出,你肯定会对博物馆的概念发生全新的认识。的确,这就是北京戏曲博物馆。

参观指南

地　　址:北京市宣武区虎坊路 3 号。

乘车路线:6、7、14、15、23、34、50、53、102、105 路公交车虎坊路下。

开放时间:9:00—16:30(参观);19:30—20:45(演出)。

票　　价:10 元;学生 5 元。

周边景观:纪晓岚故居、法源寺、陶然亭公园、牛街礼拜寺。

咨询电话:010-63518284,63510019。

The Traditional Opera Museum of Beijing

Hubei and Hunan Provincial Guild Hall was established in 1807, including many splendid buildings. It was the place where students of Hubei and Hunan province going to the capital to take part in the imperial examination live and people from these two provinces inhabited and held social activities. It enjoys a long culture, history and full of rich political connotation, really a place of galaxy of talent. In 1912, the great revolutionary forerunner Sun Yat-sen visited for five times and delivered political speeches, and on August 25th, he chaired the establishment meeting of KMT. During the period of Republic of China, many famous masters of Beijing opera, such as Tan Xinpei, Yu Shuyan and Mei Lanfang, have performed here, which made here a well-known place for traditional opera performance.

The main content of the traditional opera museum is "a brief introduction to the history of the traditional opera in Beijing", which shows the development history of the traditional opera in Beijing through various accurate and valuable literature, relic, pictures and audio and video information of the traditional opera. It is full of highly artistic and visual value.

Visitors Guide:

Address: No. 3 Hufang road in the district of Xuanwu, Beijing

Bus Route: take No. 6, 7, 14, 15, 23, 34, 50, 53, 102, 105 bus to the stop of Hufang road

Opening Hours: 9:00—16:30 (visit); 19:30—20:45 (performance)

Admission Fee: $10, $5 (student)

Tel: 86—10—63518284,
63510019

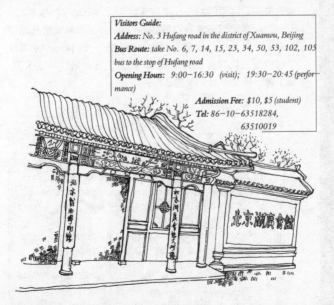

北京松堂斋民间雕刻博物馆

砖雕的笑靥

松堂斋民间雕刻博物馆坐落在北京宣武区琉璃厂东街，它的建筑在琉璃厂大街别有价值。雕花木门，棋格木窗，房基石，柱础，雕梁，房檐石等构件都是馆藏珍品，甚至门前石质台阶也是从一个废弃庙宇中收集来的。汉代的小石猴被镶嵌在外墙上，雕刻着人物形象的清代石横梁仍然气势夺人，曾在前门外大栅栏街上风光一阵的"祥光四面"栅栏围在博物馆门前，石象、八仙雕刻门墩在栅栏内尽显古风。馆内的门窗都是古建筑上的真品，古旧的窗棂或镶在墙上，或悬于房顶，立体展示藏品的效果让人叹服。

馆内，从秦砖汉瓦到明清的石、木、砖雕；从民间建筑构件装饰件到古代各式家具，1000多件（套）馆藏使博物馆蕴含丰厚。一层门厅用一架清代六扇镂空透雕木屏风隔断，厅里矗立三座门楼：山西的砖雕门楼、北京的木雕门楼、江西的石雕门楼，古韵悠悠，气势凛凛。二楼展台多是不同时期、不同地域的雕刻构件：宋代的《行孝图》砖雕、《马上封侯》的石雕、元大都时的《武士饮兽图》门墩，都是刻工精细、保存完好的镇馆之宝。

主人李松堂先生酷爱收藏，大部分藏品都是他从全国各地收集来。这里的每一件藏品背后都有一个动人的故事。

……在山西一家农户残破的门楼上，一块精美的砖雕摇摇欲坠，阵风吹过，收藏家下意识地上前一步，伸出双手接住了这块险些化作齑粉的砖雕，如今，人们在博物馆的墙上，看到了这块精美砖雕的笑靥。

参观指南

地　　址：北京市宣武区琉璃厂东街东头路南14号。

乘车路线：乘7、14、15、25、44路公交车或环线地铁和平门下。

自驾车线：琉璃厂文化街东头路南把口处。

开放时间：9：00-18：00，周一休息。

周边景观：天坛公园、西单商场、西单文化广场。

周边餐饮：水族浒记海鲜鱼菜馆、和平门正宗三千烤肉城、远东饭店。

票　　价：20元；学生10元。

咨询电话：010-83164662

Songtangzhai Folk Carving Musuem

The museum is situated on the East Street of Liulichang, Xuanwu District, Beijing. It is rich in collections ranging from the bricks and tiles in Qin and Han Dynasties to the stone, wooden and brick carvings in Ming and Qing Dynasties, and from folk construction decorations to various pieces of ancient furniture which total 1,000 sets (or items). The hall on the ground floor is sectioned by six folding screens in Qing Dynasty. Inside the hall, there are three arches over the gateway: brick arch of Shanxi Province, wooden arch of Beijing and stone arch of Jiangxi Province. They are ancient but grandeur. The exhibition on the first floor is mainly composed of carving components of different times and in different regions: brick carving entitled Filial Piety Picture of Song Dynasty, stone carving entitled Obtain an official post on horse back, and a threshold carved with the picture of warriors and animals. They are all well preserved treasures housed in the museum.

Li Songtang, owner of the museum is keen on collection. Most collections are gathered by him throughout China. Behind every collection, there is a beautiful story.

Visitors Guide

Address: No.14 east end of Liulichang East Street, Xuanwu District, Beijing

Bus Route: Bus No.7、14、15、25、44 or circular subway to the station of Hepingmen

Self-drive Route: East end of Liulichang East Street

Opening Hours: 9:00-18:00, close on Monday

Nearby Sights: the Temple of Heaven、Xidan Marketplace、Xidan Cultural Square

Nearby Restaurants: Shuizuhuji Seafood Restaurant、Hepingmen Zhengzong Sanqian Barbeque restaurant、Far East Restaurant。

Admission Fee: RMB 20 Yuan; 10 Yuan for students

Tel: 86-10-83164662

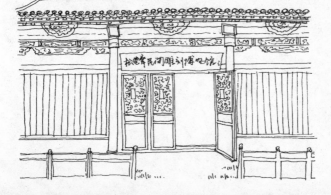

第五章 朝阳区

中国体育博物馆

中国体育博物馆

你和争金夺银连在一起

中国体育博物馆坐落在风景秀丽的国家奥林匹克体育中心东门院内，是我国唯一的一座体育专业博物馆。

作为北京市青少年爱国主义教育基地，中国体育博物馆立足于宣传中国古代、近代、现代的体育文化，尤其是新中国的体育成就，传播体育知识，教育广大群众大力发展体育事业。这里将馆藏珍品布置为基本陈列，即中国体育展览，分为四个展厅。第一展厅是中国古代体育，自先秦开始，其后秦汉隋唐宋元明清，展出古代体育文物80余件（套），壁画、拓片80余幅，另有唐代马球、宋代蹴鞠等沙盘，形象地再现中国古代体育，如射箭、狩猎、舞蹈、角抵、竞渡、马球、蹴鞠、投壶、水熄、捶丸、气功、百戏、击技、奕旗等，展现了中华民族古老而又丰富的体育文化。第二展厅是中国近代体育厅，即1840年-1949年间，这是现代体育项目传入我国的重要时期，陈列中大量极为珍贵的历史图片、文物、档案，向参观者展示中国体育从古代向现代迈进的过程，对海内外业内人士及体育爱好者极具吸引力。第三展厅和第四展厅是中华人民共和国体育成就展，根据新时代的要求，目前调整为全民健身厅和奥运争光厅。这部分展览展出500多件（套）世界冠军奖杯、奖牌、实物和广大群众开展群众体育活动的图片实物，展现了新中国体育灿烂辉煌的成就。

这里，中国体育健儿在国际赛事争金夺银的拼搏是一道鲜亮的风景，你熟悉的面孔、身影和你曾经起落跌宕的心情，把你和中国体育博物馆紧紧连在一起。

参观指南
地　址：北京市朝阳区安定路甲3号。
乘车路线：18、108、328、387、803、850路公交车。
周边景观：奥林匹克公园、元大都城垣遗址公园、北京中华民族园、亚运村。
周边餐饮：潮福源大酒楼、塞外小肥羊、太上宫大酒楼。
票　价：10元；学生、老人、残疾人5元；70岁以上老人免票。
咨询电话：010-64912167

China Sports Museum

It is China's first specialized museum centering on the collection, exhibition and research of sports materials. The museum has a central hall and four exhibition halls. China's ancient sports are a bright pearl in the cultural treasury of China. The cultural relics, paintings, rubbings and photos housed here re-emerge such activities as martial art, arrow, wrestle, ancient football, polo, I-go, breath-controlling exercise etc, reflecting the colorful sports culture of the Chinese People. The part of China's modern sports introduces the evolution of sports in China from 1840 to 1949 which include the sports activities in the revolutionary bases under the leadership of the Chinese Communist Party. The hall of sports achievements made in new China displays many pictures, models and practicalities that reflect the Party's and the State's deep concerns with the sports cause and the glorious achievements in the construction of sports areas for the public. The history of China's participation in modern Olympic Games and the development of athletics in New China are on display in the fourth exhibition hall.

Visitors Guide
Address: No. A 3, Anding Road, Chaoyang District, Beijing
Bus Route: Bus No.18、108、328、387、803、850
Nearby Sights: Olympic Park、Yuan Capital City Wall Ruins Park、China Ethnic Cultural Park、the Asian Games Village
Nearby Restaurants: Chaofuyuan Restaurant, Saiwai Xiaofeiyang Restaurant, and Taishanggong Restaurant
Admission Fee: RMB 10 Yuan; 5 Yuan for students, seniors and disabled people, free for visitors above the age of 70
Tel: 86-10-64912167

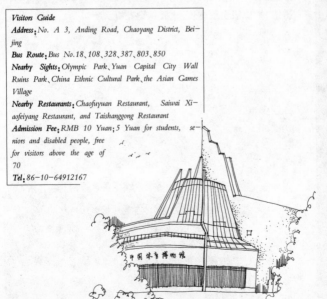

中国农业博物馆

种子向着太阳点头微笑

穿行在香灌藤蕨之中，脚畔的花香亲吻着你的衣衫。许多人是怀着朝圣的心情来参观中国农业博物馆的。中国传统农具展、中国现代科技展在倾诉着农业的古今传承，一粒种子、一株作物竟承担着支撑上天的重任，"民以食为天"真是农业的另类注释，多么深刻而又精辟的内涵啊！博物馆还设有陆生动物标本和水生动物标本展，在你倾心于农业对人类意义的时候，见识稀缺少有的水陆生动物标本，不仅仅是开阔了眼界，更使你的内心受到一种启迪：农业对社会最好的贡献莫过于它的时时更新的外延。不是么？

年轻的中国农业博物馆自建馆近 20 年以来。秣马厉兵，在收集、保护、研究、陈列藏品方面日臻精湛，一个农业文化的中心和公众终身教育的课堂已展现在这里。你看，这里的参与活动简直就是诱惑：种子辨识、认知植物、传统农事活动、果蔬 VC 测定……会让你跃跃欲试。农博恰似一颗刚刚萌芽的种子，带着泥土的芳香和雨露的润泽，向着太阳点头微笑。你先不要在环绕的回廊中驻足，也不要在通幽的竹径上匆行，只是把你的心神与湖心碧波一起荡漾，让你的身躯在岸边绿树浓荫下乘凉，你方可感到中国农业博物馆的青春在诱惑，把你吸引到这里，享受鸟语花香。

参观指南

地　　址：北京市朝阳区东三环北路 16 号。

乘车路线：乘 43、113、115、300、302 路公交车农展馆站下车。

开放时间：全年开放，周一闭馆。

票　　价：10 元；学生 5 元；学生集体参观、老人、残疾人、军人凭证免票。

咨询电话：010-65931355

The Agricultural Museum of China

There are three regular displays "China's modern technology display", "China's traditional farm tools display" and "display of terrestrial and aquatic animal samples". Besides that there is a hall for exhibiting rare aquatic animals, and near 500 specimens of aquatic animals are displayed in it, including a whale measuring 7 meters in length and 5 tons in weight with a four-month embryo, a 95-kilogram dolphin, a 150-kilogram turtle and a rare and valuable Chinese paddlefish. In the exhibition hall of rare terrestrial animals, near 200 rare specimens and large numbers of valuable picture information are displayed, including many animals enjoying the first or second class national protection, such as Manchurian tiger, golden monkey, giant panda, gibbon, snow leopard, sable, red-crowned crane, green peacock, white crane, and giant swan etc.

In the aquarium, there are more than 50 kinds of economic fish and ornamental fish peculiar to China, including Chinese paddlefish under the first-class national protection, the giant salamander under the second-class national protection. The garden with a hundred kinds of plants, located in the museum, covers above 2000 kilometers and possesses a hundred kinds of arbor, bush, vines, pteridophyte, flowers and grass.

Visitors Guide:

Address: Inside the Agriculture Exhibition Hall situated at North Road of East Third Ring Road, Beijing

Bus Route: Take Bus No.43, 113, 115, 300, 302 to the stop of Agriculture Exhibition Hall

Opening Hours: Open throughout the year except Mondays

Admission Fee: RMB 8 Yuan, 4 Yuan (student); admission is free for the organized pupil tour groups, elderly, handicapped and members of the armed forces with the relevant ID.

Tel: 86-10-65931355

炎黄艺术馆

炎黄--让我引以自豪

在京城亚运村，一座屋顶呈覆斗形体的唐代风格的建筑格外引人注目：非对称宫廷式格局，紫色琉璃瓦屋顶，青石板面墙壁，加之独具匠心的园林绿化使之愈显出古朴庄重之感。这里便是拥有3000多件艺术珍品的炎黄艺术馆。

真的要感谢黄胄先生，他在晚年为建立炎黄艺术馆倾注了全部心血，并把自己的优秀作品和古代书画藏品捐献给这里。漫步在这3000余件藏品中，你会体会到炎黄艺术的博大精深：谷牧先生的《百梅图》原作，邵宇先生的《藏童上学》，萧琼先生珍藏的蒋兆和遗作《孔明》、《苦难》（著名的《游民图》草稿之一）。也许几代人身上的一种情结对珍品的收藏已成奢望之后，目睹也成为一件幸事，于是炎黄艺术馆给了你一种满足：彦涵先生的各个历史时期的代表作，启功、黄苗子、何海霞、俞致贞、田世光、白雪石、梁树年、唐云等人的书画作品，李少言和韩国、新加坡书画家的作品以及由新华社香港分社捐赠的宋人绢本山水，都在这里熠熠生辉。而华君武等多位漫画家的近百幅代表作更让人领悟炎黄艺术的海纳百川……

实在是无法用一种介质来衡量炎黄艺术馆藏珍品的艺术价值，因为许多书画作品的作者名字成为一部部辞书的词条，因为每一幅书画作品深处都浓缩了炎黄子孙生存的山山水水和世态的炽热苍凉，因为每一位参观者都把脚步放慢放轻，怕惊起一丝尘埃让艺术蒙垢，因为这块热土上已经萌生的艺术和正在萌生的艺术都会让你更加热爱这方热土。

参观指南
地　　址：北京市朝阳区亚运村慧忠路9号。
乘车路线：108路无轨电车或328、358、380、387、406、702、713、727、849、850等公共汽车在炎黄艺术馆站下车。
开放时间：9：00--16：00。周一闭馆。
票　　价：成人5元；学生3元（寒暑假2元）。
周边景观：中国体育博物馆、中华民族博物院、奥林匹克体育中心。
咨询电话：010-64912902

Yanhuang Art Museum

The museum is located in Asian Games Village, Beijing. Huang Zhou, a famous painter is the promoter of its establishment. With great supports from the state and Beijing Municipal Government and the investment from home and abroad, China's first art museum run by the local people and sponsored by the state was established. It is a commonweal undertaking under the leadership of the Art Council. On September 28, 1991, it officially opened to the public. The museum has a construction area of 9600m², among which exhibition halls cover 3300.The main building is in the architectural style of Tang Dynasty with a funneled roof.

The museum's collections are mainly contemporary Chinese paintings, totaling over 3000 pieces at present. Mr. Huang Zhou donated his masterpieces and collections of ancient paintings, and other famous painters have also donated their representative works to the museum.

Since its establishment, the museum has held over 300 art exhibitions,including 30 national art exhibitions on a large scale and scores of significant art exhibitions for exchange between China and foreign countries. The museum also focuses its attention on art research and academic exchange, such as compilation and publication of academic series and various literatures.

Visitors Guide
Address: *Asian Games Village, Beijing*
Bus Route: *Trolley bus 108, or Bus 328、358、380、387、406、702、713、727、849、850 to the bus stop of Yanhuang Art Museum.*
Opening Hours: *9：00——16：00   Close on Monday*
Admission Fee: *RMB 5 Yuan, 3 Yuan (For students) (2 Yuan on summer and winter vacations)*
Tel: *86—10—64912902*

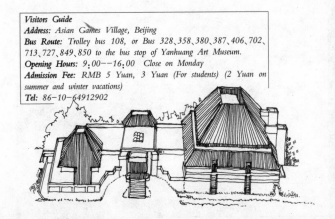

北京中华民族博物院

体会民族亲情

在古汉语中,提到少数民族,总是用"胡"、"蛮"、"夷"等,尽管此类词汇并无褒贬色彩,但让人听起来总是那么不舒服。不过这种感觉在北京中华民族博物院却变成了浓浓的亲情。在这里,你可以沐浴朝霞,与少数民族青年共唱国歌,举行庄严的升国旗仪式;在这里,你可以在欢快的鼓乐声中,与少数民族同胞翩翩起舞,把和睦温馨写到脸上,刻在心中。中华民族博物院又称中华民族园,是我国唯一展现中华各民族风情和文化遗产的大型人类学博物馆。南北两园分布着56个民族的景区,各自设有不同的专题展览,同时还有各民族1:1的民居和宗教建筑。民族地区特有的景观会使你在瞬息间感受不同民族的风情风貌:一间竹楼,你看到傣族姐妹筒裙摆起的舞姿;一座毡房,你闻到蒙古族额吉送来的奶茶飘香;一道吊桥的那边,苗族小伙子的山歌会让你觉得喉咙发痒;一片草地的尽头,哈萨克的骑手追着风从你身边闪过……还有村寨的织布、绣花、剪纸、吹木叶等民族技艺展示能让你亲身参与互动;傣族泼水节、民族集体舞大家挑、趣味体育、少数民族农耕等系列特色活动,使你忘记了谁是参观者,谁是表演者。更吸引你眼球的还有原汁原味的歌舞表演以及各民族不同的节庆活动。只要你有足够的时间,还有瀑布、梯田、植物庄稼等景区,会把你的身影融入其间。

顺便说一句,如果有人还想开阔"口"界,也请你到这儿来,酥油茶、马奶酒等各种民族美食佳肴让你尝不够呢!

参观指南

地　　址:北京市朝阳区亚运村国家奥林匹克体育中心西门对面。

乘车路线:乘55、386、407、740、804、819、849、921、941、944 等
　　　　　路公交车到北辰路站或祁家豁子站下车。

开放时间:8:30-17:30(南园每年12月至次年3月关闭)。

票　　价:分园60元,通园90元。

网　　址:http://www.emuseum.org.cn

咨询电话:010-62063647、62063646

Chinese Ethnic Museum in Beijing

In Chinese Ethnic Museum, one can appreciate the traditional national buildings and customs of various ethnic groups, watch the song and dance performance, purchase the national handicraft and can also taste the delicacies of different ethnic groups personally. The whole museum is divided into North Garden and South Garden with an area of 450,000 square meters. There are 16 national villages in the North Garden including those of Qiang, Oroqen and Hezhe ethnic groups.

There is the biggest domestic casting iron sculpture, artificial tropical banyan forest, water-eroded cave, Panlong Waterfall, rock pictures and supernatural wood of Alishan in the North Garden. There is national museum, Sculpture Square and over 20 national villages in the South Garden. All buildings adopt the proportion of 1: 1. While visiting the national villages, visitors can enjoy the water-fall, floating clouds and bonfire at grassland, they can take a view of the scenic spots of China without going out of Beijing and appreciate and participate in the song and dance, festival celebrations, production and customs of various nationalities. From various sports and performances, visitors can enjoy the distinctive culture and art of Chinese people.

Visitors Guide
Address: Opposite the west door of National Olympic Sports Center of the Asian Games Village of Chaoyang district of Beijing.
Bus Route: Bus No.55, 386, 407, 740, 804, 819, 849, 921, 941 or 944 to Beichen Road Stop or Qijiahuozi Stop
Opening Hours: 8:30 – 17:30
(The South Garden is closed from every December to March of the next year).
Admission Fee: RMB 60 Yuan for each garden, 90 Yuan for both gardens.
Tel: 86-10-62063647, 62063646

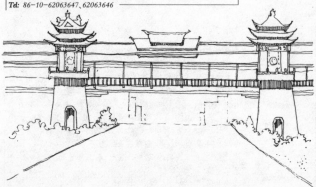

观复古典艺术博物馆

享受收藏快乐

京城知名的文物鉴定收藏家马未都先生很早就开始个人收藏,随着藏品的日益增加,他便萌发了开办私立博物馆的念头。1997年1月,马未都任馆长的观复古典艺术博物馆正式对外开放。

保存和展示民间古典艺术藏品,举办相关学术交流,传播文物鉴定知识,观复古典艺术博物馆的办馆宗旨就颇有吸引力。在国泰民安的社会中,一大批民间收藏家都有展示个人藏品的欲望,也渴望获得文物鉴定知识,而京城又是整个中华民族古典艺术的荟萃之地,这天时地利人和也许就是这座私立博物馆长盛不衰的原因吧?

博物馆藏品主要以明清传世文物为主,重点是陶瓷、古家具及小件文玩。馆内常年展出百余件明清家具,定期以专题形式展出中国古代绘画美术作品。近年来,这里举办了"17世纪青花瓷器展"、"中国古代文房用具展"、"明清箱匣展"、"宋辽金元古瓷展",除馆藏珍品以外,还将社会公私收藏珍品纳入展览中,产生了更加广泛的社会影响。其展陈方式也颇有特色,一件件展品都与四周的环境氛围相协调,把文物恢复到当年的使用状态中去,使人有身临其境的感受。在这里,参观者甚至可以动手研究,评估展品的价值;这里还为收藏爱好者提供文物鉴定服务,举办个人收藏品展览等活动。

让每一个人都享受收藏快乐,这是博物馆的办展理念。不管你的收藏兴趣或淡或浓,不管你是家藏万品还是独收一只,在这里,都会使你健谈起来,快乐起来。

参观指南

地　　址:北京市朝阳区大山子张万坟金南路18号。

乘车路线:东直门乘909路或朝阳门乘813路(开往蟹岛)张万坟站下车回行50米。

自驾车线:大山子走机场辅路过五环400米,过南皋桥600米,过高压线塔立即右拐约1500米,过不规则十字路口直行400米,路南二层拱窗白楼即到。

开放时间:9:00-17:00,春节四天休息。

周边餐饮:金三角餐厅、运福来餐厅、龙义祥餐厅。

票　　价:20元;学生10元。

咨询电话:010-64342308、64338887

Guangfu Classic Art Museum

The art museum is situated on the famous cultural street-Liulichang West Street. Entering the exhibition room, you will find yourself surrounded by classic and elegant instruments and melodious tweedles. In an instance, you will travel through the histories. The ceiling made of bast-fibre ropes, the curtain made of reed straws, the Suzhou bed made of elm in Qing Dynasty, the wooden stool at the corner, the elm chest in Ming Dynasty, the exquisite porcelains, four treasures in ancient studies, and various boxes, drawers, bags, trunks in different shapes and sizes make the exhibition room look like an old-timey living environment. All the objects in the room from the sculptured clapboard to the tool for making juices all have time-honored history.

Guangfu Classic Art Museum aims at publicizing glorious national cultures, demonstrating ancient Chinese civilization, holding classic art exhibitions and conducting relevant cultural and artistic exchanges.

Visitors Guide

Address: No. 18, Jinnan Road, Zhangwangfeng, Dashanzi, Chaoyang District, Beijing

Bus Route: Take Bus No. 909 at Dongzhimen or Bus No.813 (to Xiedao) at Chaoyangmen to the stop of Zhangwanfeng, then walk back for 50 meters.

Self-drive Route: Dashanzi Airport Assistant Way, 400 meters from 5th Ring Road, 600 meters from Nangaoqiao Bridge, and drive 1,500 meters to the right, 400 meters straight from the irregular crossing. The second-storey white building on the south of the road is the museum.

Opening Hours: 9:00-17:00, close four days during the Spring Festival

Admission Fee: RMB 20 Yuan; 10 Yuan for students

Tel: 86-10-64342308、64338887

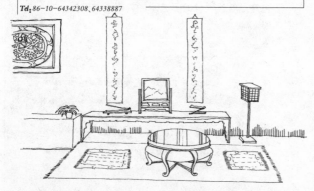

何扬·吴茜现代绘画馆

神奇的现代绘画艺术

1994年,画家何扬、吴茜夫妇到德国访问,在柏林、波恩、科隆等城市,他们看到博物馆、艺术馆和画廊比比皆是,公众素质和审美意识很高。联想到国内的情况,他们决心建立自己的艺术陈列馆。功夫不负有心人,三年后,中国第一家现代绘画馆一何扬、吴茜现代绘画馆向社会开放。

这是一座老北京平民生活的四合院,占地面积400多平方米,院中6间青砖瓦房辟作展室,展出着何扬先生和吴茜女士的现代绘画作品。主展厅有何扬的《故乡系列》、《十二生肖系列》、《宗教、世俗和文字系列》以及《新主题主义》等内容的作品,吴茜的大写意《水墨风景系列》作品。北展厅展出何扬作品《老北京的传说故事》、吴茜创作的新宫壁画《故乡系列》等作品。南展厅主要展出吴茜的《彩墨水乡系列》等作品。除此之外,绘画馆还有藏品1000多件。

也许是提供了相通的艺术语言,绘画馆建立以后,欧亚美许多国家的大使馆官员、画家、记者及现代绘画爱好者前来造访;来自德国、西班牙、克罗地亚、英国、日本、文莱、印度、伊朗、美国、墨西哥、秘鲁、智利等国家的各界人士,或参观,或来访,或文化交流,或购买画作,这里已成为现代绘画艺术的国际沙龙。

何扬先生是职业画家,吴茜女士是北京画院的画家、副教授,他们对现代绘画艺术有着独到的理解,也有着精湛的画技。他们笔下的滇南少女、汉宫靡子、洱海风情、水乡秀色都把灵秀之气表现的如痴如醉,让中外观众驻足良久,留恋不舍。

也许这就是现代绘画艺术的神奇之处吧!

参观指南

地　　址:北京市朝阳区金盏乡长店村南宫1128号。

乘车路线:703路公交车终点站下即到金盏乡郁金香花园往西500米之后往南即是。

开放时间:8:00-16:30。

周边餐饮:福运来餐厅。

票　　价:5元;学生2元。

咨询电话:010-84312537

He Yang and Wu Qian Modern Gallery

This is a typical Beijing quadrangle, covering an area of 400 square meters. The six brick rooms with grey tiles are opened as the showrooms where the visitors can enjoy the modern painting works created by He Yang and Wu Qian. The main showroom displays He Yang's series: Hometown, 12 zodiac animals, Religion, customs and characters, New themes and Wu Qian's freehand brushwork landscape ink paintings. In the north exhibition showroom, the visitors can see He Yang's Legends of Old Beijing and Wu Qian's Hometown Series. Wu Qian's Water Village Series is on display in the south showroom. In addition, the gallery houses more than 1,000 items of collection.

Mr. He Yang is a professional painter. His wife Wu Qian is a painter and a vice professor in Beijing Academy of Fine Arts. They have special understandings and outstanding skills in painting. Girls form South of Yunan Province, imperial concubines in Han Dynasty, landscape of Erhai Lake, and water villages are the themes of their painting. The grace and beauty in their works make the visitors at home and abroad reluctant to leave.

> **Visitors Guide**
> **Address**: No.25 Douban Hutong, Chaoyang District, Beijing
> **Bus Route**: Take Bus No.703 to its terminal, and walk west for 500 meters then to the south. Opening Hour: 8:00—16:30
> **Nearby Restaurant**: Fuyunlai Restaurant
> **Admission Fee**: RMB 5 Yuan; 2 Yuan for students
> **Tel**: 86—10—84312537

中国现代文学馆

中国现代文学的殿堂

这里是中国现代文学的殿堂。

这里以我国 1919 年"五四"运动前后兴起的现代文学为起点,直至目前的当代文学,所有的文学资料都在收藏之列;所有我国各民族现、当代作家以及居住在港澳台和海外的华人作家,不论其政治态度和风格流派如何,其著作和创作档案都在收藏之列。不管你是老迈年高还是垂髫稚童,都可以在这里见到你熟识的姓名和曾经阅读过的作品。

中国现代文学馆是一位历史巨人,把近百年来中国文坛巨匠名家的手稿、文物、照片、书信、音像及其他文献资料收纳到自己的襟怀之中,31 万件馆藏资料让世界重新审视中国现代文学。这里收藏的著作及各种期刊杂志完全可以重新撰写一部中国现代文学史。

文学是用语言文字塑造形象,表达作者思想感情的艺术,与其他艺术形式相比,文学反映社会生活的空间更为自由和广阔。中国现代的文学家们用自己手中的笔,弘扬美好,鞭挞丑恶,推动着社会历史不断前进,无论是风雨如晦的年月,还是阳光灿烂的日子,他们都用清醒理性的思维去面对一切,都用热爱这块土地的赤诚去迎接一切。

望着文学馆里悬挂着的 15 位中国现代大作家的肖像,人们都有一种温暖涌上心头。因为他们曾经用自己的生命做火把照亮漆黑的夜,使中国人找到光明的道路。记住他们吧!他们是:鲁迅、郭沫若、茅盾、巴金、老舍、曹禺、叶圣陶、冰心、艾青、夏衍、胡适、丁玲、田汉、沈从文、赵树理。

参观指南

地　　址:北京市朝阳区文学馆路 45 号。
乘车路线:在北三环乘 300、718、801 路公交车到和平街北口,换乘 18、62、379(高峰车)、406、419、847 到经贸大学下,或换乘 119、409、422 路到文学馆(芍药居)站下。
开放时间:9:00-16:30,周一闭馆。
周边景观:中华民族园、奥林匹克公园、太阳宫水上乐园、元大都城垣遗址公园、北京服装学院服饰博物馆、北京中医药大学中医药博物馆。
票　　价:20 元;学生 10 元。
咨询电话:010-84619011

National Museum of Modern Chinese Literature

The museum is the information center of modern Chinese literature. It performs the researching and exchanging functions as a literature museum, a literature library, and literature archives. The museum's collection covers a wide range. The new literatures in 20th century are mostly included in its collection, such as works and materials in Chinese from Hong Kong, Macao, Taiwan and abroad. The museum now houses over 300,000 items of collection, among which there are 190,000 books, 2100 kinds of magazine (90,000 volumes), 142 kinds of newspaper, 10,970 manuscripts, 8,282 photos, 7,887 letters, 453 tapes, 773 video cassettes and 2,959 cultural relics. As for those literature materials donated by some writers, libraries named after their donators are set up. Currently there are 55 libraries, including libraries of Ba Jin, Bin Xin, Tang Tao, Zhang Tianyi, Zhou Yang, Yu Pingbo, Ding Ling, Xia Yan, A Ying, Xiao Jun, Yao Xueyin, Xiao Qian, Zhang Guangnian, and Liu Baiyu etc.

Visitors Guide

Address: No.18 North Road of West Third Ring Road, Beijing

Bus Route: Take Bus No.300、718、801at North Third Ring Road to North of Heping Street, and then transfer to Bus No.18、62、379、406、419、847 to the University of Trade and Economy, or transfer to Bus No. 119、409、422 to the stop of Shaoyaoju.

Opening Hours: 9:00—16:30, close on Monday

Nearby Sights: Chinese Ethnic Cultural Park、Olympic Park、Taiyanggong Water Park、Yuan Capital City Wall Ruins Park

Admission Fee: RMB 20Yuan; 10 Yuan for students。

Tel: 86-10-84619011

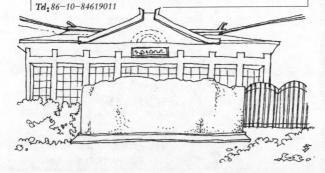

北京中医药大学中医药博物馆

将身心融入燕山秋色

西方世界在多年的猜疑和否定之后，终于摘掉了木眼镜，跨越了心理的障碍，认可了中国的中医中药。来北京的外国人中，不少人都慕名来到这里。

北京中医药大学中医药博物馆1500平方米的中药标本展厅里汇聚着中药的精华，从药用植物的标本到中药饮片，从药材实物到丸散成药，让参观者目不暇接。漫步在中国医药史的展厅里，你会感悟到它的恢弘和深邃。也许汉代画像石上扁鹊行医图带有传说的色彩，而历代名医塑像则切切实实象征了中医药的传承和发展。至于那些沙盘模型、仿宋针灸铜人、中医白铜外科用具、少数民族医药器具。还有明朝出版的医药书籍，就实实在在证明了中医中药对这个民族的生息和崛起具有怎样重大的意义。

站在宽敞的博物馆大厅，你会不知不觉融入那幅巨大的《燕山秋色图》国画中，去谛听夏商周神草疗医时是如何诊脉，去拜访在硕果累累的杏林中小憩的董奉，去感受华佗、张仲景、孙思邈、李时珍的执着和艰辛，去把握《本草纲目》科学定义以外的厚重思想。当你走出馆藏珍品的海洋时，你也许已经知道，这里已经借助网络技术构建了一个全新的中医药博物馆，无论你在世界的任何地方，移动鼠标和敲击键盘就会得到博物馆收藏、展示和教育功能的数据，从而让更多的人在观赏和研究我国古代中医药文化遗存的同时而获得助益。博物馆人已将中医药科学融会在二十一世纪那种全新的阳光里，让灿烂走遍世界。

参观指南

地　　址：北京北三环东路11号（和平街北口）

乘车路线：乘13、62、119、300、302、367、407、117、406、419、606、718、725、713、801、825、835、847、967、特8、运通104路公共汽车和平街北口下车。

开馆时间：每周二、周五　　　上午8：30-11：30
下午1：30-4：30（节假日闭馆）

票　　价：10元；学生票5元。

周边景观：现代文学馆、北京服装学院民族服饰博物馆。

咨询电话：64286845（医史部）；64286835（中药部）

Traditional Chinese Medicine Museum affiliated to Bei–jing University of Traditional Chinese Medicine

This museum was established in 1990. Mr. Shao Yifu from Hong Kong donated 3,000,000 Hong Kong dollars and the state allotted 2,500,000 Yuan for the museum's construction that was initiated in 1987.The museum is a modern building with total construction areas of 3160 square meters. It is divided into two exhibition halls: one for displaying traditional Chinese medicine samples and the other for exhibiting traditional Chinese medicine history. The former covers an area of 1500 square meters and the latter 800 square meters.

The exhibition hall for traditional Chinese medicine history is rich in collection. Under the theme, there are about 1100 cultural relics, 200 medicine books with thread binding and 6000 journals and magazines in total. The exhibition hall for medicine samples displays on a large scale every aspect of the system of traditional Chinese medicine, and the comprehensive exhibition room is the major one that opens to the public at present, which offers a systemic introduction to the basic knowledge on traditional Chinese medicine.

Visitors Guide

Address: No. 11 East Road of the North Third Ring Road, Beijing (North exit of Heping Street)

Bus Route: Bus No. 13、62、119、300、302、367、407、117、406、419、606、718、725、713、801、825、835、847、967、8(special route), 104(Yuntong) to the bus stop of North exit of Heping Street.

Opening Hours: 8:30—11:30 13:30—16:30 Tuesday and Friday (except festivals and holidays)

Admission Fee: $ 10, $ 5 (For students)

Tel: 86-10-64286845 (Dept of medicine history); 64286835 (Dept of Chinese traditional medicine)

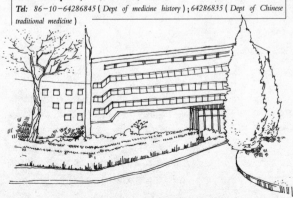

北京航空航天模型博物馆

放飞希望　　放飞心情

北京航空航天模型博物馆军事性、知识性、科学性、参与性的特点，让参观者尤其是青少年观众着迷，在这里可以参观展览，动手制作，参加训练及观摩飞行表演，度过一个欢乐的航模节日。

博物馆主体活动分三部分：一是参观展览，主要有"航空航天史话"，介绍中外航空航天首次发生的重大事件；"历史的辉煌"，介绍中国空军对外作战的历史功绩；世界战机今昔，以图片的形式介绍各国主要作战飞机的参数造型以及中国航空航天成就展和航空航天模型展。二是航模制作与竞赛，向每人赠送简易模型飞机套材一副，在教练的指导下现场组装并参加比赛，博物馆免费提供奖品。三是观摩模型飞机的飞行表演，主要机型有初教五飞机、AH-1 武装直升机、J3联络机、CAP-21 飞机、运十二飞机、"巨嘴鸟"双机编队，可以进行特技飞行、空投表演、投放彩花彩带、机枪扫射、对地进攻等各项飞行表演。你可以乘坐电动滑翔机飞上天空，体验飞行感受。还可以亲手操纵长二丙火箭模型的发射，当你按动电钮，火箭拖着长长的尾烟扶摇直上，刺向青天的时候，你的心潮会波涛翻滚，无比激动。为了让人们亲眼目睹大型飞机编队的飞行气势，博物馆每年 5 月至 10 月举办规模浩大的仿真飞行表演，让你的感官和心灵同时获得一种震撼。

也许，你会在这里购得一架航模飞机，并且学会了放飞。于是，你为你的飞机系上红领巾或装满心愿，发动引擎，放飞于蓝天白云之间。其实你不正是放飞了希望，放飞了心情吗？

参观指南

地　　址：北京市朝阳区大山子环铁内。

乘车路线：403、813 路环线总站；402、418 路南皋总站需步行 20-40 分钟。

开放时间：8：30-17：00，周一闭馆；5 月至 10 月每周六上午 10：30，大型仿真表演（恶劣天气，另有任务除外）。

票　　价：日常参观 20 元，学生 10 元；飞行表演 40 元，学生 25 元。团体参观价格另议。

咨询电话：010--64372990、64373015

Beijing Museum of Aeronautic and Astronautic Models

Beijing Museum of Aeronautic and Astronautic Models is China's first model museum. Open to the public on September 9, 1999, the museum has been successively designated as Beijing Patriotism Education Base, Beijing Science Popularization Education Base, Scientific and Technological Education Base for Primary and Middle School Students in Chaoyang District, Science Popularization Education Base in Chaoyang District. Located in Dashanzi, Chaoyang District, the museum has activity zones represented by "the small airport", exhibition halls, workshops and teaching halls with a total coverage of 26,000 square meters. There are 92,000-square-meter green belts with beautiful rural landscapes.

The facilities inside the museum are suitable for international contests. The museum is an ideal place for those keen on aeronautic models to fly their models. At present, there is considerable discrepancy between China and foreign countries in conducting this activity. We hope that men of insight make concerted efforts to promote this cause and let our children's dreams fly from here.

Welcome to this museum. Welcome your visit and participation in flying the aeronautic models.

Visitors Guide

Address: *Dashanzi Huantie, Chaoyang District, Beijing*

Bus Route: *Bus No. 403, 813 to their destination; Bus No. 402, 418 to the stop of Nangao, then walk 20−40 minutes*

Opening Hours: *8:30−17:00, close on Monday; large−scaled simulation performance begins at 10:30 a.m. on Saturday from May to October (except in bad weather and on special tasks)*

Admission Fee: *RMB 20 Yuan(adults), 10 Yuan (students) for regular exhibition; RMB 40 Yuan (adults), 25 Yuan (students) for aerobatic flight. Price will be discussed for group visitors.*

Tel: *86−10−64372990、64373015*

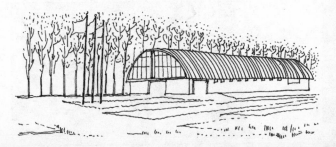

北京民俗博物馆

从"祈福"到"戴福"

在高楼林立，霓虹闪烁的现代化气息的掩映下，一座红墙绿瓦的古老建筑静悄悄地坐落在车水马龙的街道上，她以古朴苍劲的气势和传统文化的神韵，迎接着每一位到这里参观游览的客人。

北京民俗博物馆自 1999 年正式开放以来，以举办富有民俗特色的展览为主要内容。北京民俗风物展、中国百年民间服饰展、老北京人的生活展、荷包收藏展等大型展览，吸引着许许多多参观者。老人在这里找到回放的童心，中年人在这里把稚趣又带回梦里，孩子们在这里看到快乐还有这么广阔的天地。只是参观"人生礼俗展览"感觉有些疲惫：那么多繁文缛节，人得多累啊！不过，中国自古有"礼多人不怪"之说，尽管累点儿，但那种暖融融、乐陶陶的氛围不是更加珍贵吗？

春节是中华民族的第一大节日。民俗博物馆适时构建了京城春节民俗文化活动的一个景观。以"祈福迎祥，戴福还家"为主题的"走福路"、"挂福牌"、"绕福树"、"画福部"、"系福条"活动使许许多多京城百姓的节日情怀更加浓郁。春节后人们相见，似乎能看到对方眉间跳动的那个"福"字。从"祈福"到"戴福"，一个"福"字的功劳何止万语千言。

博物馆坐落在国家一级保护文物东岳庙内。这座历史文化深厚、文物观赏价值极高的东岳庙是北京民俗文化的积淀与传承的一个完美的载体，有形的民俗文化瑰宝和无形的民俗文化神韵相映成辉，凡是到过这里的人都会有这样的思考：是东岳庙选择了民俗文化，还是民俗文化选择了东岳庙？

参观指南

地　　址：北京市朝阳区朝外大街 141 号。

乘车路线：乘 101、109、110、112、750、846、858、846 路公交车到神路街站下车。

开放时间：8：30-16：30。

周边餐饮：陶然居、水上人家。

票　　价：10 元。

咨询电话：010-65510151、65514148

Beijing Folklore Museum

The museum is a place of interest which stores treasures of folk-custom cultures in Beijing. Situated in Dongyue Temple, a cultural site under the first-class protection of the state, the museum is composed of grand and exquisite buildings which look especially spectacular.

Since it opened to the public in 1999, the museum has put on exhibitions characterized by distinct folk style. Such exhibitions as Beijing Folklore Exhibition, China's Centenary Folk Costume Exhibition, Old Beijingnese Life Exhibition, Etiquette and Custom Exhibition and Pouch Collection Exhibition enjoy great popularity among the people in Beijing. The folk cultural activities along with the festivals also attract every visitor to the museum. The activities like "walk the blessing road, round the blessing tree, draw the blessing cloth, and tie the blessing ribbon" under the theme of "pray blessing and carry the blessing home" have become a famous ceremony to celebrate the Spring Festival in the capital.

Visitors Guide
Address: No.141, Chaowai Street, Beijing
Bus Route: Bus No.101、109、110、112、750、846、858、846 to the bus stop of Shenlu Street
Opening Hour: 8:30—16:30。
Nearby Restaurants: Taoranju Restaurant, Shuishangrenjia Restaurant
Admission Fee: RMB 10 Yuan
Tel: 86—10—65510151、65514148

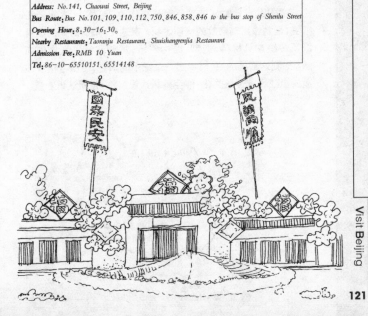

北京中国紫檀博物馆

认识紫檀

中国紫檀博物馆本身就称得上是一件完美壮观的工艺品，气势宏大而又处处精巧，古色古香而又不乏现代气息。1000多平方米的馆前广场采用海漫斗板地面——大青砖铺设后再浸润桐油，要知道，过去只有皇家才使用这种方法呢！抬望眼，看看博物馆纯木结构的大门，横竖叠砌用了400多立方米木材，那支撑门楼的4根立柱，高8米，直径0.6米，无论是规模还是材质，在北京的仿古建筑中都是极为少见的。博物馆五层大楼主体建筑使用磨砖对缝工艺，也许你用放大镜才能见到其中的缝隙。在博物馆建筑工程中，一些曾在故宫博物院工作过的木、瓦、画等行业专家亲临指导，这些专家一向被人们称为"活国宝"。

在近一万平方米的展厅里，你可以领略到紫檀木创作的那种神韵：故宫的角楼、紫禁城御花园中千秋亭与万春亭显尽了皇家气派；山西五台山龙泉寺320条蛟龙姿态各异；玲珑剔透的北京四合院；飞翘天空的山西飞云楼，这些传递着东方神韵的艺术珍品，都是用紫檀木雕刻而成，众多的圆雕、浮雕、透雕作品，无不在熠熠生辉地展示着紫檀所创造的艺术魅力。

紫檀因为它的红棕颜色而被统称为"红木"，木质坚重细腻，是制作高档家具的优质木材。在这里，明清时期的家具以及传统家具材料、造型、结构展示，重新演绎了家具的内涵。来到这紫檀的海洋，拂起一朵细小的浪花，感悟紫檀所传递的中国民族传统文化，你会重新认识紫檀，重新认识自我。

参观指南

地　　址：北京市朝阳区兴隆西街9号。

乘车路线：乘312、728路公交车或小公共汽车至高碑店；乘115、718路或康恩专线至康家沟下车，往南部步行至高速路口再往东200米；乘342、382、846、859、908路至太平庄下车往南400米；乘一线地铁到四惠站向东500米；乘城铁在高碑店下车向西100米；乘游船在高碑店湖下即可。

开放时间：8:30—17:00（16:30停止售票）。周一休息。

周边景观：红领巾公园、兴隆公园、团结湖公园、大黄庄苗圃、定福庄福利艺园、北京朝阳高尔夫俱乐部。

周边餐饮：华润饭店。

票　　价：50元，团体、老人、学生凭证30元，学生团体20元；1.2米以下儿童免费参观。

咨询电话：010-85767320

China Red Sandalwood Museum

This museum itself is a perfect craftwork. It looks spectacular, exquisite, archaic but modern.

The exhibition room covers an area of 10,000 square meters. Here you will touch the essence of red sandalwood culture. The corner tower of the Palace Museum and the Qianqiu Pavilion in the imperial garden assume an imperial air. 320 dragons carved in the Longquan Temple in Shanxi Province are in different postures. The delicate Beijing quadrangles and the Feiyun Building in Shanxi Province are representatives of red sandalwood arts. They are all artistic treasures in the Orient made of red sandalwood. Numerous basso-relievo, sculpture-in-the-rounds, fretworks give full display to the charms of red sandalwood.

Sandalwood is called the red wood because of its color. Its texture is hard, which makes it excellent material for making furniture. Here, the furniture made in Ming and Qing Dynasties, traditional furniture materials, designs, structures give a brand-new interpretation of the meaning of furniture.

Visitors Guide

Address:

Bus Route: *Bus No. 312、728 to the stop of Gaobeidian; Bus No.115、718 to Kangjiagou, walk south to the exit of expressway, and then walk east for 200 meters; Bus No.342、382、846、859、908 to Taipingzhuang, and walk south for 400 meters; subway to the station of Sihui, and walk east for 500 meters.; urban railway to Gaobeidian, and walk west for 100 meters; Take boats to Gaobeidian Lake.*

Opening Hours: *8: 30–17: 00(16: 30 stop selling tickets), close on Monday*

Nearby Sights: *Honglingjin Park、Xinglong Park、Tuanjiehu Park、Dahuangzhuang Nursery、Dingfuzhuang Welfare Art Garden、Beijing Chaoyang Golf Club*

Admission Fee: *RMB 50 Yuan、30 Yuan for students, senior citizens and group visitors.*

Tel: *86–10–85767320*

北京服装学院服饰博物馆

用花朵打扮

现代人把服饰当作审美的重要内容，而多民族构成的中华民族大家庭又是缤纷服饰的硕大花园，牡丹与月桂连理，腊梅与芙蓉并蒂。

北京服装学院民族服装博物馆里，一万余件中国 56 个民族的服装、饰品、织物、蜡染、刺绣等传统民族服饰向参观的人们展示炎黄子孙五千年服饰的演进和神州大地各民族服饰的绚烂多彩。博物馆设综合服饰厅展示中国南北方各民族精美的服饰；苗族服饰厅展示苗族各支系的不同服饰；金工首饰厅展示中国各民族的金工首饰；民族考察图片厅展示著名民族学家、摄影家庄学本先生于 20 世纪 30 年代初拍摄的一批民族考察图片；多功能厅用于现代化的民族音像资料的演示，内置先进的电化教学设备，既可展示馆藏珍品，也可用于教学和学术交流。从这里走向香港的《银装盛彩 — 中国少数民族服饰展》，从这里走向巴黎的《百年时尚 — 中国衣饰展》，都赢得国内外人士的极大赞誉，成为北京市乃至全国服装服饰对外展示的一个窗口。

西子湖畔的织锦，姑苏城里的刺绣，苗寨瑶山的蜡染是中国传统民间纺织、印染工艺，这些具有民族风格的艺术品在这里都有精品展示，参观者可以在博物馆里亲自动手学习织、绣、染的各种手工技术。当你捧着自己的艺术佳作时，一定会对我们中华民族织染和服饰文化产生深厚的感情。

人们把这里比作中华民族服饰的苗圃，辛勤的园丁采撷 960 万平方公里土地上的花朵，装点中华民族的容貌，酿造我们生活的甜蜜。

参观指南

地　　址：北京市朝阳区和平街北口樱花路甲 2 号。

乘车路线：乘 13、62、117、119、361、367、379、416、419、422、606、713、725、730、807、847、特 8、运通 101 路公交车到和平街北口、樱花东街或中日医院站。

开放时间：每周一、二上午 8：30-11：30；

　　　　　每周四、五、六下午 1：30-16：00；

　　　　　每周三、日、节假日及寒暑假闭馆。

票　　价：20 元；学生 10 元。

周边景观：现代文学馆、北京中医药大学中医药博物馆。

咨询电话：010-64288261

Museum of Ethnic Costumes in Beijing Institute of Clothing Technology

Museum of Ethnic Costumes in Beijing Institute of Clothing Technology is a cultural research institution integrated with collection, research and teaching. It has Comprehensive Displaying hall, Miao Ethnic Group Trappings hall, Golden Jewelry hall, Fancyworks and Dyed Products hall, Old Photos hall and Folk Traditional Trappings room.

This museum boasts more than 10 thousand excellent works of traditional ethnic costumes including clothes, trappings, fabrics, batiks and bredes of China's 56 nationalities. The level of Miao ethnic group costume collection in this museum is first-class among such kind of research institutes. It has collected over 1000 wonderful costumes including silver trappings of more than a hundred branches of the Miao ethnic group and has taken a lot of photos concerned. This museum also pays much attention to the collection and research of golden jewelry, folk fabrics and batiked craft and forms different series. Meanwhile, the museum houses a group of precious pictures taken in 1930s for ethnic investigation.

Visitors Guide:

Address: A2, Yinghua Road, northern entrance of Heping Street , Chaoyang District, Beijing

Bus Route: Bus No. 13, 62, 117, 119, 361, 379, 416, 419, 422, 606, 713, 725, 730, 807, 847, special 8 and Yuntong 101 to northern entrance of Heping Street, east Yinghua Street or China-Japan Hospital

Opening Hours: Mon and Tue   8:30 ———11:30
                   Thu, Fri and Sat 13:30———16:00
                   Closed during Wed, Sun, vacations and holidays

Admission Fee: RMB 20 Yuan; 10 Yuan for students; 5 Yuan for groups; free for middle and primary school students, retired carders, senior citizens, teachers and students of Beijing Institute of Clothing Technology, overseas Chinese who have been in China for more than 50 years.

Tel: 86-10-64288261

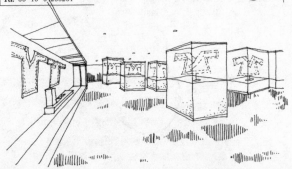

北京金台艺术馆

相通的人类艺术心灵

在邻近旧时燕京著名的八景之一"金台夕照"的地方，一座建筑风格独特的艺术馆格外引人注目，典雅的五台状外形，错落的五座金字大屋顶，艺术馆外朝阳湖碧波浩淼，湖畔绿树浓荫，在湖馆之间，是由党和国家领导人亲手栽种的大片松林以及外国政要种植的国际友谊林。越湖远眺，艺术馆的金字山顶掩映在葱郁之中，如同一幅优美的风光画作。这里就是由全国政协委员、著名画家袁熙坤先生集资创建的金台艺术馆。

国家逢盛世，文化亦昌隆。作为国内迄今最大的民间艺术博物馆，以其独特的艺术创意和文物收藏为媒介，将中国传统文化的底蕴与魅力推向国际，又将世界许多国家五彩缤纷的艺术送进国人的视线。近期举办的"哥伦比亚工艺作品展"上，430件珍奇的家具、装饰、器皿、服装、礼仪用品以及玩具，涵盖了这个国家的风貌与民俗。"保加利亚当代艺术展"中，50多幅充满艺术前瞻、抽象风格的油画吸引着文化部、外交部人士和东欧一些国家大使馆的外交官。由以色列知名艺术家设计的有关家具和灯饰等方面艺术的数十件作品以及众多的摄影作品构成"当代以色列艺术设计展"，让参观者了解了这个国家当代艺术风采和自然风光名胜。

袁熙坤先生擅长用水墨丹青刻画人物，并对油画民族化进行了成功的探索。馆内陈列着他应邀为国际100多位政要和知名人士写生创作的肖像。人们参观艺术馆，望着这些地球村村落领袖和名人的肖像画以及肖像的主人签名题词致信时的高度赞誉，会深深地感到，人类艺术心灵的相通必将会创造一个更加美好的地球。

参观指南

地　　址：北京市朝阳公园内（西门）。

乘车路线：乘302、710、805路公交车朝阳公园下。

开放时间：10：00-16：00，不定期举办展览。

票　　价：朝阳公园门票。

咨询电话：010-65019441

Beijing Jintai Art Museum

Jintai Art Musuem is founded by Yuan Xikun, a famous painter and a commissioner of national committee of the CPPCC. As China's largest folk art museum, it relies on its unique art originality and cultural collections to present China's profound traditional culture and its charms on the international stage, and introduce the colorful arts of foreign countries into China. On the current Columbia Arts and Crafts Exhibition, there are 430 precious decorations, furniture, wares, costumes and ceremonial necessities and tolls which reflect the folk customs in Columbia. On Bulgaria Contemporary Arts Exhibition, 50 avant-guard and abstract oil paintings attract many experts from the Ministry of Culture and the Foreign Ministry, and also attract some diplomats from East European countries' embassies. Contemporary Israel Art Design Exhibition composed of furniture and light decorations designed by famous Israeli artists and scores of photographic works help the visitors know more about the artistic charms and natural beauty of Israel.

Visitors Guide

Address: Inside Chaoyang Park (west gate)

Bus Route: Bus No. 302, 710, 805 to the stop of Chaoyang Park

Opening Hours: 10: 00—16: 00, hold irregular exhibitions

Admission Fee: included in the ticket price of Chaoyang Park

Tel: 86—10—65019441

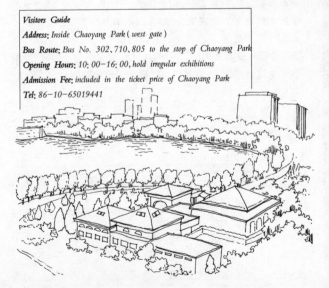

中国铁道博物馆

中国铁路在风驰电掣

　　1881 年筑成的唐山至胥各庄铁路,是我国第一条标准轨距铁路,120 多年来,铁路在中国大地上不断延伸,通向了沙漠深处,通向了世界屋脊,不久的将来,这钢铁巨龙将驶进西藏拉萨,掀开中国铁路史新的一页。也许就在这一天,将会有大批的参观者涌进中国铁道博物馆。

　　中国铁道博物馆是铁路系统的国家级博物馆,是铁路文物、科研成果的收藏、保管、陈列、展示及编辑研究的专门机构,是保护铁路历史遗产,传播铁路科技知识,宣传铁路建设成就的公益性文化场所。在博物馆 16500 平方米的机车车辆展厅里,展出了 40 余台(辆)不同年代,不同型号的机车车辆。其中有国内现存最早的"0"字号蒸汽机车,旧中国使用的多种外国机车,新中国自行设计制造的首台蒸汽、内燃和电力机车,著名的"毛泽东号"、"朱德号"机车,党和国家领导人使用的公务车及多种铁路客车和货车。在 4000 多平方米的综合展厅里,向观众展示中国铁路发展史、铁路建设成就和铁路科普知识。大量的实物、模型、照片、图表以及多媒体生动地再现了中国铁路一个多世纪以来的发展变化和铁路在国民经济中的重要作用。

　　中国铁道博物馆还有着展览设计制作业务的传统优势和雄厚实力。20 多年来,以全新的设计、制作手段,独立承办了国内外许多大型展览会,如在日本举办的"中国铁道展",在加拿大举办的"世界交通通讯博览会","全国铁路'八五'改革与发展成果展"等,通过这些展览会,人们看到中国铁路的风驰电掣,也看到铁道博物馆的飒爽英姿。

> **参观指南**
> 地　　址:北京市朝阳区酒仙桥北路 1 号院北侧。
> 乘车路线:乘 403、629、813 路终点站下车向东。
> 开放时间:9:00-16:00,周一休息。
> 周边餐饮:品中品大酒楼、蓝宝石商场、龙樽酒楼。
> 票　　价:20 元;学生 10 元。
> 咨询电话:010-64381317

China Railway Museum

The museum is the national museum of the railway system. It specializes in collecting, storing, displaying, exhibiting and studying the cultural relics concerning railways. It is a cultural site for protecting the railway heritages, publicizing the railway technologies, and popularizing the railway construction achievements. In the exhibition hall covering an area of 16,500 square meters, there are about 40 locomotives on display. Among them, there is China's earliest steam engine locomotive with number series beginning with O, foreign locomotives used in old China, the first domestic steam engine, gas engine and electric engine locomotives manufactured since 1949, the famous Mao Zedong Train, Zhu De Train, the special trains for state leaders, various railway carriages and wagons etc. The 4,000-square-meter comprehensive exhibition room presents in front of the audience Chinese railway development, railway construction achievements, and railway scientific knowledge. A large number of real objects, models, photos, charts and multi-media give a vivid introduction to the development of China Railway in the past century.

Visitors Guide
Address: No.1 Courtyard, Jiuxianqiao North Road, Chaoyang District, Beijing
Bus Route: Bus No.403、629、813 to the terminal and then walk east.
Opening Hours: 9:00—16:00, close on Monday
Nearby Restaurants: Pingzhongping Restaurant、Sapphire Market-place, Longzun Restaurant
Admission Fee: RMB 20 Yuan; 10 Yuan for students
Tel: 86—10—64381317

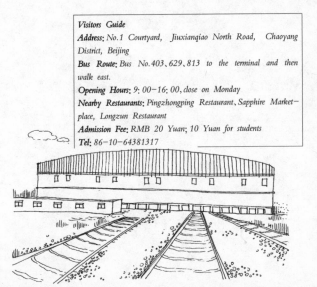

第六章 丰台区

中华航天博物馆

祝福，中国航天

随着天文望远镜的改进和观测技术的提高，于是可观测的范围日益扩大。20世纪末，人类可观测到的最远的天体距地球约200亿光年。面对如此浩瀚的宇宙空间，人类飞行其中，探索其奥秘的梦想与愿望与日俱增。阿姆斯特朗在登上月球时说：这对一个人来说是走了一小步，但对人类来说是跃出了一大步。杨利伟在太空中手捧中国国旗和联合国旗，其实正是表达了人类一个共同的心声：到地球以外的空间去航行，到星际和行星际去航行。

中华航天博物馆作为中国航天事业最大的展示窗口，越来越受到国内外各界人士的青睐。前来参观的人中，不乏肩负考察洽谈任务的官员、企业家、专家、学者、自费出行的旅游者，更有期望增长科学知识的大中小学生和着意领略中国航天业绩的各阶层人士。这里的每件展品都是中国航天事业艰辛和辉煌的写照。人们从这里看到中国第一枚运载火箭飞越万里长空，准确地落入南太平洋预定海域；看到长征二号捆绑火箭发射澳大利亚卫星的立体模拟沙盘及其演示；看到标志着长征系列火箭50次发射成功的五星红旗。"中华航天火箭卫星展"、"航天之魂展"的系列展览，众多的实物和图片让世人看到中国航天事业的昨天、今天和明天。

看到许许多多的飞行器在宇宙中穿梭，中国人更看重那神舟五号飞船，当每晚月亮升起的时候，中国人在期盼不久的将来嫦娥奔月的那一天。

祝福，中国航天！

参观指南
地 址：北京市丰台区东高地南大红门路1号。
乘车路线：742、729路公交车六营门站下车。
开放时间：9:00-16:30。
周边景观：南苑机场、北京麋鹿生态实验中心、北普陀影视城。
周边餐饮：肯德基、大公鸡餐厅等。
票 价：30元；学生、老人、残疾人凭证半票。
咨询电话：010-68384456

China Spaceflight Museum

The museum is located on the axis of Beijing city, 10 km south of Tian'anmen Square. It was opened in October 1992, with a coverage of 10,000m², among which the exhibition areas are 5,000m². It is the biggest display window for China's spaceflight technology. Beijing Municipal Government and the people's government of Fengtai District successively rated the museum as Youth Education Base.

The museum is composed of preface hall, comprehensive main hall, high-tech application hall, specialized halls etc. On the first floor, the main hall displays major products in the field of China's spaceflight, including carrier rockets, satellites, models, lamp boxes and pictures. Inside the museum, there are well-equipped academic report hall, advanced technological negotiation hall, VIP room, which are available for various academic and technological exchanges, interior and exterior cooperation and all kinds of exhibition.

Visitors Guide

Address: *No.1 Dahongmen Road, South of Donggaodi, Fengtai District, Beijing*

Bus Route: *Bus No. 742, 729 to the stop of Liuyingmen*

Opening Hours: *9:00−16:30*

Nearby Sights: *Nanyuan Airport, Beijing Elk Zoological Experimentation Center, Beiputuo Moovie Town*

Nearby Restaurants: *KFC, Big Roaster Restaurant*

Admission Fee: *RMB 30 Yuan, 15 Yuan for students, seniors and disabled people with relevant cards.*

Tel: *86−10−68384456*

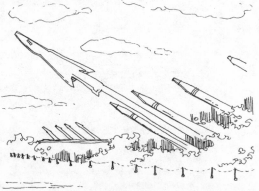

中国人民抗日战争纪念馆

卢沟桥抒情

卢沟桥的石栏上，精刻着485个石狮，每当夜幕降临，月上西山，狮影月色构成了一幅动人的画卷，清乾隆皇帝所题"卢沟晓月"碑立于桥东碑亭内。在这醉人的美景中，中华民族开始遭受人类历史罕见的灾难，中国人民也由这里开始了不屈不挠的战斗。坐落于卢沟桥旁宛平城的中国人民抗日战争纪念馆向人们讲述着这段血与火的历史。

作为全国唯一一座全面反映中国人民抗日战争历史的综合性大型纪念馆，建筑面积2万平方米，展览面积6000平方米，藏品达1万余件，基本陈列为《中华民族的抗日战争》展览。3个编年史陈列展馆和"日军暴行馆"、"人民战争馆"、"抗日英烈馆"专题馆。采用文物与景观、照片与影视、音乐与解说、参观与参与相结合的方式，再现了从1847年日本帝国主义侵略中国，到日军投降以及中日建交的历史过程，突出表现了在中国共产党倡导的抗日民族统一战线的旗帜下，全民族团结抗战和中国共产党的中流砥柱作用，讴歌了无数个革命先烈为民族解放、国家独立而英勇牺牲的感人事迹，深刻地揭露了日本侵略者在侵华战争中犯下的滔天罪行。600幅珍贵照片，500件实物，8个大型景观及一组模拟地道，全面、具体、深刻地再现了历史，给观众以强烈的震撼。

中国人民抗日战争纪念馆把"以史为鉴、勿忘国耻、振兴祖国"为永恒的教育主题，立足于增强公众的民族意识，培养爱国主义精神。如今，当人们来到卢沟桥抗战遗址，沐浴"卢沟晓月"美景时，心中还有对历史的追忆和奋发的豪情。

参观指南

地　　址：北京市丰台区宛平城内街101号。

乘车路线：624、709、748、937支3、964、964支、971、983路公交车。

开放时间：8:00-16:30(16:00停止售票)。

票　　价：15元；大学生8元；中小学、残疾人、60岁以上老人凭证免票。

周边景观：卢沟桥、宛平城、中国人民抗日战争纪念雕塑园、长辛店二·七纪念馆。

咨询电话：010-83893163

The Memorial Hall of the Chinese People's Anti-Japanese War

The museum is situated in Wanping County near the Lugou Bridge where the July 7th Event took place. Set up in 1987, the museum is composed of three comprehensive halls, three specialized halls (atrocities of Japanese army, the People's war, and the anti-Japanese heroes) and one half-panorama art gallery. It houses 3800 photos and materials, and 5000 cultural relics. The comprehensive halls display the whole process of Anti-Japanese War. The specialized exhibition on Japanese army's atrocities includes the recovered scenes of notorious 731 bacteria army and Nanjing Massacre. The exhibition on the people's war retrieves the grand scenes of the brave struggles and the movements to save the nation from extinction. Introductions to the famous Taierzhuang, Pingxingguan and 100-Battalion campaigns can also be found on the exhibition. In the hall of heroes in anti-Japanese war, the brave stories of Yang Jingyu, Zhao Yiman, Zuo Quan, Peng Xuefeng, Zhang Zizhong, Tong Linge, and Zhao Dengyu are introduced. In the gallery, modern video-audio technologies are adopted to vividly simulate the battle field of July 7th Event.

Visitors Guide

Address: No. 101, Wanping County, Fengtai District, Beijing

Bus Route: Bus No.624、709、748、937(branch),3、964、964(branch)、971、983

Opening Hours: 8:00—16:30 (16:00 stop selling tickets) renovation period is from January 17, 2005 to July 7,2005

Nearby Restaurants: Hualing Household Recipe Restaurant 、Jingchuan Restaurant、Fumannian Dumpling Restaurant

Admission Fee: RMB 15 Yuan; 8 Yuan for college students; Free for primary and middle school students, the disabled and the seniors over 60 years old with relevant proofs.

Tel: 86—10—83893163

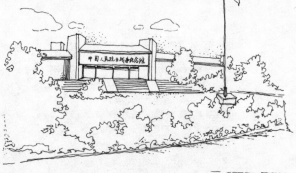

北京辽金城垣博物馆

汩汩水关已千年

1990年,北京发现了金中都南城垣水关遗址,被评为当年全国十大考古发现之一。水关遗址是现在北京除部分金代城墙外仅存的金中都建筑遗迹。水关是古代城墙下河水进出的水道建筑,又称水门。金中都城内的河水即通过这里流入南护城河。1995年,北京辽金城垣博物馆在这里建成并对外开放。

馆内布置着《首都之始》的基本陈列,介绍了北京城的发展史。第一单元以照片、线图、复原图及水关遗址出土文物为主,介绍水关遗址的发现、发掘经过及水关建筑的结构、价值和中国城市水关建筑的演变过程。第二单元为辽金以前的北京。展出的文物有战国、汉代的陶井圈,北朝的铭文砖——北魏"熙平元年"砖以及史思明墓出土的珍贵文物等。第三单元展示辽代北京城即辽南京的面貌。第四单元详细展示金中都的城垣、宫城、城市布局、漕运等。第五单元是金以后的北京,展示由于元大都城址向东北迁移,金中都城作为南城就逐渐衰败以至消亡的过程。此外,还有以辽金为主题的展览,"辽代墓葬壁画及文物精品展"、"京城辽金佛教遗址摄影展"和"契丹女真碑刻拓片精品展"等都深刻系统地反映了辽金的历史演变和文化艺术情况。

近几年来,博物馆千方百计地扩大馆藏,金代铜辟邪、木桌椅、磁枕、契丹小字墓志、木版画等一大批文物成为馆藏珍品。它们与金中都南城垣水关遗址交相辉映,使参观者更加深入地了解了千年以前辽金王朝的时代风貌。如果在这驻足倾听,水关遗址过水涵洞里,是否依稀传来汩汩水声?

参观指南

地　　址:北京市丰台区右安门外玉林小区甲40号。

乘车路线:特3、19、49、59、122、361、716、717、744、800路菜户营或大观园下。

自驾车线:商务会馆东侧向南玉林小区内。

开放时间:9:00-16:00,周一闭馆。

周边景观:大观园、商务会馆。

票　　价:10元。

咨询电话:010-63054992

Beijing Liao and Jin City Wall Museum

Situated at Yulin Neighborhood, Fengtai District, Beijing, the Liao Jin City Wall Museum is built on the ruins of a water gate in Zhongdu, the capital of Jin Dynasty (1153 - 1215).

The Museum consists of the underground part and the historical displays. The underground part is the protected Watergate Site, and its volume is the greatest among all the ancient city wall water pass sites which have ever been found in China. Built to allow sewage to flow out under the city wall, the gate lies five meters underground and connected via a culvert with the Liangshui River, 50 meters to the south. Built of wood and stone, the lowermost layer is pine, over which lies a layer of stone slabs, fixed with iron brackets. The basic exhibition entitled "Development of Capital Beijing" is divided into several sections: Beijing before Liao and Jin Dynasties, Nanjing in Liao Dynasty, City Walls of Jin Zhongdu, Palaces, Urban Layout, Canal Transportation, and Beijing after Jin Dynasty etc. Various cultural relics, the discovery and excavating course of the site, practicalities, photos and charts about the structure of the water-gate are on display.

Visitors Guide

Address: No.40 Yulin Community, You'anmenwai Road, Fengtai District, Beijing

Bus Route: Bus No. special 3、19、49、59、122、361、716、717、744、800 to the stop of Caihuying or Daguanyuan

Self-drive Route: Inside the Yulin Community, east of Commerce Assembly Hall

Opening Hours: 9:00-16:00, close on Monday

Nearby Sights: Daguanyuan Garden、Commerce Assembly Hall

Admission Fee: RMB 10 Yuan

Tel: 86-10-63054992

北京大葆台西汉墓博物馆

古墓随笔

汉宣帝本始元年（公元前 73 年），高祖刘邦的嫡孙刘建被封为广阳王，其领地亦称广阳国。1974 年发现的大葆台一号汉墓的墓主人就是刘建。在其后对一号墓进行扩大发掘的过程中发现的二号墓的墓主人即为其王后。大葆台一、二号墓是目前北京地区考古发掘规模最大的两座汉墓，也是新中国成立后首次发现的"黄肠题凑"墓，墓葬形制和棺椁结构保存得十分清楚和完整，为研究我国汉代"梓宫，便房，黄肠题凑"的帝王葬制提供了重要而珍贵的资料。大葆台汉墓虽早年被盗，但仍出土了千余件文物，其中有许多工艺水平较高的珍品，体现了 2000 多年前工匠的高度创造才能。1983 年12 月，在一号墓原址上建立的大葆台西汉墓博物馆正式对社会开放。

从这座古墓的结构来看，刘建墓室严格遵循西汉帝王的葬制。大葆台西汉墓博物馆设有广阳王刘建墓室复原陈列厅，再现了"梓宫，便房，黄肠题凑"的墓葬结构，以及当时随葬的车马遗址。出土文物陈列室，展出两墓随葬的陶器、铁器、铜器、玉器、漆器以及丝织物，从中可以了解当时人们的生活轮廓。

西汉王朝的强盛体现在许多方面。大葆台西汉墓博物馆陈列的帝王御用的最高级别的葬具体系，就从一个侧面展示了这种强盛。地宫里用几百方柏木、楠木等珍贵木材累成的椁室更足以看出 2000 年前那种奢华，那种辉煌。

参观指南

地　　址：北京市丰台区郭公庄世界公园东南。

乘车路线：特 7、744、905、937（西线）、967、905 路公交车至世界公园站下车，南行 10 分钟可见"西汉古墓"路标。

开放时间：9：00-16：00。

参与项目：模拟考古　30 元／探方。

周边景观：世界公园景区、世界著名景观微缩展出。

票　　价：10 元；学生 5 元。

咨询电话：010-83612852

Museum of Western Han Dynasty ancient tombs at Dabaotai of Beijing

It is a distinctive imperial tomb site museum, built on the former underground palace site of King Liu Jian (73 B.C.-45 B.C.) in Western Han Dynasty with an area of 18000 square meters. The underground palace is of large-scale and special structure with "the standard of emperor" of Han Dynasty, namely the highest emperor-burying system in the Western Han Dynasty. The underground palace was completely constructed by such precious trees as cypress and nanmu, etc. It is 23.2 meters long from north to south, 18 meters wide from east to west and 4.7 meters from the earth's surface. There are 3 carriages, 11 horses in the tomb, which were for the crown prince and kings according to history record. There are over thousands of unearthed relics, including bronze, ironware, jade article, lacquer ware, agate article, the pottery and silk fabrics. Underground palace site is the only large domestic intact tomb site of Han Dynasty and the carriages and horses are valuable materials for the study of Chinese culture and Beijing history.

Visitors Guide

Address: The south of Guogongzhuang of Fengtai district of Beijing.

Bus Route: Take Bus No. 7 (special), 744, 905, 937 (west line), 967 or 905 and get off at World Park Stop, then walk for 10 minutes towards the south and the signpost " Western Han Dynasty ancient tombs " can be seen.

Opening Hours: 9:00−16:00

Participate−in Project: Simulation archaeological activities 30 Yuan for each visitor.

Nearby Sights: World Park, world−famous sights in miniature.

Admission Fee: RMB 10 Yuan; 5 Yuan(students)

Tel: 86−10−83612852

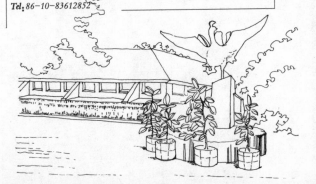

北京御生堂中医药博物馆

精缩中医药的历史

商代的龙骨、战国的九针,上迄宋、元下至民国时期的上百件不同式样的陶瓷药罐,明、清时期制作的如今尚未启封的中药……北京御生堂中医药博物馆珍藏着3000余件"宝贝"。门前矗立着手捧灵芝的明代神农雕像,生了锈的铁钩上挂着木色斑驳的药幌,旧式柜台上摆着医家出诊用的木药箱。展厅里陈列着各类展品:从刻着"内府"二字的药酒缸到《内经》中记载的九针;从熊胆、虎骨等珍贵药材到给同治皇帝开的宫廷御方。那幅标注着各个穴位图文并茂的练功图让人们想起武侠小说中的武林秘籍;那胡庆余堂的药罐让人们想起了胡雪岩曾有的慷慨曾有的悲怆;就连那满墙的草药标本也有百年的历史。

始创于明万历36年(1609年)的山西榆次的御生堂药铺后转至河北、北京,至今已有近400年的历史。今天,清代御生堂后人将药铺的老物件以及多年来收藏的中国历代中医药文物聚集一堂,择其精华,创办了北京御生堂中医药博物馆。馆长柏杨先生是御生堂的后世传人,他向观众娓娓叙说着药铺的历史和博物馆创建的过程。历经战火和浩劫,很多文物保存下来非常不易。"文革"期间,这个宋代的黑釉药坛子上面白色的"内府"二字被刮下来,然后里外抹上泥土,佯作腌咸菜的缸子才保存下来。这种药坛在国内只存三个,这一个为最大最完整的。

数千件展品不仅展现了御生堂药铺的兴衰历程,也精缩了中国中医药6000年发展变化的历史。人们有理由相信,从御生堂药铺到御生堂中医药博物馆,是时代的跨越,是认识的飞越,是思维的超越。

参观指南

地　　址:北京市丰台南路69号四合庄园内。

乘车路线:乘351、353、747、804路公交车丰台南路站下
　　　　　车。

开放时间:9:00-16:00。

周边餐饮:丰和轩、君子阁酒家、玉福麟酒家。

票　　价:20元;学生10元。

咨询电话:010-63712176

Beijing Yushengtang Herbal Medicine Museum

The museum houses over 3,000 pieces of collection, among which include a statue of Shennong (a legendary ruler of ancient China who introduced agriculture and herbal medicine) in Ming Dynasty mottled color camouflages on rusty iron hooks, statue of the medical king on an old-style medicine-chest, and wooden medicine boxes on counters. One can envision the bustling business of the drugstore with its golden and silver medical utensils, old account books as well as rare herbal medicines like fossil fragments with inscriptions of the Shang Dynasty arranged as they were in the past.

From the "nine needles" and stone needles in the Eastern Zhou Dynasty when the Classic of Internal Medicine was compiled, to the big black vat for producing medicine, you can trace Chinese medical science back to ancient times. The fossil fragments with inscribed characters of the Shang Dynasty, bamboo slips of the Han Dynasty, the prescriptions for Emperor Tongzhi of the Qing Dynasty, and herbal samples with a history of more than 100 years, indicate the countless ties between the Chinese herbal medicine and the traditional culture. The vicissitudes of the drugstore and the 6000-year-old history of ancient Chinese medicine have been reflected through these collections.

Visitors Guide
Address: *No.69, Fengtai South Road, Sihe Manor, Beijing*
Bus Route: *Bus No.351、353、747、804 to the stop of Fengtai South Road.*
Opening Hours: *9:00—16:00*
Nearby Restaurants: *Fenghexuan、Junzige Restaurant、Yufulin Restaurant*
Admission Fee: *RMB 20 Yuan; 10 Yuan for students*
Tel: *86-10-63712176*

第七章 石景山区

中国第四纪冰川遗迹陈列馆

神奇的冰川擦痕

也许"第四纪"、"冰川擦痕"之类词语过于专业化,使许多人对坐落于北京石景山区的中国第四纪冰川遗迹陈列馆颇有陌生之感。其实,"第四纪"即为地质历史的最后一个分期,大约为250万年以前至今;"冰川擦痕"就是冰川的运动造成山体岩石出现状貌相似、与山坡倾斜方向基本一致的条痕,这是由于冰川内沙砾或石块的棱角在运动中刻画出来的。当这多少万年以前山体运动的遗迹呈现在眼前时,你会有什么样的感慨呢?的确,这就是中国第四纪冰川遗迹陈列馆向你展示的实景。

这里的展览共分四部分。第一部分是"地球 — 人类的家园",主要介绍地球的产生、地球的位置、太阳对地球自然环境的影响以及地球的构成等内容。第二部分是"李四光关于第四纪冰川学说的创立和发展",主要介绍冰川的基本知识和李四光创立中国第四纪冰川学说的过程。第三部分是"冰期形成的假说",主要介绍当今科学界关于冰期形成原因的理论和假说等。第四部分是"当代地球科学的前沿 — 全球变化研究",主要介绍第四纪冰川研究等一系列关于把地球科学的最新理论联系起来进行研究的内容。在这些展览中,你还会认识这个熟悉或陌生的人物 — 中国地质学家李四光,人们用语言或文字表述自然科学的时候,总是很难脱离枯燥艰深的窠臼。但是当你站在科学奇景面前时,才会感觉到语言文字功能的单薄和无力。因此,这冰川擦痕的遗迹只用神奇来表述是远远不够的。

参观指南

地　　址:北京市石景山模东28号。

乘车路线:乘311、336、396、746、747、959、965、972、977、运通112、运通206路公交车在模式口或首钢口下;乘地铁到苹果园站换乘336、396路公交车至首钢小区,311路至模式口东口。

开放时间:9:00-17:00。

周边景观:法海寺、承恩寺。

周边餐饮:天外天、百姓坊。

票　　价:5元;学生3元。

咨询电话:010-88722585、88724148

China Display Hall of Quaternary Glacier Relics

The display hall is situated beside the Quaternary glacier site at Moshikou, Shijingshan District. Facing the Yongding River and leaning against the Cuiwei Mountain, it is the world's only display hall of glacier relics.

Inside the hall, you will get access to the basic knowledge about the Quaternary glaciers, the establishment and development of the Quaternary glacier theory initiated by Li Siguang, the application of glacier research in national economic construction and the distribution and the review of China's Quaternary glaciers. Most of the exhibits are photos and stone samples of glacier relics. The scientific popularization is the display hall's advantage. Influences of weather and environment on man's survival and development, how should man continue the civilization in future ice age, glaciers offer man opportunities in storing energies and pose grave challenges to human civilizations and other specific exhibitions will help us further know about the Quaternary glacier theory.

Visitors Guide

Address: No.28 Modong, Shijingshan District, Beijing

Bus Route: Bus No. 336,747,959,992 to the stop of Shougang Xiaoqu; Bus No. 337,354 to the stop of Shijingshan or Bus No. 337 to the general station

Opening Hours: 9:00—17:00.

Nearby Sights: Fahai Temple, Cheng'en Temple

Nearby Restaurants: Tianwaitian, Baixingfang

Admission Fee: RMB 5 Yuan; 3 Yuan for students

Tel: 86-10-88722585,88724148

法海寺

松柏壁画法海寺

古语说,有山便有水。北京石景山区模式口东北的翠微山,高不过几百米,每当春夏来临,清冽的泉水汇成小溪,潺潺地流过幽静的山谷。苍松巨柏掩映了一座古老的寺庙,这就是著名的北京法海寺。

坐北朝南的法海寺由南往北顺山势而建。主要建筑分别设置在三级平台上,第一级是山门殿,第二级有四大天王殿,第三级坐落着大雄宝殿,环绕宝殿东西南三面是回廊式祖师堂。法海寺建成于明正统八年(1443年),英宗朱祁镇亲赐寺额,在北京众多寺院中名垂一时。

法海寺以壁画闻名于世。五百多年的岁月沧桑丝毫没有剥蚀大雄宝殿六面墙上明代壁画的精美。三世佛身后的祥云图,东西墙壁上的佛众赴会图,龛背的三大士图和后墙壁的帝释梵天礼佛护法图,均采用工笔重彩卷轴画法,构图严谨,笔法细腻,技巧纯熟,用色考究,是北京历史古迹中在壁画方面的杰出代表,与甘肃敦煌的壁画和山西永乐宫壁画相比各有千秋,可与欧洲文艺复兴时期的壁画相媲美。

有时候,到峰峦绵亘、松柏葱郁的名胜古迹去旅游,不仅仅是访古问今,也不完全是游山玩水,而是信马由缰,随情遂意,让身心和生命都去松弛一刻,也许会别有一番滋味。假如你来法海寺,先不要思量这里柏林和壁画的内在精髓,只让林中的微风在耳边轻拂,只把壁画的美丽当作过眼烟云,你会感觉如何呢?

参观指南

地　址:北京市石景山区模式口。

乘车路线:乘311、336、337、396、746、747、959、965、972、977路公交车;乘地铁到苹果园站换乘336、396路公交车至首钢小区,311路至模式口东口。

开馆时间:9:00-17:00(冬季9:00-16:30)。

参观内容:明代壁画真迹,明代壁画录像,敦煌、永乐宫壁画图片展。

周边景观:八大处,田义墓,冰川遗迹,慈善寺。

票　价:成人20元,学生10元。

咨询电话:010-88715776

Fahai Temple of Beijing

Fahai Temple is located on the Cuiwei Mountain, two kilometers northeast of Moshikou, Beijing. The main constructions are respectively built on three terraces. On the first terrace is the Hall of Gateway; on the second is the Hall of Four Gods, and on the third is the Grand Hall of Buddha, around which is the Hall of Masters. Fahai Temple's construction was completed in 1443. Emperor Zhu Qizhen inscribed the stele of the temple, which makes it famous among numerous temples in Beijing.

Fahai Temple is noted for its murals, which are represented by the mural painting the auspicious clouds behind the three-life Buddha, the mural painting the Buddhists attending a meeting, the mural behind the shrine painting the three Masters and the mural on the back wall depicting Brahma worshiping the Buddha. They all adopt the traditional Chinese realistic painting method characterized by fine brush work and close attention in detail. Fine, delicate strokes, meticulous painting and exquisite coloring have made the murals distinguished among murals found in Beijing. Compared with Dunhuang Murals and Yongle Palace Murals in Shanxi Province, murals in Fahai Temple have their own merits, which could match the beauty of renaissant murals in Europe.

Visitors Guide:

Address: Moshikou, Shijingshan District, Beijing

Bus Route: Bus No.31 1,336,337,396,746,747,959,965,972,977; Underground railway to the station of Pingguoyuan, transfer to Bus 336 or 396 to Shougang Xiaoqu, then take Bus.311 to Moshikou Dongkou.

Opening Hours: 9:00–17:00 (winter 9:00–16:30).

Visit Contents: Authentic works and video programs about murals created in Ming Dynasty, Pictures of Dunhuang Murals and Yongle Palace Murals.

Nearby Sights: Badachu Park, Tianyi Tomb, Glacier Vestige and Philanthropy Temple

Admission Fee: RMB 20 Yuan (For adults), 10 Yuan (For students)

Tel: 86–10–88715776

第八章 海淀区

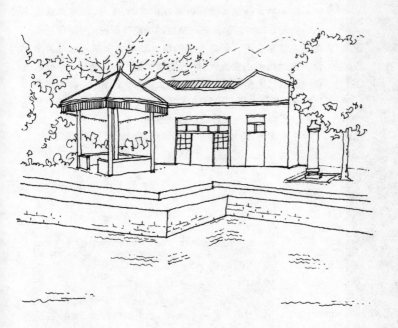

中国人民革命军事博物馆

那镏金的八一军徽

镏金的"八一"军徽在蓝天下熠熠生辉,永远显示着中国人民革命军事博物馆的辉煌和自豪。

走进军博,请放慢你的脚步,因为一丝一毫声响都会将那些展品惊醒:土地革命战争馆,井冈山黄洋界的炮声仍在无声地轰鸣;抗日战争馆,青纱帐里传来游击队员低沉有力的歌声;全国解放战争馆,百万雄师的樯橹樯帆正挟电携风;抗美援朝战争馆,上甘岭坑道里的志愿军战士已无唾液滋润一下干渴的喉咙……

从古代战争馆的刀枪剑戟,到现代战争馆的激光制导,还有兵器馆、礼品馆和程允贤雕塑艺术展等展馆,仿佛让你置身于金戈铁马的洪流之中,置身于兵家谋略和战争风云之中,去探究社会历史的变迁和民族军事文化的精粹。于是,你就看到了成吉思汗挽弓射雕的威武身影和横扫亚欧大陆的蒙古铁骑;于是,你就会领略了康熙大帝三战雅克萨的非凡魄力和郑成功收复台湾的民族豪情;于是,你就把列强入侵的罪行和鸦片战争失败的耻辱铭记在心;于是,你就将辛亥革命的艰辛和南昌起义第一声枪响的震撼深深体味。你还会对工农红军二万五千里长征的惊世壮举和中华儿女艰苦卓绝的抗战历程由衷赞叹,你还能感受到"三大战役"空前紧张的决战气氛和朝鲜三千里江山上血与火的洗礼。你还想得到什么?是不是还想了解琳琅满目的武器世界和兵器知识介绍?这里会让你的兴趣得到极大的满足。

走出军博,再回头望一望楼顶那镏金的八一军徽吧!

参观指南

地　　址:北京海淀区复兴路9号。

乘车路线:地铁一号线及长安街沿线各路公交车。

票　　价:成人20元,学生10元。

周边景观:中华世纪坛、玉渊潭公园、北京西客站。

周边餐饮:上海莺莺酒家、麦当劳、梅地亚中心。

咨询电话:010-66866114

Military Museum of the Chinese People's Revolution

Please slow down your paces when entering the Museum, for any noise will awaken those exhibits. The cannons' roaring from Huangyangjie, Jinggangshan Mountain still resounds in the Hall of Land Revolution War; the guerrillas' singing rising from green mountains still echoes in the Hall of Anti-Japanese War. In the Hall of National Liberation War, the exhibits will help you retrieve the scene that millions of soldiers sail across the Yangtze River like storms sweeping headlong. And in the Hall of War to Resist US Aggression and Aid Korea, items on display will remind you of the story that the voluntary army men at the Shangganling Tunnel have no saliva to wet their thirsty throats···

From swords displayed in the Hall of Ancient War to the laser weapons in the Hall of Modern War, from the exhibits in the Hall of Weapons to those in the Hall of Gifts, all the exhibits will lead you into a different world: horses, valiant soldiers, insightful strategists and smokes of gunpowder ··· they constitute a spectacular picture recording social and historical vicissitudes which reflect the essence of national military culture.

Visitors Guide

Address: Fuxing Road, west of Chang'an Street, Beijing

Bus Route: No. 1 Underground Railway, buses along Chang'an Street

Admission Fee: $ 20 (For adults), $ 10 (For students)

Nearby Sights: China Centenary Altar, Yuyuantan Park and Beijing West Railway Station

Nearby Restaurants: Shanghai Lulu Restaurant, McDonald, Media Center

Tel: 86-10-68518165

大钟寺古钟博物馆

子夜听钟　　祈福迎祥

　　元旦子夜时分,北京大钟寺古钟博物馆的永乐大钟轰鸣着,给首都市民送去了福音、带来了吉祥。大钟寺新年鸣钟活动已成为北京人辞旧迎新、祝愿祈福的一大品牌。

　　铸于明朝永乐年间的大铜钟悬于觉生寺的钟楼内,人们也就把觉生寺俗称为"大钟寺"。清乾隆时期,大钟寺成为皇家举办为民祈雨、消灾、降福法事活动的重要场所。几百年流传下来,聆听钟声已是人们心中最美好的愿望之一。钟声响起来的时候,人们把所有幸福齐聚心头,把所有烦恼抛至天外,尽情享受这美好的一刻。钟声还是传递友情的一种语言,不同肤色、不同信仰的人们在聆听钟声前那一刻的寂静,正是心灵的沟通和默契。

　　大钟寺古钟博物馆是我国唯一一座古钟文化类专题性博物馆,古钟文化的独特内涵吸引着海内外广大观众。东邻日本、韩国的客人来了,西方法兰西、意大利、挪威的朋友也来了。古钟文化是桥梁,是纽带,把友谊连结起来;古钟文化又是一粒种子,在世界各地开满钟铃艺术的鲜花。可以把永乐大钟的铭文中所记叙的内容看成是古钟文化的一个侧面,而人们用口用心传说的古钟故事,却是古钟文化最宝贵的财富。古钟文化随钟声而远播,一切尽在钟声里。

　　2003 年的元旦,大钟寺古钟博物院首次采用中科院声学所提供的气动扬声器扩音,几公里之外也能听到新年的钟声。此时,人们耳际的轰鸣,心头的震撼,脉搏的跳动都预示着明亮灿烂的未来。

参观指南

地　　址:北京市海淀区北三环西路甲 31 号。

乘车路线:乘 361、367、422、425、601、718、727、730 内环、836、836 支、367、967、运通 101、运通 201、小 73 路到大钟寺车站下。

开放时间:8:30—16:30。

周边景观:动物园、北京石刻艺术博物馆、北京艺术博物馆。

周边购物:双安商场。

票　　价:10 元;学生 3 元;北京市老年人、北京市中小学生、残废军人持有效证件免票。

咨询电话:010-62550843

Ancient Bell Museum in Great Bell Temple

The Ancient Bell Museum is located in the famous temple of the Great Bell. The Temple built in 1733 was originally called Jue Sheng Temple with coverage of 30 thousand square meters. With exquisite structures and great atmosphere, it was an important venue for the royal family to pray for rain and hold Buddhist activities. Because there is an enormous Buddhist bell made in the Ming Dynasty in the temple, it is also called Great Bell Temple.

The Ancient Bell Museum was founded in October, 1985. It is the sole special museum in China with the theme of collecting, exhibiting, studying and exploring the resources of ancient bells and the data concerned, as well as publicizing cultural knowledge about ancient bells. This museum treasures up hundreds of ancient bells with various kinds and thousands of data about ancient bells. It holds all kinds of ancient bell exhibitions regularly and conducts consultation, research and exchange on ancient bell culture. The unique exhibits and graceful environment have attracted a lot of visitors at home and abroad. Now on every New Year's Day, Spring Festival and significant ceremonies, the Yongle Bell will produce sound.

Visitor Guide:

Address: A31, West Beisanhuan Road, Hai Dian District, Beijing

Bus Route: Take Bus 361, 367, 422, 425, 601, 718, 727, 730(inner ring), 836, 836 (branch), 367, 967, Yuntong 101, Yuntong 201, 73 to Great Bell Temple stop.

Opening Hours: 8:30---16:30

Nearby Sights: Zoo, Beijing Stone Carving Art Museum, Beijing Art Museum

Nearby Shopping Center: Shuang'an Mall

Admission Fee: RMB 10 Yuan ; 3 Yuan (student); free for the senior citizens, middle school and primary school students and disabled armymen of Beijing.

Tel: 86-10-62550843

北京艺术博物馆

另一种京华

古老的万寿寺如今已经成为一座艺术的殿堂 — 北京艺术博物馆。馆内的万寿寺历史沿革、佛教艺术展、明清工艺品展、明清瓷器展和福寿文化艺术展等五项固定展览使这里名声大噪，其中明清工艺品展、瓷器展和佛教艺术展更是凝聚着北京的人气。倒不是说外地人或者北京的年轻人不喜欢京城的"料器"、"物件"，而能够真正看懂这些展品，了解它们深邃内涵的只有地地道道的老北京人。

"明清工艺品展"集中了近百件中国工艺美术发展鼎盛时期的宫廷和民间工艺品，用翡翠制成的酒杯、玉石雕成的香熏、天然犀牛角雕刻的酒具、象牙雕成的臂搁等等，每一件都构思巧妙，工艺精湛，美不胜收。"明清瓷器展"展出了百件瓷器，分为青花、釉里红、彩瓷、单色釉、仿古和鉴真几个部分，人们在这里一边欣赏精美绝伦的陶瓷艺术品，一边了解它们的历史演进过程，领略中国古代文明的灿烂风姿。"佛教艺术展"更是集中展示近百尊明清时期的各类佛造像，分诸佛、菩萨、护法神、罗汉、祖师、法器等几类，尽善尽美地反映汉传佛教和藏传佛教两大体系的并行发展，着重展示在造型、神态、服饰、技法等方面体现出的艺术创作成就。

如果说，高楼大厦、车水马龙和灯红酒绿、流光溢彩显出京华的繁盛，那么，北京艺术博物馆里，浓郁的文化氛围和深厚的文化底蕴不正显示了另一种京华吗？

参观指南

地　　址：北京市海淀区苏州街万寿寺内。

乘车路线：乘 300、323、374、730、830、831、817、944、967 路公交车万寿寺站下车。

参与项目：触摸屏，内容包括万寿寺景观介绍、艺术博物馆藏品介绍、知识问答题。

周边景观：紫竹院、石刻博物馆。

票　　价：20 元；北京市中小学生免票；持北京市老年证者免票。

咨询电话：010-68413380

Beijing Art Museum

Beijing Art Museum lies in the old Wanshousi temple. "Exhibition of the handicrafts of Ming and Qing Dynasties " has collected nearly one hundred imperial and folk handicrafts in the prime period of Chinese industrial arts. There are various categories including the emerald wineglass, jade incense-holder, wineglass made of natural rhinoceros horns, arm-holder made of ivory and so on.

"Porcelain Exhibition of Ming and Qing Dynasties " exhibit nearly one hundred porcelains, which are divided into QingHua, YouLiHong, color porcelain, single color glaze and archaized ceramics which can make people have a taste of the magnificent and graceful bearing of China's ancient civilization during the process of understanding superb ceramics of this period and the ceramic progress.

"Buddhism Art Exhibition" has shown nearly one hundred various Buddhism statues of the period of Ming and Qing Dynasties which are mainly divided into Buddha, Bodhisattva, doctrine-defending god, arhat, founder and instruments used in a Buddhist mass. They all reflect the parallel development of the two systems of Han nationality and Tibet as much as possible and show emphatically the artistic creation achievement embodied by design, expression, dress, skill and technique.

Visitors Guide

Address: Wanshousi, Suzhoujie, Haidian District of Beijing.

Bus Route: Take Bus No.300, 323, 374, 730, 830, 831, 817, 944 or 967 and get off at the stop of Wanshousi.

Participate—in Project: Touch—sensitive screen on which there are introductions to the view of Wanshousi temple and art museum collection as well as question & answer.

Nearby Sights: Zizhuyuan Park, Stone Engraving Museum.

Admission Fee: RMB 20 Yuan; students in middle and primary schools of Beijing

Tel: 86—10—68413380

北京石刻艺术博物馆

北京石刻艺术博物馆

噢，石刻艺术离我们的生活这么近!

红墙灰瓦，古树石塔，好一番宁静清幽的古刹浓韵。

跨入北京石刻艺术博物馆，只见千百年来的历朝历代的石刻精华，环绕着庄严的金刚宝座五塔高低错落地矗立着，俨然就是一个历史演进的里程铭碑。人们从这里回望明朝永乐年间，真觉寺在此处拔地而起，200余间大大小小的殿宇楼阁使之成为京畿第一大寺院，虽然清末的大火把寺院焚毁，但金刚宝座塔却奇迹般地未损丝毫。塔座、亭罩和五座四角密檐式佛塔，内砖外石，周身镌满佛教题材的雕像，使它成为年代久远、结构独特的大型古代艺术品。

也许你曾去过我国大型的石窟和著名的碑林，对石刻艺术产生着浓厚的兴趣，那就再请你到北京石刻艺术博物馆来看看吧!《汉故幽州书佐秦君志神道柱》及石阙构件，北朝的造像，唐朝以来的历代墓志，金元石雕，清代石享堂以及纳兰性德夫人卢氏墓志等众多的名家书法刻石，件件都会让你驻足流连。于是你会看到北京地区的汉唐雄风，辽金元各民族的交流融通以及明清时代的帝都风华。700年间的石雕艺术精品会使你时时产生抑制不住的激动，这是石刻艺术的神奇功力。

来这里自己动手试做一份拓片吧，服务员会免费为你讲解和指导，试做一件深黑闪光的乌金拓，色淡匀净的蝉翼拓，还是红色的朱拓，然后珍藏其自己操作成功的拓片，不管是工整还是参差，你都能体会到:噢，石刻艺术原来离我们的生活这么近!

参观指南

地　　址:北京市海淀区白石桥五塔寺24号。

乘车路线:105、107、111、808、804、814、904、320路公交车白石桥站下车，穿过首都体育馆，沿长河往东即到;运通104、105、106及727、804路，国家图书馆下车，沿长河往东即到。

开放时间:9:00—16:30(周一休息)。

票　　价:成人20元;学生10元;北京市中小学生免门票。

周边景观:北京动物园、北京天文馆、中国古动物馆、国家图书馆、中央民族大学民族博物馆。

咨询电话:010-62173543

The Stone Sculpture Museum of Beijing

The Stone Sculpture Museum of Beijing is located in the Zhen-jue Temple Ruins. Zhenjue Temple, commonly known as Wuta Temple is one of the older and uniquely structured tower among those existing in China. It is a rare piece of ancient art.

Inside the Museum, "Beijing Stone Sculpture Cultural Exhibition", "Zhenjue Temple Jingang Seat Historical and Cultural Exhibition" and the "Open-air Stone Sculpture Exhibition" display the gallantry of the Han and Tang Dynasties, the interaction among ethnic groups during the Liao, Jin and Yuan Dynasties and the charisma of the capital city during the Ming and Qing Dynasties. In particular, the stone sculptures spanning 700 years of the Yuan, Ming and Qing Dynasties are without equals. The important pieces exhibited include the earliest stone sculptures existing in Beijing, the stone carvings, figurines of the Northern Dynasty, tombstones since the Tang Dynasty, stone sculptures from the Jin and Yuan Dynasties, the exquisitely carved stone stands from the Qing Dynasty, the unique tombstone of Nalanxingde's wife, the model calligraphy of "Yejinzhai" and "Jinghetang" and the engraved stones of many calligraphy masters. Visitors will enjoy those charming sights so much as to linger on with no thought of leaving for home.

Visitors guide

Address: 24 Wutasi, Baishiqiao Bridge, Haidian District, Beijing

Bus routes: Take Buses 105, 107, 111, 808, 804, 814, 904 and 320 and alight at Baishiqiao Stop. Go through the Capital Stadium and walked along the river towards the east; Take Yuntong Buses 104, 105 and 106 as well as Buses 727 and 804 to alight at National Library stop. Walk along the river eastwards to reach the Museum.

Opening hours: 0900~1600 hrs (closed on Mondays)

Admission fee: RMB 20 Yuan (adult); 10 Yuan (student), admission is free for secondary and primary students from Beijing schools.

Tel: 86-10-62173543

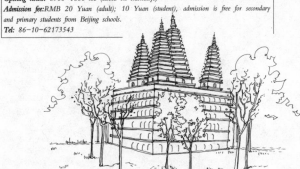

北京大学赛克勒考古与艺术博物馆

考古与艺术

赛克勒先生是一位美国医学博士,也是一位著名的收藏家和慈善家,一生钟爱中国的传统文化,对中国文物的保护和发展做出了有益的贡献。在赛克勒先生的慷慨帮助下,北京大学赛克勒考古与艺术博物馆于1993年5月落成并对外开放,这是我国高校中第一所考古专题博物馆。

北京大学历来有很浓厚的人文色彩。当年这所考古与艺术博物馆只有一个唯一的理由建在北京大学校区,那就是文化的相互契合。博物馆坐落于鸣鹤园旧址的南部,中国古典式建筑的结构与风格,既庄严宏伟,又典雅古朴,与燕园昔日的园林建筑十分和谐。只要你站在博物馆的门前,就可以感受到那种独特的流风余韵,重新构思古典美的真正含义。

赛克勒考古与艺术博物馆有两大展出内容:一是辅助中国考古学教学的标本,按时代和考古学文化顺序陈列;二是北京大学考古文博学院的师生历年考古发掘取得的重要收获,按工作地点集中陈列。"金牛山人"、"山东长岛北庄新石器时代聚落遗址"、"山西曲沃曲村晋文化墓葬"、"河北磁县观台窑址"等展品在中国考古文化中占有极其重要的地位。旧石器时代的出土石器,新石器时代的典型器物,商代的甲骨文,西周墓葬和遗址出土的铜器、玉器及陶瓷、钱币和封,无论是标本还是文物,其价值都远远超过其本身。置身在这两万多件展品当中,浓厚的学术气氛和艺术化的治学理念会时时浸润你的脑际。

参观指南

地　　址:北京大学西校区。

乘车路线:乘332、718、732、808路,运通106、114路,320支路、332支路、355支路等公交车到北大西门站下车步行5分钟。

开放时间:9:00-17:00(16:30停止售票);正月初一至初五休息。

周边景观:中关村高科技园、圆明园遗址公园、颐和园。

票　　价:5元;学生1元。

咨询电话:010-62751667

Sackler Museum of Art and Archeology at Peking University

The museum was completed and officially opened to the public on May 27. Situated in the beautiful west campus of Peking University, it is the first of its kind to be established in China's institutions of higher learning. In 1986, the construction of the museum was started by digging for the foundation with the investment of Mr. Sackler, who is a medical doctor, a famous collector and a philanthropist. He loves Chinese cultures and makes great contributions to the cause of protecting and developing Chinese cultural relics. The exhibitions are divided into basic displays and temporary exhibitions. The former is arranged chronologically into seven periods: Paleolithic Age, Neolithic Age, Xia Shang Zhou Dynasties, the Period of Warring States, Qin Han Dynasties, Three kingdoms, Double Jin Dynasties, South and North Dynasties, Sui Tang Dynasties, and Song Liao Jin Yuan Ming Dynasties. In addition, the museum holds an annual special exhibition which mostly gives instructions to the major archeological findings in recent years.

Visitors Guide

Address: *West campus of Peking University*

Bus Route: *Bus No. 332、718、732、808, 114, Yutong 106, 320(branch), 332(branch), 355 (branch) to the bus stop of West Gate of Peking University, then walk for 5 minutes.*

Opening Hours: *9:00-17:00 (16:30 Stop selling tickets);Close from the first to the fifth of the first month of the lunar year*

Nearby Sights: *Zhongguancun High-tech Park、Yuanmingyuan Park、the Summer Palace*

Admission Fee: *RMB 5Yuan;1 Yuan (Students)*

Tel: *86-10-62751667*

李大钊烈士陵园

英魂浩气长存

一座通体洁白的汉白玉塑像矗立在万年青、美人蕉的花圃中间。塑像前，鲜花绽放，香气四溢，好像在向主人表达崇高的敬意和深切的缅怀。

李大钊烈士陵园建于1983年，当时利用万安公墓的老建筑，年代久远，破损严重，因而进行了大规模的翻修改建工程。如今，一座仿古庭院式的木结构四合院建筑呈现在参观者面前。陵园正西房是李大钊生平事迹陈列室，第一展室通过大量的图片、实物资料展示李大钊烈士在天津法政专门学校读书及在日本早稻田大学留学及后来接受和传播马列主义的经历。重点展示李大钊在任北京《晨钟报》总编辑和《新青年》杂志编辑期间，发表的《庶民的胜利》、《布尔什维克主义的胜利》等文章，创办《每周评论》，积极领导五四运动，在北京发起组织马克思学说研究会和共产主义小组的情况；陈列室还展出了李大钊在中国共产党成立以后的一系列工作活动经历，歌颂了李大钊作为中国最早的马克思主义者，中国共产党早期领导人，为中国革命事业所做出的伟大贡献。第二展室展出陵园20多年的发展历史、党和国家领导人及各界人士参观陵园的照片及资料。

在众多的图片资料中，有一幅李大钊站在绞刑架下的照片，让参观者心中热浪翻滚。那种坦然自若、大义凛然的神情，表现出了革命烈士坚定不移的共产主义信念。通过这幅照片，人们感受到烈士的英魂和浩气长存于天地之间。

参观指南

地　　　址：北京市海淀区香山东万安里1号。

乘车路线：360、737路公交车。

自驾车线：香山东南侧万安公墓内。

开放时间：8：00-15：30。

周边景观：香山公园、北京植物园、卧佛寺。

周边餐饮：香山饭店、东岳酒楼、双清别墅。

票　　　价：免费。

咨询电话：010-62591044

Li Dazhao's Memorial Park

Li Dazhao's Memorial Park is located in the Wan'an Cemetery, southeast of Fragrant Mountain. With coverage of 2,200 square meters, the park is a courtyard in ancient styles, which was officially open to the public on October 29, 1983. Li Dazhao was one of the founders of the Communist Party of China (CPC). He made considerable contributions to the New Cultural Movement, the establishment of the CPC and the first cooperation between the CPC and the Kuomingtang Party. Li was killed by a reactionary warlord. In 1933, the CPC buried him inside the Wan'an Cemetery. In the newly built memorial park, the white marble statue of Li Dazhao is erected. Behind the statue is Li and his wife Zhao Renglan's tomb. Deng Xiaoping inscribed the characters on the monument behind the tomb. North to the monument is the epigraph written by the central committee of the CPC. The west room of the courtyard is for exhibition on Li Dazhao's Revolutionary Activities. A large number of materials with pictures give a detailed introduction to Li Dazhao's life journey and his great achievements.

Visitors Guide

Address: No.1 Wan'anli, east of Fragrant Mountain, Beijing

Bus Route: Bus No. 360、737

Self—drive Route: Inside the Wan'an Cemetery, southeast of Fragrant Mountain

Opening Hours: 8:00—15:30。

Nearby Sights: Fragrant Mountain Park、Beijing Botanic Park、Sleeping Buddha Temple

Nearby Restaurants: Fragrant Mountain Hotel、Dongyue Restaurant、Shuangqing Villa

Tel: 86—10—62591044

中央民族大学民族博物馆

舒展心情的好地方

有位诗人说，如果你想在任何时候都嗅到春天的气息，那就请你欣赏中国少数民族的服饰。真佩服诗人的语言，当你走进民族博物馆《少数民族服饰展》的时候，一股春天的暖意向你拥来，那么艳丽，那么绚烂，那么五光十色，那么多彩多姿。你如同坠入花的海洋，周身被芬芳的泡沫包围着。然而，这样的展览在民族博物馆只是展陈中的一部分。

中央民族大学民族博物馆藏品极为丰富，有各民族的生产工具，历史和革命文物、文献资料、锦旗、古扇、古文经典、生活用具、乐器、宗教器物、漆器、银器、铜鼓及各种民族服饰2万多件，绝大部分为珍品、稀品、罕见品。这里是全国收藏民族实物文化较多、较全、影响较大的博物馆。

民族博物馆是一座仿古建筑，琉璃瓦脊的悬山式屋顶在太阳的照耀下迸发着道道金光。拱形大门两旁，塔松侧柏葱葱郁郁，好像是敞开绿色的怀抱欢迎参观者的到来。走进博物馆的展厅，《中国少数民族服饰及生活用品展》的展品使你进入了一个五彩缤纷的世界：藏族的铜鼓、锦旗；黎族的织锦；土族妇女的头饰；蒙古族的佛像造型等展品，让你领略中国少数民族的生产、生活、娱乐的种种风采和神韵。在这里，你还可以了解高山族的建筑，鄂伦春日的桦树皮文化，仫佬族风情。无论你有没有艺术细胞，在这里都会产生艺术灵感，或亮开歌喉，或挥毫作画，或赋诗高诵，或与友阔谈，总之，这里是让你舒展心情的好地方。

参观指南

地　　址：北京市海淀区中关村南大街27号。

乘车路线：特4、特6、运通105、运通106、320、332路公交车于民族大学站下。

开放时间：周二至周五　9：00-12：00；周一、二、四14：00-17：00；周三、五下午闭馆；寒暑假、节假日闭馆。

周边景观：北京石刻艺术博物馆、国家图书馆、首都体育馆、紫竹院公园。

票　　价：10元；学生5元。

咨询电话：010-68932390

Museum for Nationalities of Central University for Nationalities

Situated inside Central University for Nationalities, No.27 Baishiqiao Road, Haidian District, the museum is a comprehensive ethical museum for academic teaching.

The museum houses over 30,000 cultural relics, books, costumes, production instruments which are identified into 14 categories. The basic display of the museum centers on the ethical costumes which reflect the skills and traditional techniques of nationalities in weaving, dyeing, making leathers etc. Here, you can see the Mongolian gowns, boots, Hani Nationality's jewelry cats and colorful dresses, Tibetan silver plates and pots, and other wares such as figures of Buddha and wooden sculptures etc. All these exhibits play a positive role in helping the people study the history and culture of nationalities and facilitating their mutual exchange. Meantime, the museum frequently holds exhibitions at home and abroad. Wherever it comes, it is greeted by warm welcome.

Visitors Guide

Address: No.27 Baishiqiao Road, Beijing

Bus Route: Bus No. special 4, special 6, yutong 105, yutong 106, 320, 332.

Opening Hours: Tuesday—Friday 9:00—12:00; Monday, Tuesday, Thursday 14:00—17:00; close on Wednesday and Friday afternoons, summer and winter vacations and holidays.

Nearby Restaurants: Red Sun Restaurant、Bostan Restaurant、Xinjiang Entertainment City, Laosichuan Restaurant, Jintan Chicken Soup and Shark Fin Restaurant and Jiangxue Restaurant.

Admission Fee: RMB 10 Yuan; 5 Yuan for students

Tel: 86—10—68932390

北京航空馆

心灵起飞

北京航空馆地处北京航空航天大学校内,其前身是北京航空学院飞机设计教研室的陈列室和停机坪。为了加强航空科普阵地建设,充实北京航空学院教学实验内容,1986 年 10月,中国航空学会北京航空馆正式开馆。

航空科技是一个国家经济发展的标尺之一。北京航空馆作为新中国成立以后第一座综合性的航空科技馆,牵动着业内人士和广大观众的心。20 年来,这里承担着对内教学,对外进行科普宣传的任务,并在保证教学科研的前提下,敞开大门,面向社会和大众,进行科技兴国、航空航天科普知识教育。据统计,建馆以来接待各类观众 200 多万人次,许多国内国际知名人士和大型跨国集团的代表也前来参观。

北京航空馆用大量的实物、模型和图片、照片布置多项陈列展览:30 多架飞机构成的"实体飞机精品"展,60 多件模型构成的"中国航空工业之窗"展,150 多件展品构成的"世界航空模型"展以及"中国航天技术图片"展等,都向人们展示中国和世界航空事业的竞争与合作,推动与促进的历程。"航空发展史"展把人类在飞行中梦想与尝试的座谈,跋涉与成功的今天,辉煌与灿烂的明天展示给观众。

展厅里,一架人称"鹞式"飞机的英国垂直短距起落战斗机和一架中国制造的歼八 Ⅱ 战斗机木制样机比肩而立,使参观者浮想联翩。人们的眼前,蓝天白云之间,飞机画出一道美丽的白线;人们的心中,航空强国的愿望正在一步步实现。只有在这里,你的心灵才会跟着飞机一起起飞。

参观指南

地　　址:北京市海淀区学院路 37 号。

乘车路线:到学院路的公交车都能到达。

开放时间:8:00-12:00;14:00-17:00(周一休息)。

票　　价:4 元;外宾 10 元;大中小学生、老人、残疾人 2 元。

咨询电话:010-82317512、82317513

Beijing Aviation Hall

Beijing Aviation Hall is located inside Beijing University of Aeronautics and Astronautics. It is a scientific and technological museum integrating science popularization and university teaching. The exhibition area of the hall is 9,000 square meters, including two showrooms and an outside parking apron. The aviation gallery in the eastern showroom employs vivid pictures, models and detailed data to describe the path of human's aviation exploration. The two exhibitions entitled Window on China's Aviation Industry and Achievements on China's Aviation Technologies give a comprehensive introduction to the development of China's aviation since 1949. Beijing Aviation Hall is a window for the public to know about China's great achievements in aviation as well as a patriotism education base for the youth.

The outside parking apron is the most attractive place, where about 30 aircrafts made in different countries and different periods are on display, including combat planes, fighter planes, bombers, scouts, helicopters and various civil planes etc.

Visitors Guide
Address: No.37 Xueyuan Road, Haidian District, Beijing
Bus Route: Buses to the stop of Xueyuan Road
Opening Hours: 8:00－12:00; 14:00－17:00; close on Monday
Admission Fee: RMB 4 Yuan; 10 Yuan for foreign guests; 2 Yuan for students, the disabled and the senior citizens
Tel: 86－10－82317512、82317513

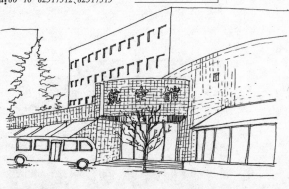

团城演武厅

震天吼声在耳畔

乾隆 13 年（公元 1748 年），清军在川滇地区与少数民族作战时遇到了麻烦。当地少数民族部落在关口路隘和地势险要之处用石头修建起许多高高的碉楼以抵抗清军，致使清军伤亡惨重，大败而归。乾隆皇帝震怒，亲自从八旗兵中挑选了 2000 名军士组建健锐营，进行用云梯攻碉特技训练。这支部队在后来的战斗中表现出色，显示了神威。随着健锐营的建立，京西象山南麓出现了一座集城池、殿宇、亭台、碉楼、校场为一体的武备古建筑群，这就是团城演武厅。

团城演武厅是健锐营的大练兵场，每月在固定的日子集中在这里进行合练，乾隆皇帝曾多次在演武厅的"松堂"检阅、奖励有功的将士。历经数百年沧桑岁月，团城演武厅仍巍然屹立在这块美丽的土地上，它背倚西山群峰，东对玉泉佛塔，场面宏大，气势恢弘。团城、演武厅、校场、实胜寺碑亭、松堂等建筑从北向南依次排开，北城楼卧碑上铭刻着健锐营平定准噶尔的战功；碑亭里的《御制实胜寺碑记》记述了金山战役的经过。从城门门额到卧碑碑文，均为乾隆皇帝亲笔手写，可见他对团城演武厅寄托着多么厚重的冀望。

1979 年，这里被列为北京市重点文物保护单位，经过整理和复建，团城演武厅恢复了往日的神采。200 多年前，宫廷画家、意大利人朗世宁曾绘制《健锐营演武图》，把当时演练的场面呈现给世人。如今你站在这椭圆形的团城城池里，还仿佛能听到演武兵士震天的吼声。

参观指南

地　　址：北京市海淀区香山南路红旗村 1 号。

乘车路线：运通 112、318、360、630、714、733、854、小 23、小 66、小 80 路到红旗村站下车向北 200 米；331、737、904 路卧佛寺站下车向南 800 米。

开放时间：9：00—16：00（周一闭馆）。

票　　价：3 月至 11 月 10 元；12 月至次年 2 月 5 元；中小学生免票。

周边景观：香山公园、卧佛寺、碧云寺、樱桃沟、植物园、曹雪芹纪念馆。

咨询电话：010-62591609

Tuancheng Exhibition Hall

Tuancheng Exhibition Hall, built in 1749, is the only ancient building complex for arms and equipment kept in Beijing, and those building include towns, palaces, pavilions, blockhouses and exercising grounds.

Tuancheng Exhibition Hall was the venue where Emperor Qianlong of Qing Dynasty watched parades and the Jianrui Scaling Ladder Battalion practiced martial arts. The hall is elliptic with a diameter of 50.2m from east to west and 40m from north to south. The wall has a height of 11m and a width of 5m. Bowlder steles on the southern and northern gates are engraved "martial walls" and "firm guard" written by Emperor Qianlong. The southern town was built with green tiles with colored glaze, surrounded by many corridors; in the northern town, there is a large stele lying on the ground, on which engraves important historical materials of Qing Dynasty, written by Emperor Qianlong.

The exhibition hall includes 5 main rooms with a pavilion and a platform. The western gate is built with green and white stones, with a height of 11.2m and a width of 24m. To the north and south of this archy gate, there are bluestone pavements.

Visitor Guide:

Address: 1, Hongqi Village, South Xiangshan Road, Hai Dian District, Beijing

Bus Route: Bus Yuntong 112, 318, 360, 630, 714, 733, 854, 23, 66, 80 to Hongqi Village, then walk to the north for 200m; 331, 737, 904 to Lying Buddha Temple stop, then walk to the south for 80m.

Opening Hours: 9:00---16:00 (except Monday)

Admission Fee: RMB 10 Yuan from Mar to Nov, 5 Yuan from Dec to next Feb; free for middle school and primary school students.

Tel: 86-10-62591609

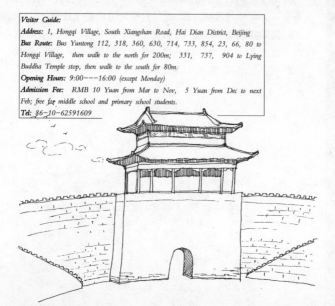

圆明园展览馆

讲述圆明园故事

只有在圆明园展览馆里才能从微缩模型上看到圆明三园，欣赏着"园中之园"的瑰丽景色。这既是圆明园的悲哀，也是中华民族的悲哀。就在1860年仲秋的一天，英法联军在大肆抢掠之后，纵火将圆明园烧毁，从此圆明园从国人的视线中消失。120年以后，圆明园展览馆按原貌制作了微缩模型并以大量的珍贵文物、图片和影视资料详细介绍圆明园的景观，再现了一代名园曾有的芳容英姿。

展览馆位于圆明园遗址公园的长春园西洋楼遗址景区内。这座建筑像学富五车的师长，每天不知疲倦地向参观者讲述着这里过去的故事。清康熙四十八年（1709年），朝廷筹措大量钱款，在北京西郊修建环绕福海的圆明、绮春、万春三园，开湖堆山，种植奇花异木，设置罗列国内外名胜40余景，亭台楼榭150多处，其中除造型独特、结构精巧的庭园建筑外，长春园中还有海晏堂、远瀛观等西洋风格的建筑群。这些建筑用长廊、墙垣、甬道、桥梁连接，并与自然景物结合，构成人间的仙山琼阁，其艺术价值、审美价值无法衡量。站在展览馆的微型模型面前，人们的思绪时断时续，英法联军的残暴行径似乎又闪现在人们眼前，冲天的火光中，魔影在狞笑，作为全人类宝物的圆明三园，此时只有哭泣而别无选择。

圆明园的故事说完了，展览馆里一片寂静。参观者默默地走出展厅，周身立刻被灿烂的阳光所包围，虽然如此，但有一丝莫名的郁闷，像一片阴云笼罩在心头，总也挥之不去。

参观指南

地　　址：北京市海淀区清华北路圆明园公园内。

乘车路线：特4、特6、22路专线、运通104、运通105、运通205、301、303、330、331、332、333、346、355-365专线、362、375、384、394、716、717、718、801、808、810、814、951路公交车。

开放时间：7:00-17:30。

票　　价：10元；学生5元。

周边景观：清华大学、北京大学、颐和园。

咨询电话：010-62543673

Exhibition Center of Yuanmingyuan Park

The Exhibition Center is located in the northeastern part of Changchunyuan (Garden of Eternal Spring). It is like a knowledgeable teacher, tirelessly telling the stories that happened here to the visitors. In 1709, the imperial court raised a large amount of money to build Yuanmingyuan (Garden of perfect splendor), Changchunyuan (Garden of Eternal Spring), and Qichunyuan (Garden of Blossoming Spring) around Fuhai Lake in western suburb of Beijing. Man-made lakes, rockery formations, exotic trees and flowers were in place. About 40 famous scenes and 150 buildings were arranged. In addition to those uniquely designed and exquisitely structured courtyards, there are also some western architectural buildings such as Haiyantang (Hall of National peace), Yuanyingguan (Immense Ocean Observatory) in Changchunyuan. Corridors, walls, passages and bridges linked the building complexes with natural landscapes. All contribute to forming a picture of fairy land. The artistic and esthetical values of these buildings are immeasurable. Standing in front of the mini models, the visitors will travel back in history. The atrocity of the Anglo-French army reappeared in front of our eyes. Facing the towering flames set by the fleering devils, the three gardens as all human beings' treasures had no other choice but to weep helplessly.

Visitors Guide

Address: Inside the Yuanmingyuan Park, North Qinghua Road, Haidian District, Beijing

Bus Route: Bus No. special 4, special 6, 22, Yuntong 104, Yuntong 105, Yuntong 205, 301, 303, 330, 331, 332, 333, 346, 355 —365, 362, 375, 384, 394, 716, 717, 718, 801, 808, 810, 814, 951.

Opening Hours: 7:00–17:30

Admission Fee: RMB 10 Yuan; 5 Yuan for students

Tel: 86–10–62543673

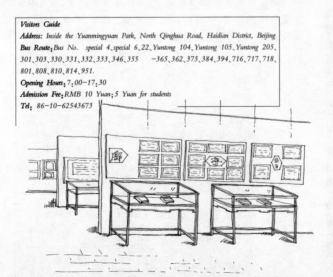

大觉寺

赏花、听琴、品茗的地方

始建于辽代的大觉寺是京西著名古刹。最早历史记载见于寺存《阳台山清水院藏经记》碑，古寺初名清水院，后又称灵泉寺，明宣德三年（公元1428年）重修，改称大觉寺。

大觉寺是一座社科类专题遗址博物馆，它地处阳台山麓，坐西朝东，依山而建。寺前平畴沃野，景界开阔；寺后层峦叠嶂郁郁葱葱，每天庙门洞开，一抹朝阳照亮殿宇屋脊，辉煌与希望一起蒸腾；夕阳落下，傍晚余晖笼罩山林与寺院，寂静中的神秘愈加迷人。大觉寺的大雄宝殿、戒堂、憩云轩、领要亭、功德桥等建筑都恢复始建原状，同时对缺失的殿堂铜钟、香炉进行复制，对"无去来处"的匾额和南路水道进行恢复，对断裂的庙产碑进行修复并重新安立，对南海观音悬塑进行抢救性修缮。修旧如旧，古庙古风，大觉寺的建筑是其沧桑岁月的见证。今天的大觉寺及其周围山色，仍如碑文所记："阳台山者，蓟壤之名峰；清水院者，幽都之胜概。"

近几年来，大觉寺立足于对馆藏文物的考证和整理，寺内旧存文物得以充分利用，辽代的碑记，元明清的木刻经板让参观者的心绪回溯到历史的那个春秋，体味其中艺术的价值和科学的价值。这里的园林胜境和文化内涵吸引着众多中外游客参观游览，探古访幽。

站在大觉寺的青砖甬道上，坐在参天古树下，玉兰芬芳弥漫在你的鼻喉，筝瑟古韵缠绕在你的耳畔，香茗清幽浸润你的肺腑，噢，生活原来还有这样的一番滋味啊！

参观指南

地　　址：北京市海淀区苏家坨大觉寺路9号。

乘车路线：颐和园乘330、346路公交车至温泉，换乘903路大
　　　　　觉寺站下车。

自驾车线：（1）颐和园—温泉—大觉寺；（2）八达岭高速
　　　　　（北安河出口）—北清路—北安河—大觉寺；
　　　　　（3）肖家河路—百望山—温泉—大觉寺；肖家
　　　　　河路—北清路—北安河—大觉寺；（4）阜石路
　　　　　—三家店—军庄—杨坨—大觉寺。

开放时间：8：00—17：00。

票　　价：10元；学生5元。

咨询电话：010-62456163

Da Jue Temple

Da Jue Temple, built in 1068, is located at the foot of Yang Tai Mountain, northwestern suburb of Hai Dian District of Beijing. It was first called Qingshui Court, and then Lingquan Temple. In 1428, it was rebuilt and called Da Jue Temple. It is composed of Tianwang Hall, Daxiong Hall, Wuliangsi Hall and Dabei Hall.

Da Jue Temple is a famous temple with a long history. Many lively and vivid Buddhist sculptures are worshiped there. The stele that recounts the sutra treasured up in this temple is a precious cultural relic, built in 1068. Da Jue Temple has an elegant environment, with a large field in the front and many mountains and trees at the back. Clear and sweet spring water runs in small channels through the temple grounds. Umbrageous old trees that reach the sky have various postures, with yulans and gingkoes as the best in Beijing. Da Jue Temple is a cultural relic unit under state-level protection. After nearly a thousand years of refit, it has become a new tourist destination at the suburb of Beijing.

Visitors guide

Address: 9, Dajuese Road, Sujiatuo, Hai Dian District, Beijing

Bus Route: *Take Bus 330/346 from the Summer Palace to Hot spring, then transfer to 903 to Da Jue Temple*

Self-drive Route: *a) the Summer Palace---Hot spring---Da Jue Temple; b) Badaling Highway---Beiqing Road---Beian River--- Da Jue Temple; c) Xiaojiahe Road---Baiwang Mountain---Hot spring--- Da Jue Temple; Xiaojiahe Road---Beiqing Road---Beian River---Da Jue Temple; d) Fushi Road---Sanjiadian---Junzhuang---Yangtuo--- Da Jue Temple*

Opening Hours: *8:00---17:00*

Admission: *RMB 10 Yuan; 5 Yuan (student)*

Tel: *86-10-62456163*

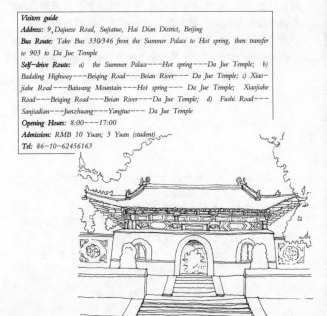

中国蜜蜂博物馆

蜜从这里来

也许你对香山的红叶是那么熟悉，但是在美景深处，在卧佛古刹的西侧由一个神奇的"蜜蜂王国"，那就是中国农业科学院蜜蜂研究所内的中国蜜蜂博物馆。请你走进这神秘而又甜蜜的世界吧，看看你眼前的这古蜜蜂化石以及六、七千年前古人攀崖采集野生蜂蜜的岩画，你会深深体悟到蜜蜂与人类文化及生活的历史渊源；面对相态大小不同的蜂种和硕大罕见的野生大蜜蜂蜂巢，你会被那种种引人入胜的生物学特性和生活习性的奥秘牢牢吸引；看到蜜蜂那有趣的"圆圈舞"和"摆尾舞"以及耸人听闻的"杀人蜂"的来龙去脉，你会对昆虫世界的种种奇妙而感到无比震惊……小小的蜜蜂以及它们奉献给人类的产品向我们展示了无尽的蜜蜂的知识。

"蜜蜂是人类的朋友"，请你不要认为这句话过于哲理。当你看完以此为主题的科普展览，你会在心中重新诠释这句话的含义。500 多幅图片和图表，700 余件标本、模型和实物演绎了我们身边另一个王国的春秋：蜜蜂的起源与演化、中国古代养蜂史、蜜蜂与文化艺术、中国养蜂业发展成就、世界养蜂业概况和国际科技交流。也许从这个时间开始，你呷一口蜂蜜的时候，心中的甜美远远超过嘴里的韵味。也许从这个时间开始，你会对身边的槐树、枣树、油菜、荞麦等许许多多不起眼的小花产生异样的感觉：蜜从这里来。

参观指南：

地　　址：北京香山卧佛寺西侧北京植物园内。

乘车路线：331、904、833、733、360、318 路公交车北京植物园或卧佛寺站下车，进北京植物园。

开放时间：除冬季(11 月 15 日—次年 3 月 5 日)闭馆外，全年开放。

票　　价：2 元；学生 1 元。

周边景观：香山公园、地震博物馆等。

咨询电话：010-82594910、82590094

The Bee Museum of China

When entering "the kingdom of bee", you will find yourself wandering in ancient times. Before your eyes are bee fossils and rock drawings which record the scene that people living 6,000 or 7,000 years ago are climbing the cliff to get the wild honey. At the sight of them, you will understand how bees relate to our life in culture and in history. Bee species in various sizes and extra-large wild honey-combs will tell you the biological characters of bees and the secrets of their living habits. You could also get access to the secrets of "round dance" and "waggle dance" of the bee and listen to the story of "killer bee". Little bees and their labor fruits contain endless knowledge. In the museum, an exhibition entitled "Bees are our friends" is put on all year around. The exhibition hall covers an area of 150 square meters which is devoted to three exhibition rooms where 506 pictures and charts are on display.

Visitors Guide
Address: Beijing Botanic Garden, west of Sleeping Buddha Temple, Fragrant Mountain
Bus Route: Bus No. 331、904、833、733、360、318 to the bus stop of Beijing Botanic Garden or Sleeping Buddha Temple
Opening Hours: All year around (except November 15— March 5 the next year)
Admission Fee: $ 2, $ 1 (For students)
Nearby Sights: Fragrant Mountain Park, Earthquake Museum etc.
Tel: 86—10—82594910、82590094

曹雪芹纪念馆

只有一个黄叶村

只有在黄叶村曹雪芹纪念馆，你才能触摸到这位伟大文学家沉闷的脉搏。无论是他一生变故带来的对社会的深刻认识，还是命运多舛造就了他对自己生命取向的执着；无论是他通过笔墨纸砚把自己的愤懑向苍天倾诉，还是一壶酒一杯茶一**抔**土把自己隅居在荒村茅舍，曹雪芹都给后人留下难以破解的谜团，于是人们来到这里，想了解在这远离荣宁二府的地方到底发生了什么，竟让他"字字看来都是血，十年辛苦不寻常"。

这是一组低矮院墙环绕的长方形院落，前后两排共 18 间房舍。前排展室陈列曹雪芹生活及创作环境的模型以及 200 年来有关曹雪芹身世重大发现的书籍和文章。后排六间展室主要陈列曹雪芹生平家世和《红楼梦》影响两大部分。展品有再现旗人民风民俗的八仙桌、躺柜墩箱、青花瓷器，还有《红楼梦》中提到的萨满教全套祭器、银锁、拂尘等，这些泛着幽幽光泽的器物，会让人想起那个让曹雪芹出生和消逝的时代，那个曾经酿造美酒和调制苦药的时代，不是有人说《红楼梦》就是一杯美酒和一剂苦药的混合物吗！

纪念馆的这面墙壁，就是旗下老屋西小间的西墙壁，扇面形、菱形的题壁诗仍然清晰可读。1971 年，一座古老民居屋内的墙皮脱落，露出了这里的一层灰白墙皮，竟有墨书的文字出现。经过房主人的细心剥揭，最后露出了满墙排列有序的八组诗文。这无疑是关于曹雪芹千万传说中最激动人心的发现了。后来随着曹雪芹书箱书稿的发现，人们把目光倾注在这里。随目光而来的，还有为《红楼梦》魂牵梦萦，为曹雪芹饮泣滴血，为宝黛悲情舍生忘死的一个个身影。

世界上，只有一个黄叶村。

参观指南

地　　　址：北京香山北京植物园内黄叶村

乘车路线：乘 737、904、331、833、360、854、特 6、112 等路公交车。

开馆时间：8：00--16：30（冬季 8：30--16：00）

票　　　价：成人 5 元，学生、老人凭证 2 元。

咨询电话：010-62591561 转 2028、010-62595904

Cao Xueqin Memorial Hall

The memorial hall is inside Beijing Botanic Garden at the foot of Fragrant Mountain. Cao Xueqin is China's great master in literature in 18th century. His masterpiece named A dream of red mansions is renowned throughout the world.

The memorial hall is a rectangle courtyard surrounded by low walls. There are 18 rooms in architectural style of Qing Dynasty at the front and the back rows. The front exhibition rooms display the living environment of the eight-banner people living in Qing Dynasty, the creation environment of Cao Xueqin at Xishan, discoveries about Cao's life experiences in the past two centuries, and relevant books and articles. The six back exhibition rooms mainly display the life experiences of Cao Xueqin and the influences of A dream of red mansions. The exhibits include old fashioned square table for eight people, chests and trunks, porcelains and other religious wares, silver lock, hand warmer, and horsetail whisk that appear in the novel. In addition, the museum specially opens a room for the exhibitions on research achievements on Cao Yueqin and various versions of A dream of red mansions.

Visitors Guide

Address: *Huangye Village inside Beijing Botanic Garden*

Bus Route: *Bus No. 737、904、331、833、360、854、special 6、112*

Opening Hours: *8：00－－16：30（winter 8：30－－16：00）*

Admission Fee: *RMB 5 Yuan、2 Yuan for students and senior citizens with relevant proofs.*

Tel: *86－10－62591561－2028、62595904*

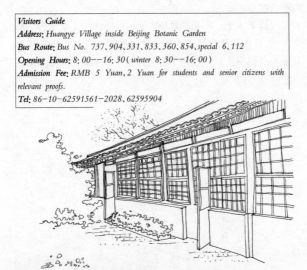

香山双清别墅

只有一个黄叶村

香山双清别墅原为清代皇家园林香山宜园"松坞云庄",1920年,原北洋政府国务总理熊希龄辟为私人宅邸,改为今名。1949年3月,中共中央、人民解放军总部从河北省平山县西柏坡迁至香山,当时毛泽东就住在香山双清别墅。就在这半年的时间里,毛泽东等老一辈无产阶级革命家成功地进行了国共和谈,指挥了渡江战役,筹备了中国人民政治协商会议,为新中国的成立做了大量准备工作。

双清别墅纪念馆坐落在香山公园南麓的半山腰,三面青山环绕,院内松青竹翠,碧水红莲相映,曲径连接廊榭。不知道毛泽东当年有无闲暇欣赏这醉人美景,只知道在离开西柏坡往北京行进的路上,他对他的同事们说过一句意味深长的话:"我们这是进京赶考,合格不合格就看我们自己了。"纪念馆有一幅照片吸引着人们的目光:毛泽东正坐在双清别墅的回廊上,聚精会神地阅读登载有人民解放军占领南京消息的报纸。

纪念馆还举办"毛泽东在双清别墅陈列展",大量的文物、工作生活用具和图片、照片等展品生动形象地再现了伟人在这里工作生活的情景,毛泽东的办公室、卧室等都恢复原貌,使参观者能够亲身体验出当年的氛围气息,感受伟人的不朽精神。

1949年9月,毛泽东离开这里,迁入中南海丰泽园的菊香书屋,开始他革命生涯的又一个新阶段。但是香山双清别墅里那铿锵有力的脚步声,那高大伟岸的身影,将会回荡在今天,映现到永远。

参观指南

地　　址:北京市海淀区香山公园。

乘车路线:特5、318、331、360快、630、714、733、737、818、854、904路公交车。

开放时间:8:30-16:00。

周边景观:香山公园、北京植物园、卧佛寺、团城演武厅。

周边餐饮:恒洋酒家、香山饭店。

票　　价:5元;学生3元。

咨询电话:010-82590297

Shuangqing Villa on Fragrant Mountain

Shuangqing Villa is the former imperial garden named Song-wuyun Manor in Qing Dynasty. In 1920, Xiong Xiling built the manor into a private villa and changed its name into Shuangqing Villa (Literarily means two clear fountains). In March 1949, the Central Committee of the Communist Party of Pingshan County, Hebei Province removed here. Mao Zedong, with other leaders, commanded at the villa the battle of crossing the Changjiang River, and discussed plans to construct the country. A great deal of preparation work was done here for the founding of the People's Republic of China. An exhibition in the courtyard entitled "Mao zedong at Shuangqing," displays a large number of cultural relics, work and life necessities, photos and pictures which record the working and living scenes of Chairman Mao in Shuangqing Villa. The office and the bedroom of Chairman Mao reserve its original looks. Visitors can feel the atmosphere of that period and touch upon the immortal spirits of the great man.

Visitors Guide

Address: Fragrant Mountain Park, Haidian District, Beijing

Bus Route: Bus No. Special 5、318、331、360(fast)、630、714、733、737、818、854、904

Opening Hours: 8：30—16：00

Nearby Sights: Fragrant Mountain Park、Beijing Botanic Garden、Sleeping Buddha Temple、Tuancheng Exhibition Hall

Nearby Restaurants: Hengyang Restaurant、Xiangshan Restaurant

Admission Fee: RMB 5 Yuan；3 Yuan for students

Tel: 86—10—82590297

中国电信博物馆

电信创造着人类文明

在中国电信博物馆的近代通信厅，一幅纵贯台湾、连接海峡两岸的通信线路图特别引人注目。这是台湾首任巡抚刘铭传1887年在台湾主持架设的中国第一条电报水线。它的一端纵贯台湾南北，另一端连接着福州闽江口和台北淡水口，这是中国电信史上第一条海底电缆，表明在100多年以前，海峡两岸就有密切而又便利的联系。讲解员摁动开关，这条长长的水线上立刻亮起了一串绿色的小灯。

中国电信博物馆作为中国唯一以国家通信为内容的大型专题博物馆，展示了中国从甲骨文记录的古代通信活动萌芽到当地通信近3000年的通信发展历史，1000多件展品汇集在通信史厅，其中清末挪威进献给清王朝的龙图案电话机、韦斯登重锤式电报机、供电式人工交换机等都是难得一见的珍品。令人瞩目的展品还有两封分别寄于1949年5月和6月的信件。当时，中国政局动荡，物价飞涨，旧中国的邮政也不可避免地衰落，展出的两封平信上所贴邮票都有40多枚，邮资已超过2000万元。

科技科普厅里，在"电路交换路由显示图"前，观众拿起代表北京市区的电话拨打一个西藏拉萨的电话号码，当这一号码的电话机在展桌的另一端响起时，墙上线路密布的中国地图上，刚刚拨打的电话所经过的交换线路就逐次亮起，形成一条美丽的灯线。

中国电信业百年发展历程精缩在这里的展台上，国内外电信发展的最新成就展示在观众面前。无论是记载历史，还是沟通未来，无论是传播信息，还是发展科技，一切都是为了创造人类文明。中国电信博物馆无比自信。

参观指南

地　　址：海淀区学院路42号。

乘车路线：331、375、386、706、722、743、748、810路公交车到北京航空航天大学站下。

周边景观：奥林匹克公园、中华民族园、圆明园遗址公园、北京航空馆。

周边餐饮：万博达美食娱乐城、滕王阁酒家。

票　　价：成人10元，学生5元。

开放时间：9:00-16:30，周二至周日开放。

咨询电话：010-62303665、62301958

China Telecom Museum

China Telecom Museum is a comprehensive museum on telecom industry; it is the special institution on China's telecom culture relics' collecting, propagating, education and research. It is also the social commonweal culture base for academy and technology exchange

China Telecom Museum is located at be Northeast of XueZhi Road, Haidian District, which is in the Zhongguanchun Science and Technology Developing Zone. The exhibition area is more than 7000sq. More than 17000 culture relics and 4 exhibition halls are available in the museum.

China Telecom Museum is making great effort to become the window for showing China's telecom achievement and communicate history and culture. China Telecom Museum is going to become the collecting place for the advanced telecom products; the second science propagation classroom for the kids and teenagers; the bridge for linking enterprises and users & audiences; the tie for linking the telecom operation and manufacture enterprises; the base for international exchange. Now China Telecom Museum is ready to welcome the visitors from home and abroad with its new spirit.

Visitors Guide
Address: No.42, Xueyuan Road, Haidian District
Bus Route: Bus No.331、375 (branch)、386、902 to Beijing University of Aeronautics and Astronautics
Nearby Sights: Olympic Park、Chinese Ethnic Cultural Park、Yuanmingyuan Ruins Park
Nearby Restaurants: Wanboda Diet and Entertainment City、Tengwangge Restaurant
Admission Fee: Adults 10 Yuan, students 5 Yuan
Tel: 86-10-62303665、62301958

北京上庄纳兰性德史迹陈列馆

谁人遗珠翠湖边

北京海淀区翠湖旅游度假区,波平水清的上庄水库。这里河道宽阔,湖面舒展,两岸垂柳依依,条条石甬弯弯,荷塘摇曳出几只惊鸿,稻浪推涌出一片软玉。浸润在大自然中的人们,忽然想到,一个成长在这里,又长眠在这里的人物,是偶然的机缘,还是恒久的命运,把他与这块土地紧紧相连?

纳兰性德贵为清代大学士明珠的长子,立身审慎、勤奋好学,阅历丰厚,学识超人,经史子集无所不窥,以文进士的身份做到武官正三品御前一级侍卫,不幸在 31 岁时英年早逝。更重要的是他的词作成就,他的词注重刻画人心与社会,情调伤感婉艳、隽永清丽。以至著名学者王国维在其《人间词话》中评价纳兰性德:"北宋以来,一人而已"。

纳兰性德陈列馆主体建筑是典型的四合院格局,沿铺砌的小径,首先进入院落的垂花门,门内为抄手游廊。穿山而过,廊壁锦窗点缀,檐下彩画生辉,具有传统的园林风格。正厅是陈列馆的主体,大量的历史文献、图片表格、实物构成七部分内容:家世、生平、著作、纳兰性德的词、纳兰性德的交游、纳兰性德与海淀及京西北各地和纳氏研究简史。在展品中,清代著名画师禹之鼎为词人做的肖像,弥足珍贵的镇馆之宝纳兰性德墓志盖,上面有陈廷敬篆书"通议大夫一等侍卫进士纳兰君墓志铭",可谓是国宝级的文物了。

在这个美丽幽雅的庭院里,多种复杂的感受交织在参观者的心头。一股神奇的力量吸引你推门入院,与这位词坛俊杰把盏共叙三百年的故事。此时,翠湖粼粼,波光映照着岸边草叶上的露滴,晶莹亮丽。你不禁信口拈来:"谁人遗珠翠湖边?"

参观指南

地　　　址:北京市海淀区上庄翠湖水乡旅游度假区内

乘车路线:乘 303、933 路上庄水库站下路西,过星通培训中心往西即到。

开放时间:9:00-16:00

票　　　价:10 元;学生 5 元。

咨询电话:010-80713599

Nalan Xingde Memorial Hall at Shangzhuang

Nalan Xingde Memorial Hall at Shangzhuang is built in memory of Nalan Xingde, a great poet and litterateur in Qing Dynasty.

The main body of the hall is a typical Beijing quadrangle. The display is composed of a large number of historical records, pictures, charts, real objects and articles, which give a comprehensive introduction to Nalan Xingde's creation and life experiences as well as the research achievements on Nalan Xingde in the past century. The exhibition is divided into seven parts: Nalan's family, Nalan's life experiences, Nalan's works, Nalan's poems, Nalan's communications, Nalan's footprints at Haidian and northwest of Beijing, and researches on Nalan.

The visitors can see the portrait of Nalan Xingde painted by Yu Zhiding, a famous imperial painter in Qing Dynasty and see the precious treasure in the memorial hall-Nalan Xingde's gravestone with epitaphs.

Visitors Guide

Address: *Shangzhuang Cuihu Water Village, Haidian District, Beijing*

Bus Route: *Bus No.303、933 to the stop of Shangzhuang Reservoir, walk west past the Xingtong Training Center.*

Opening Hours: *9:00—16:00。*

Admission Fee: *RMB 10 Yuan; 5 Yuan for students*

Tel: *86—10—80713599*

中华世纪坛艺术馆

精美绝伦　天工叹服

　　用象征着我国960万平方公里土地的960块花岗岩方砖铺砌的广场中央，升腾着一簇2000年1月1日零时世纪之交点燃的永不熄灭的圣火，这就是北京中华世纪坛圣火广场上的一景。走过广场北侧的青铜甬道，就是坛体内部的中华世纪坛艺术馆。

　　驻足艺术馆的世纪大厅，中央直径5.8米的锻铜贴金圆柱上，龙凤呈祥、日月光华为主题的柱体图案透出温馨祥和的气氛。四壁镶有国内最大的环行浮雕壁画《中华千秋颂》。壁画周长117米，高5米，采用产自国内的15种彩色花岗岩雕刻而成。壁画按历史编年浓缩了中华民族5千年文明史，268位人物形象栩栩如生，其中有名有姓的历代杰出人物62位。壁画汇集众多大师手笔，可谓是精美绝伦，天工叹服。

　　中华世纪坛艺术馆世纪大厅两侧的东西方艺术馆是国内一流并达到国际水平的艺术展厅。文明系列展中的"世纪国宝展 — 中华的文明"、"神秘的玛雅 — 墨西哥古代文明"，大师系列展中的"黑白意向 — 毕加索版画展"、"狂想的旅程 — 大师达利互动展"等都是具有国际水平的东西方文物艺术大展。位于一层的现代艺术馆经常展出近现、当代的各种流派的艺术作品，如"世纪风骨 — 中国当代艺术名家展"，"美国国家地理百年摄影作品精选"等。地下一层的多媒体数字艺术馆以现代化数字技术为基础，向观众提供更加丰富详尽的图像信息，巨大的屏幕配之以环绕立体声，其强烈的视听觉冲击效果和震撼力让你感受人类创造现代文明的伟大力量。

参观指南

地　　址：北京市海淀区复兴路甲9号。

乘车路线：地铁一号线军事博物馆站；1、4、32、57、65、320、337、414、617、728、827、特1、特5、特6路公交车军事博物馆下车。

开放时间：夏季 8:00-18:00；冬季 9:00-17:30。

票　　价：30元；大学生、60岁以上老年人20元；中小学生15元；离休干部及75岁以上老年人免费。每周一为中小学生集体参观免费日。

周边景观：中国人民革命军事博物馆。

咨询电话：010-68527108

China Millennium Art Museum

China Millennium Art Museum provides a self-contained environment for high-level art exhibitions, with its modern displaying equipment and high-tech system integration progressing with the world. The audience can not only appreciate all kinds of artistic works of excellent quality, but also can feel the visual shock brought by the digital image technique and enjoyment produced by the perfect combination of art and scientific technology.

The "Centurial National Treasure Display" was a centralized exhibition of top national artistic works and unprecedented archaeological discoveries, after these works had been displayed in the U.S. and Japan. The "Mysterious Mayan civilization---Mexican Ancient Civilization" was a specific display of Mayan civilization, while "the Black and White---Picasso Prints" and "Rhapsodic Journey---Mutual Interaction Display of Master Darly" brought you the mien of the masters. Besides, the Millennium Art Museum will hold several displays of excellent artistic works of other famous museums at home and abroad as well as modern artistic works.

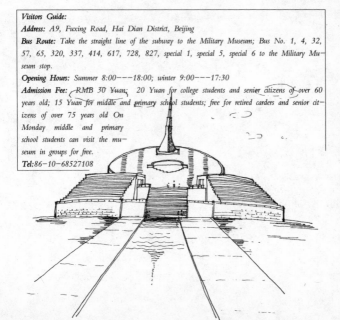

Visitors Guide:

Address: A9, Fuxing Road, Hai Dian District, Beijing

Bus Route: Take the straight line of the subway to the Military Museum; Bus No. 1, 4, 32, 57, 65, 320, 337, 414, 617, 728, 827, special 1, special 5, special 6 to the Military Museum stop.

Opening Hours: Summer 8:00---18:00; winter 9:00---17:30

Admission Fee: RMB 30 Yuan; 20 Yuan for college students and senior citizens of over 60 years old; 15 Yuan for middle and primary school students; free for retired carders and senior citizens of over 75 years old On Monday middle and primary school students can visit the museum in groups for free.

Tel:86-10-68527108

第九章 门头沟区

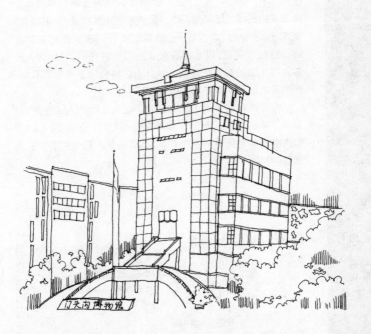

门头沟博物馆

门头沟区博物馆

情思门头沟

很久以来，是戒台寺、潭柘寺让门头沟声名远播，人们垂青于京西这块美丽的地方，就像穿境而过的永定河水，把众多的目光和踪影带到这里，又把门头沟的历史、文化、经济连同煤炭送往远方。门头沟区博物馆 3400 多件馆藏文物生动地描绘着永定河的潮起潮落，描绘着百花山的花开花谢。

这里的基本陈列分为三个部分。第一部分"门头沟区简史"，展现了从新石器时代到清末这个地区人民创造的古代灿烂文化。包括在北京史上占有重要地位的"东胡林人"墓葬遗物、商周战国的贝币、刀币、青铜剑戈、辽三彩菩萨像、斋堂辽墓壁画以及明清时期京西煤炭业资本主义萌芽等珍贵史料。第二部分"革命斗争史"，展示了自 1924 年秋开始中国共产党就在这个地区宣传马列主义，领导农民、学生、煤矿工人开展革命活动，抗日战争时期斋堂成为京西抗日根据地的中心，解放战争时期这里的人民同国民党反动派进行针锋相对斗争的历程。第三部分"民俗陈列"，全面系统地展示京西山野的民间风情画卷。许多民间早已失传的油灯、窑灯、拉煤床子、水嘟噜、老虎帽子、绣花鞋以及成套的民间文艺乐器、道具、服装等，显示出在漫长的历史进程中，门头沟人民与京城生活的紧密相连，又独具山区特色的生产生活习俗、传统工艺以及丰富多彩的民间娱乐形式。

逶迤连绵的京西山脉，造就了这块土地的人杰地灵，风霜雨雪中门头沟人创造了曾有的辉煌；青山秀水之间，门头沟人续写着前所未有的灿烂篇章，以至让人们产生了许多缠绵的情思。

参观指南

地　　址：北京市门头沟新桥向东小区 4 号楼北。

乘车路线：从石景山区苹果园地铁站换乘通运 101、336、370、
　　　　　921、931、959 路公交车到河滩下车向西 100 米。

开放时间：9：00-16：00，周一休息。

周边景观：滨海公园。

票　　价：5 元。

咨询电话：010-69852446

Mentougou Museum

The construction of the museum was initiated in August 1982. In September 1984, Mentougou Museum was officially open to the public. As Beijing's first county-level comprehensive museum, it is a public service unit with 11 working staff affiliated to Mengtougou Cultural Bureau.

The original museum was built in the style of gardens in the Qing Dynasty. Covering an area of 15,100 square meters, the museum has a construction area of 1,464 square meters. The museum was removed to No.4 Building in Xiangdong Living Area, Xinqiao Street in July, 1996. The first floor of the building has been rented by the museum for routine works and temporary exhibitions.

The museum houses 3,400 pieces of collection represented by folk-custom items. The basic displays include History of Mentougou, Revolutionary History, and Folk Customs. Additionally, the museum holds 12 temporary exhibitions on various subjects such as cultural relics, revolutions, folk customs, painting, and photographing etc. The forms include circular exhibitions and the regular exhibitions.

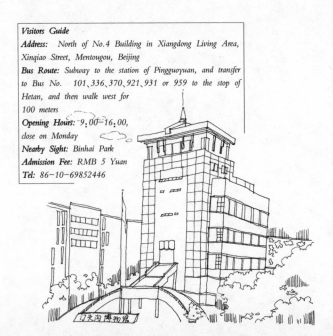

Visitors Guide

Address: North of No.4 Building in Xiangdong Living Area, Xinqiao Street, Mentougou, Beijing

Bus Route: Subway to the station of Pingguoyuan, and transfer to Bus No. 101、336、370、921、931 or 959 to the stop of Hetan, and then walk west for 100 meters

Opening Hours: 9:00—16:00, close on Monday

Nearby Sight: Binhai Park

Admission Fee: RMB 5 Yuan

Tel: 86—10—69852446

第十章 房山区

北京西周燕都遗址博物馆

北京，3050 年前

北京建城起始于哪一年？这是许许多多老北京人心中的疑问。北京西周燕都遗址博物馆回答了人们的疑问。公元前1045 年，周武王灭商并封召公奭于北燕，故这一年作为燕国都城建城的起始。从北京市房山区琉璃河商周遗址中发掘出的大批青铜器及其他文物证明，这里就是西周燕国的都城。以此算来，2005 年是北京建城 3050 年。

北京西周燕都遗址博物馆在原遗址古城东墙外，坐东朝西，占地 28 亩，建筑面积近 3000 平方米。主体建筑呈方形，顶部由一高四低的五组攒尖式大屋顶覆盖，屋顶呈红色色调，四壁为月白色，形成庄重肃穆的结构风貌。馆内基本陈列为"灿烂的古燕都文化"，设有序厅、青铜礼器厅、墓葬车马坑厅、青铜酒器兵器厅、陶器玉器漆器厅等 7 个展厅，以大量的西周燕国文物展示古燕国文化的风貌神韵。展厅内陈列设计古朴庄重，红色色调体现了周代崇尚赤色的审美意识。

琉璃河燕都遗址面积广阔，东西 3.5 公里，南北 1.5 公里，遗址范围内有广泛的西周文化遗存分布。在遗址中发掘出土的文物中，最重要的是青铜器堇鼎、伯矩鬲、克盉、克罍。堇鼎重达 41.5 公斤，铭文记载西周初年燕侯派堇去宗周向召公奭奉献珍馐，召公赏堇贝、堇铸鼎以示纪念。伯矩鬲上下铸造大大小小的 7 个牛头，造型精美绝伦，艺术水平高超，形象地反映了商周时期的铸造技术。这些珍品也成为北京西周燕都遗址博物馆的镇馆之宝。

3050 年的概念已无法用文字诠释，人们只能用思绪来构筑这个历史空间。琉璃河遗址以其独特久远的文化面貌和重要的历史价值，默默地为北京这座历史文化名城增添着辉煌和厚重。

参观指南

地　　址:北京市房山区琉璃河办事处董家林村。

乘车路线:天桥乘 917 支线（韩村河方向）至上周遗址下往南 1500 米。

自驾车线:京石高速路窦店出口。

开放时间:8:30-16:30。

咨询电话:010-61393412、61393049

Yan Capital Site Museum of Western Zhou Dynasty

The title of the museum was inscribed by Su Binqi, a master in the circle of archeology. Covering an area of 3,000 square meters, the museum has a basic display entitled "Glorious Ancient Yan Capital Culture" divided into eight parts. Over 1,000 cultural relics, replicas, materials, models, tombs and horse carriage tunnels give a systemic and vivid introduction to the range, pattern and panorama of the ancient Yan Capital. The glorious culture and advanced civilization of Yan Kingdom have been retraced. Ancient Chinese people's creativity and their significant contributions to the world's civilization are on display. The most attractive exhibits are the well preserved tombs and horse carriages tunnels. Their original looks have been presented in front of the audience's eyes through high-tech means. You will see what the earliest city built in Beijing looks like and know the vicissitudes of the famous ancient city of Beijing.

Visitors Guide

Address: *Dongjialin Village, Liulihe, Fangshan District, Beijing*

Bus Route: *Take Bus No. 917 branch at the Tianqiao stop (to the direction of Hancunhe) to the stop of Shanzhou Site, and then walk south for 1500 meters*

Self-drive Route: *Doudian Exit of Jingshi Expressway*

Opening Hours: *8:30-16:30*

Tel: *86-10-61393412、61393049*

北京房山云居寺石经陈列馆

感悟石经

　　释迦牟尼以自己的言行赢得无数佛家弟子的信仰和崇拜,于是佛祖及其弟子生平事迹和讲学说道内容变成浩如烟海的经典文字,经众人口手相传,遍及世界的各个角落,潜移默化在皈依之人的心中。

　　北京房山云居寺石经陈列馆内,1122部3572卷14278块篆刻佛经向人们展示着隋唐辽金元明六个朝代一千多年的寺藏石经。刊刻规模之大,历史之长久,确是世界文化史上的罕见壮举,堪与万里长城、京杭大运河相媲美,这稀有而珍贵的文化遗产不愧为北京的敦煌再现、世界佛经奇观。石经、纸经、木板经、佛祖舍利无不显示佛教曾有的辉煌,显示僧侣信徒的虔诚和坚韧,显示佛学文化的博大精深。除僧尼之外难怪还有那么多人在"净名事理人难解"的情况下"身不出家心出家"。

　　云居寺始建于隋朝末年,坐西朝东,环山面水,距今已有1400年的历史。僧人静琬大师为使佛经永存世间,遍访中国名山大川后,选中白带山取石刻经。以后的一千多年,无数僧人用执著和毅力把世界最古老最完整、数量最多的石刻藏经奉献给后人,成为研究佛教、政治历史、社会经济、文化艺术等方面的重要资料,其经文的准确性、经末题记的范围,以及书法艺术等许多方面堪称佛经之绝唱。此外,佛家的广阔襟怀与云居寺的石经及文物容量真是一种契合:重约400吨的《龙藏》木经;石经山腰的9个藏经洞;千年隋唐塔群和佛祖舍利,让人们为这里为佛家喝彩。

参观指南

地　　址:北京市房山区南尚乐乡云居寺。

乘车路线:天桥乘917支云居寺站下车;节假日在前门乘游10路或在北京南站乘游7次列车至云居寺。

开放时间:夏季8:30-17:00;冬季8:30-16:30。

参与项目:"三学"(学印刷、学拓裱、学书法)活动;打金钱眼、投吉祥包;撞云居古钟。

票　　价:云居寺40元;石经山10元。

咨询电话:010-61389612、010-61389142

Stone Scriptures Display Museum in Yunju Temple of Fangshan County

Yunju Temple has a 1400-year history. It houses valuable stone scripture, paper scripture, wooden scripture, Buddha sarira, towers of the Tang and Liao Dynasties. It is a museum blending architecture, relics, religion and natural scenery.

The scripture in the temple was engraved in the Daye Year of the Sui Dynasty (605). Reverend Jingwan and other monks engraved scripture on stone to maintain the proper law. The engraving went through the six dynasties of Sui, Tang, Liao, Jin, Yuan and Ming over 1039 years. The seal character Buddhist scripture totals 1122 books, 3572 volumes and 14278 pieces. The scale of the engraving and the history enables the project to rival the world-renowned Great Wall of China and the Beijing-Hangzhou Grand Canal. It is a rare cultural relic of the world. It is the Dunhuang (historical relic site) of Beijing and one of the world's best. In the 9th second of the 9th minute on 9 September 1999, Yunju Temple stored 10082 stone scripture of the Liao and Jin Dynasties completely in nitrogen-filled airtight cellars with constant temperature and humidity. To facilitate tourists' viewing, the cellars have 9 observation windows for direct viewing of the grand spectacle of the 10082 pieces of stone scripture.

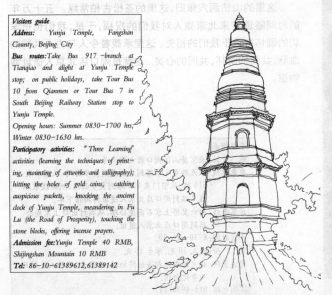

Visitors guide

Address: *Yunju Temple, Fangshan County, Beijing City*

Bus routes: *Take Bus 917 –branch at Tianqiao and alight at Yunju Temple stop; on public holidays, take Tour Bus 10 from Qianmen or Tour Bus 7 in South Beijing Railway Station stop to Yunju Temple.*

Opening hours: Summer 0830–1700 hrs; Winter 0830–1630 hrs.

Participatory activities: *"Three Learning" activities (learning the techniques of print-ing, mounting of artworks and calligraphy); hitting the holes of gold coins, catching auspicious packets, knocking the ancient clock of Yunju Temple, meandering in Fu Lu (the Road of Prosperity), touching the stone blocks, offering incense prayers.*

Admission fee: *Yunju Temple 40 RMB, Shijingshan Mountain 10 RMB*

Tel: *86–10–61389612,61389142*

周口店北京人遗址博物馆

走过五十万年的时间隧道

1929年12月2日，我国古人类学家裴文中在京郊房山区龙骨山下发现北京猿人头盖骨化石，此后又相继发现大量古人类化石，5万件石器，近200种动物化石，还有20世纪震惊世界的重大考古发现 — 北京猿人丰富的用火遗迹，这就是中国人引以为自豪、世界为之赞叹的周口店。它凝结了太多的中国人热爱自己国家的情结：第一批全国重点文物保护单位、全国百家爱国主义教育示范基地、一个响亮而又凝重的名字 — 北京人遗址博物馆。这里也汇聚了世界各地不同肤色的人们的惊诧与景仰：1987年，联合国教科文组织将这里列入世界文化遗产名录，从此，它不仅属于中国，也成为全世界人民的一笔丰厚的科学文化财富。

当然，你也许不是古人类学家、古生物学家、考古学家、地层学家或年代学家，但你来到周口店北京人遗址博物馆，了解五十万年前在这块苍茫土地上一群顽强的古人类生活的环境与状态：窥探我们祖先的第一次直立行走，第一次钻木取火，第一次用石块抛击野兽的那许多奥秘；体味那一群在原始条件下繁衍生息的人群的坚强品性。也许你能够获得许多对今天美好生活的感悟与启迪。

这里的山峦洞穴依旧，这里的苍松古柏常绿。五十万年的时间隧道传来北京猿人对我们的祝福，于是，我们也把深切的缅怀寄往于我们的祖先。这里承载着今人与古人共同的血脉，共同的胸怀，共同的心灵。这就是周口店北京人遗址博物馆。

参观指南

地　　址：北京房山区周口店大街1号。
乘车路线：从天桥乘917路到房山或到良乡西门、从西单乘616路、从前门乘922路到良乡西门，然后改乘环线2路到周口店北京人遗址博物馆下车。
自驾车线：由六里桥上京石高速公路，从阎村出口上京周公路到周口店北京人遗址。
开馆时间：8：30—16：30。
票　　价：成人30元，学生15元。
周边景观：北京西周燕都遗址博物馆、云居寺、平西人民抗日斗争纪念馆。
咨询电话：010-69301287

北京文化之旅

Peking Man Site at Zhoukoudian

Here is the hometown of Peking Man who lived 500,000 years ago, also the former residence of Upper Cave Man. Since the 1920s, 27 locations of high academic research values such as Upper Cave and New Cave have been discovered and excavated at Zhoukoudian. The findings include numerous hominid fossils, thousands of stone wares, nearly 200 kinds of fossil faunas and thick traces of fire use, which represents a significant archeological achievement that shocked the world in 20th century. Zhoukoudian is not only a treasure house of hominid fossils, but also a multidisciplinary education and research base for palaeoanthropology, paleontology, archaeology, stratigraphy and chronology.

Peking Man Site at Zhoukoudian was designated Youth Education Base by Beijing Municipal Government in 1992 and one of China 100 demonstration bases for patriotism education in 1997. It was listed among the first group of China's historical and cultural heritage sites to be placed under special state protection in 1961 and among the first group of China's cultural heritages included in UNESCO World Heritage List in 1987.

CULTURAL TOUR IN BEIJING·MUSEUM VOLUME

Visit Beijing

Visitors Guide:
Address: Fangshan District, southwest of Beijing
Bus Route: Take Bus 917 at Tianqiao to Fangshan or Ximen of Liangxiang, or take Bus 616 at Xidan or Bus 922 at Qianmen to Ximen of Liangxiang, then transfer to Circular Route Bus 2 and get off at Peking Man Site Museum at Zhoukoudian.
Self-drive Route: Drive onto Beijing - Shijiazhuang Expressway from Liuliqiao, and exit at Yancun to Jingzhou Highway, then drive directly to Peking Man Site at Zhoukoudian.
Opening Hours: 8:30—16:30
Admission Fee: $ 30 (For adults), $ 15 (For students)
Tel: 86—10—69301287

平西人民抗日斗争纪念馆

用先烈的业绩撞击心扉

通过纪念馆的沙盘，参观者认识了北京（旧称北平）以西的这块土地。桑干河、永定河、拒马河从这里流过，百花山、东灵山、小五台山在这里耸立。险要的地势使这里成了拱卫京畿的战略要地。抗日战争时期，中国共产党领导平西人民进行艰苦卓绝的战斗，创造了不朽的光辉业绩。平西人民抗日斗争纪念馆里众多的文物、照片资料向人们讲述着平西人民这段光荣的历程。

展览分七个部分："党领导的平西抗日战争"，展示平西党组织从播撒革命火种到展开全民族抗战的史实；"平西抗日根据地创建和发展"，再现了在艰苦条件下的政权建设、军民团结、发展教育事业的场景；"日寇的残暴罪行"，通过惨不忍睹的尸体、被烧毁坍塌的房屋和蒙受屈辱的泪水揭露日寇蹂躏平西的暴行；"艰苦岁月，平西人民坚持斗争"，再现了军民结合、劳武结合、开荒种地、自制枪炮、自制纸张、克服经济困难的场景；"转入反攻，争取抗战胜利"，展示这里的英雄儿女前仆后继、艰苦斗争，终于迎来抗日战争的胜利；"平西部分烈士英名录"和"缅怀先烈，继承遗志"，分别介绍了牺牲的英烈的事迹和平西人民筹建烈士纪念碑、碑亭和纪念馆的过程，各界人士凭吊先烈的情况。

纪念馆位于风光秀美的十渡风景区，拒马河水在连绵的群山中蜿蜒流淌。当你来这里踏春秋游、享受大自然的同时，走进纪念馆，让历史的警钟震动自己的耳膜，用先烈的业绩撞击自己的心扉，你的心灵也受到了一次净化。

参观指南

地　　址：北京市房山区十渡村。

乘车路线：游10路公交车直达；在天桥乘长途汽车或乘6路到终点站下车，到莲花池换乘长途汽车直达十渡；北京南站乘火车到十渡站下。

开放时间：8：00至17：00。

周边景观：十渡西湖港风景区。

票　　价：10元。

咨询电话：010-61340814

Pingxi Memorial Hall of People's Resistance against Japan

The exhibition is composed of seven parts: Pingxi Anti-Japanese War under the Leadership of the CPC, which demonstrates the history that the party scattered the revolution kindling and organized the national war against the Japanese invasion; the Establishment and Development of Pingxi Anti-Japanese Citadel, which demonstrates the scenes of political construction, the solidarity between the people and the army, and the educational development in hard times; the Atrocity of the Japanese Army, which demonstrates the ferocities the Japanese committed: numerable corpses, burnt houses and helpless tears···; Pingxi People Persisted in the Struggle in Hard Times, which demonstrates the scenes of opening up wasteland, making firearms and paper, integrating the production with the struggle, combining the people and the army and overcoming the economic difficulties; Turn into Counterattack to Strive for the Final Victory over Anti-Japanese War, which demonstrates that the heroic Pingxi People won the final victory through hard struggles; List of Some Martyrs in Pingxi and Recall the Martyrs and Inherit their Unfulfilled Wishes respectively give introductions to the heroes' deeds, the processes that the Pingxi people built the monument, the stele and the memorial hall, and people's visit to the hall to show their respect to the heroes.

Visitors Guide
Address: Shidu Village, Fangshan District, Beijing
Bus Route: Bus No 10 (for tourists) to Shidu; take long-distance buses at Tianqiao or take Bus No.6 to its terminal, and then transfer long-distance buses at Lianhuachi to Shidu; take trains at Beijing South Railway Station to Shidu
Opening Hours: 8:00—17:00
Nearby Sight: Shidu Xihugang Scenic Spot
Admission Fee: RMB 10 Yuan
Tel: 86-10-61340814

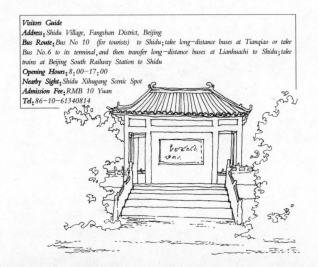

第十一章 通州区

通州区博物馆

明珠在这里闪光

通州博物馆作为社科类地方性综合博物馆,固定陈列着"古代通州"和"漕运与通州"两大部分馆藏展品,向人们讲述这块古老土地上衰弱与兴盛的历程,反映着通州的京畿文化和大运河文化交相辉映的内涵。

自西汉置县到清代2000多年,通州的区位优势在历史进程中发挥了重要作用。通州博物馆展出的114件(套)有代表性的文物,展示了通州曾有过的繁荣与辉煌,把自新石器时代至20世纪初期的悠久历史精缩在文字、图片和实物之中。

通州扼守京城的东大门,又是京杭大运河的北起点,这就决定了通州在中国漕运史上的重要地位。元明清时期,东南地区的几百万漕粮都要经贯通南北的大运河运往通州。试想当年帆樯如林,车水马龙,人头攒动,古老通州的繁华犹如一幅画卷,永远留存在人们的记忆中。博物馆里在运河两岸出土的铁锚、城砖和瓷片,都生动而翔实地反映出通州与漕运那种相互依存的关系。

京杭大运河已成了历史的遗迹,漕运也把昔日的辉煌定格在20世纪初年。可是通州向前迈进的历史脚步仍是那么豪迈。尤其是改革开放的春风吹来,通州向着文化城、科技城的目标奋进着,通州博物馆记录着它的每一个前进的步伐。1992年以来,这里举办展览近百个,其中2000年的"通州美协作品展"、2002年的"大运河文化五夷花园杯中国书画获奖作品展"都把通州文化建设的成就呈现给广大观众。通州作为首都北京的卫星城,像一颗灿烂的明珠,在京东大地熠熠发光。

参观指南

地　　址:北京市通州区西大街9号。

乘车路线:乘312、342路公交车道新华大街。

开放时间:8:00—11:30;14:00—17:30(周一闭馆)。

票　　价:3元;学生1元;老年人、现役军人、残疾人持有效证件免票。

咨询电话:010-69546442

Tongzhou Museum

Tongzhou, the northern starting place of the Great Beijing-Hangzhou Canal, is the eastern gate of Beijing, China's capital. Tongzhou's advantage of location and its role in history decide that it is not only an important part of the canal culture, but also an insepararble part of Beijing's culture. As a local comprehensive museum of social science, Tongzhou Museum has two parts of display: "Ancient Tongzhou" is composed of 114 representative cultural relics, among which there are 2 first-class, 9 second-class and 57 third-class pieces. The display introduces the long history of Tongzhou from neolithic age to the Republic of China, with the period from Western Han to Qing Dynasty as the key. "Water Transportation and Tongzhou" mainly displays pictures hanged on the wall. In addition, there are such cultural carriers as iron anchors, wall bricks and china pieces excavated from underground. All the relics and pictures lively show the relationship between Tongzhou and water transportation and the important position of Tongzhou in China's water transportation history.

Visitors Guide:

Address: 9, West Street, Tongzhou District, Beijing

Bus Route: Bus No. 312, 342 to Xinhua Street

Opening Hours: 8:00---11:30; 14:00---17:30 (except Monday)

Admission Fee: RMB 3 Yuan; 1 Yuan for students; free for senior citizens, active armymen and the disabled

Tel: 86-10-69546442

北京崔永平皮影艺术博物馆

皮影与崔永平

13 世纪中叶,西亚地区及欧洲被华夏古国的一种艺术所痴迷,这就是皮影戏。600 多年以后的 1988 年,中国的一台戏剧《西游记》获日本政府文艺嘉奖,这也是皮影戏。

北京崔永平皮影艺术博物馆于 2004 年 4 月 22 日正式开馆,为我国古老的濒临失传的民间艺术 — 皮影戏创建了一个生存与传承的空间。人们从这里看到两千多年前皮影戏的发明创造过程和 500 多个生动别致的皮影头像。无论是善美的还是恶丑的,都有一种熟悉亲切之感。熟稔的故事情节和人物形象都向人们展示着皮影戏曾有的辉煌。《山羊与狼》、《哪吒闹海》、《宝莲灯》、《水漫金山》、《小英雄雨来》等诸多剧目都曾获艺术奖励。这一切,都与一个带有传奇色彩的人物息息相关。

崔永平先生是我国著名的北京皮影西派艺人,他历任北京皮影剧团演员、演出队长、艺术主任等职,又是中国戏剧家协会会员、北京戏剧家协会理事、中国皮影木偶学会理事。崔永平成就了皮影艺术,皮影艺术也成就了崔永平,从艺 45 年的历程使他把自己的挚爱投入到这座博物馆;6 年多小贩生涯的积蓄,11 年中风病患的意志与毅力连同那一万多件珍贵馆藏展品都带有一种苍凉的意味。"皮影艺术家"这个称号,崔永平当之无愧。

北京崔永平皮影艺术博物馆以它的独辟与神奇,填补了我国博物馆的空白,那种苍凉的意味使人们对这古老的艺术形式产生了无尽的思念与景仰。

参观指南
地　　址:北京通州区马驹桥金桥花园 16 楼 4 单元一层。
乘车路线:732、927 路公交车马驹桥站下车到金桥花园。
自驾车线:沿永定门、木樨园、成寿寺、亦庄、马驹桥线路到金桥花园。
开馆时间:9:00—17:00。
票　　价:外宾 50 元(包括表演);成人 10 元;学生 5 元。
周边餐饮:口福居、亦海情饭庄、玉林烤鸭店。
咨询电话:010-60502692、13681223653

Beijing Cui Yongping Art Museum of Leather–Silhouette Show

The establishment of Cui Yongping Art Museum of Leather-Silhouette Show fills in a gap of Beijing museums. The museum is reconstructed by three apartments in the ground floor, and the area covering about 250 square meters. More than 10,000 pieces of leather-silhouette works of different periods such as Ming dynasty, Qing Dynasty, Republic of China, Anti-Japanese War, in different places such as Hebei, Shangdong, Sichuang and Shaanxi province, as well as part of the works Cui Yongping designed by himself are collected in the museum. In order to collect the leather-silhouette works in various places and the related historical materials, Cui left his footprints on the most of the ground of China.

The collected leather-silhouette works in the museum cover a wide range of subjects, including historical novels, folklores, fairy tales, fables and modern stories. On a wall of the museum, 500 leather-silhouette head portraits are displayed according to the four roles in traditional Chinese opera: male role, female role, painted-faced role and comic role. In addition, there are introduction of working procedures, the historical materials, stage property, scripts and the live performance of leather-silhouette shows in the museum.

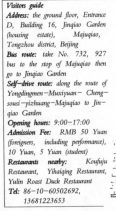

Visitors guide
Address: *the ground floor, Entrance D, Building 16, Jinqiao Garden (housing estate), Majuqiao, Tongzhou district, Beijing*
Bus route: *take No. 732, 927 bus to the stop of Majuqiao then go to Jinqiao Garden*
Self–drive route: *along the route of Yongdingmen—Muxiyuan— Chengsousi—yizhuang—Majuqiao to Jinqiao Garden*
Opening hours: *9:00–17:00*
Admission Fee: *RMB 50 Yuan (foreigners, including performance), 10 Yuan, 5 Yuan (student)*
Restaurants nearby: *Koufuju Restaurant, Yihaiqing Restaurant, Yulin Roast Duck Restaurant*
Tel: *86–10–60502692, 13681223653*

第十二章　顺义区

焦庄户地道战遗址纪念馆

地道奇兵话古今

　　地道战是依托地道工事开展对敌斗争的作战方法，抗日战争时期，华北平原抗日根据地军民成功地运用并发展了这一战法。北京顺义区焦庄户村的地道在全国堪称经典之作。1964 年秋，这里建成了"焦庄户民兵斗争史陈列室"，后来对焦庄户地道战遗址进行维修和扩建，命名为"北京焦庄户地道战遗址纪念馆"，1987 年夏，新馆落成并对公众开放。

　　纪念馆门口的广场上，一尊雕塑形象地刻画了焦庄户人们利用地道同日寇进行斗争的场面。纪念馆的地道入口掩映在苍松翠柏之中，长达数百米的地道里，生活、战斗、防水防毒设施一应俱全，出入口和对敌射击孔的开设和伪装极为巧妙。地道与地面上的暗堡和房屋上的作战工事相结合，构成消灭敌人的天罗地网。展览室里，众多的实物和图片形象生动地再现了焦庄户人民英勇斗争和善于创造的历史功绩，纪念馆还设有吃"抗战饭"的凉棚和放映抗战题材影片的电影厅，地道里，奇兵布阵，地道外，神兵天降，一个个场面如在眼前。参观者可以在这里亲生经历那枪林弹雨的氛围。

　　走出地道，参观者被国槐、松柏、鲜花簇拥着，阳光洒在身上，连同心情都是一片灿烂。远处，一座抗战时期敌人的炮楼和一颗枯干的树木立在那里，与身边的景色是那么不协调。也许，这就是北京焦庄户地道战遗址纪念馆让你永远铭刻在记忆中的故事。

参观指南

地　　址：北京市顺义区龙湾屯镇焦庄户村。

乘车路线：在东直门长途汽车站乘 934 路东直门到焦庄户专列。

自驾车线：京顺路到枯柳树环岛向右直行至潮白河彩虹桥之后第一个红绿灯路口向左行。

开放时间：8：00-17：00。

周边餐饮：安利隆山庄。

票　　价：20 元；初三以下学生、1.2 米以上儿童、老人、残疾人凭证 10 元；1.2 米以下儿童免费。

咨询电话：010-60461906

Jiaozhuanghu Memorial Hall of Tunnel Warfare Site

In Jiaozhuanghu Village of Shunyi District, northeast of Beijing, there is a special place-Jiaozhuanghua Tunnel Warfare Site. In the anti-Japanese war, how could we better protect ourselves and give a heavy blow to the enemies under the circumstances that the enemies were stronger than us? The intelligent people in North China found a new way for struggles: Tunnel Warfare. Tunnel is the major object for your visit. It has a length of 23 li. At present, about 600-meter-long tunnel has been renovated. The five-storey cannon tower where the militia watched and combated has also been repaired. Inside the tunnel, you can find individual blindages, planks, meeting rooms, headquarters, gunshot holes, warehouses etc. The entrances of the tunnel are out of your expectations, such as the kangs, kitchen ranges, hogpens, donkey slots, wardrobes etc. The tunnel site displays the immortal achievements the Chinese people made in anti-Japanese war and the great and magic power of the people's war.

Visitors Guide
Address: Jiaozhuanghu Village, Longwantun Town, Shunyi District, Beijing Bus *Route*: Take long-distance buses from Dongzhimen to Jiaozhuanghu
Self-drive Route: Drive onto the Jingshun Expressway to Kuliushuhuandao, and then walk straight to the right to Rainbow Bridge over Chaobaihe River, and then turn left at the first traffic light.
Opening Hours: 8:00-17:00
Nearby Restaurant: Anlilong Restaurant
Admission Fee: RMB 20 Yuan; 10 Yuan for students under 15, children above 1.2 meters, the disabled, the senior citizens with relevant proofs; free for children under 1.2 meters
Tel: 86-10-60461906

第十三章 昌平区

北京市昌平区博物馆

地道奇兵话古今

军都山从东北向西南，横亘在北京昌平城区的西北方向。山上松柏长青，泉水长流，山脉象一道天然的屏障，为这座繁华的城区遮挡住西北沙尘和凛然寒风，使这里风和日丽，气候宜人。这里就是北京市昌平区。

昌平始建于汉代，除个别朝代曾短期更名以外，昌平之名沿用至今，是北京区县中使用时间最长的名称。明朝选皇陵兆域于昌平，于是这里又因皇陵而名声远扬，一度曾升州辖县，可见昌平与皇陵的关系是多么重要。永安城、巩华城成为护卫京城与陵寝的重要防御建筑。清朝以后昌平依然是王公贵族的趋骛之地，纷纷将归西吉壤选择在昌平，以弥补生身享受的不足。

走进昌平博物馆，你还可以了解到距今五千年前依靠自然条件而生存的原始部落人群，他们选择了这块地方生活、繁衍、生息，可见昌平的适宜的气候和丰饶的地产。人们常说，时间和空间是人类回溯历史和展望未来的隧道，在这个隧道里，五千年只是倏然一瞬。宛如一轮弦月的大厦把文物留载的信息揽在胸前，像是嫦娥在向前来参观的人们微笑发问：你可曾在历史星空仲裁协议没经验的星星？

走出昌平博物馆，无论是那众多展品勾起你往事记忆中的幸福与辛酸，还是那几十年前的老物件带给你流失岁月曾有的矜持与孟浪，都将使你更加自信与坚强，哪怕是你未曾经历过的故事，就像原始部落人群刀耕火种的劳作，也让你无比感谢前人的贡献和大自然的滥觞。

参观指南

地　　址：北京市昌平区府学路东段南侧。

乘车路线：345支线至昌平东关总站；314、357、376、845、912路至昌平东关站。

自驾车线：出德胜门沿京昌高速路北行，大约35公里出13C昌平西关环岛出口右行进入昌平城区，向东直行驶过政法、石油大学、亢山广场后道路南侧即是。

闭馆时间：周一。

周边景观：明十三陵、中国航空博物馆、坦克博物馆、居庸关、银山塔林、小汤山温泉。

票　　价：5元(暂定)。

咨询电话：010-69741095

Changping Museum

Changping District of Beijing has agreeable weather because Jundu Mountain like a natural barrier stops all the dust and cold wind for it. Many princes and princesses of the royal family in Ming and Qing Dynasty have chosen Changping as the place where their tombs were built. In the Changping Museum, you will know aboriginal tribes that depended on natural conditions to live chose this place five thousand years ago, from which you can see the good weather and rich agricultural products. Although five thousand years are only a twinkling to history, you can still look back to history and look forward to the future. After your visit to Changping Museum, you will appreciate the contribution of our ancestors and the bestowment of the nature.

Visitors Guide:

Address: *South of the east Fuxue Road, Changping Distria, Beijing*

Bus Route: *Bus 345 (branch) to Dongguan general stop of Changping; 314, 357, 376, 845, 912 to Dongguan stop of Changping*

Self—drive Route: *From Deshengmen to the north for about 35km along Jingchang high way until Changping District, then to the east until the back of the University of Petroleum*

Closing Time: *Monday*

Nearby Sites: *Ming Tomb, China Aeronautic Museum, Tank Museum, Juyongguan, Yinshanta Forestry and Xiaotangshan Hotspring*

Admission Fee: *RMB 5 Yuan (temporary)*

Tel: *86—10—69741095*

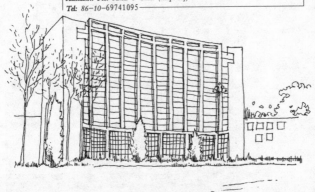

明十三陵博物馆

风水十三陵

北京市昌平区天寿山南麓，埋葬着明朝迁都北京以后的13位皇帝及皇后和部分皇妃。这里是世界上埋葬皇帝最多，保存较为完整的帝陵。除帝陵外，还有七座妃子墓和一座太监墓，为帝后谒陵服务的行宫、园圃等各式建筑，在陵区周围还因山设险，山口筑城垣，水口垒水门等军事防御设施。

明十三陵博物馆负责十三陵范围内的文物安全、管理和接待参观游览等工作，下设定陵、长陵、昭陵、神道等四个分馆。定陵埋葬着明神宗朱翊钧及两皇后。墓室由五个高大宽敞的石筑殿堂联结而成，前中后殿装有三重雕刻精美的石门，馆内陈列有众多随葬品及其他文物；长陵是明成祖朱棣和皇后徐氏的合葬陵寝，在明十三陵中营建的时间最早，规模最大，保存也最为完整。主体建筑祾恩殿全部用金丝楠木加工而成，古香古色。殿内陈列的金银玉器、金冠、凤冠及帝后服饰等130套(件)，工艺精湛，价值连城；昭陵内葬明穆宗朱载垕及皇后。现在宰牲亭、东西配殿、祾恩殿等处设有基本陈列；神道是进入陵区的主要通道。由石牌坊、大红门、碑楼、石像生、龙凤门等建筑组成，碑亭以北共矗立36座石像生，均用整块巨石雕刻而成，堪称"石刻艺术博物馆"。

明代帝王选择此处作为陵寝之地，自然是看重这里的风水：北倚天寿山，南有龙虎二山左右对峙，势如门户，温渝河水自西向东奔流不息，成为一道天然护陵河。如今，人们漫步在明十三陵博物馆，似乎也感觉到了吉祥和福祉的温暖。

参观指南

地　　址：北京市昌平县十三陵特区。

乘车路线：西直门乘845路或安定门乘912路直达水库；游1、2、3、4、9路；德胜门919东昌平站下车；由德胜门乘坐345支线到昌平，换乘314路或立水桥乘22路到达。

开放时间：4月-10月　8:00-17:30；11月-次年3月8:00-17:00(神道博物馆16:00)。

周边景观：十三陵水库、银山塔林、居庸关、云台。

票　　价：淡季20元，旺季30元；60岁以上老年人、残疾人、学生(不含研究生、成人教育系列)凭证半票；现役军人、离休干部凭证免票。

咨询电话：010-60761424

The Ming Tombs

The museum consists of Dingling Mausoleum, Changling Mausoleum, Zhaoling Mausoleum and the Devine Road. Dingling is the grave of Zhu Yijun and his two empresses. Five spacious stone halls constitute the grave chamber. Exquisitely carved stone gates were installed in the front, middle and back halls. Inside the chamber, there are many funerary objects and other cultural relics on display. Changling is Zhu Di and his empress's grave, also the earliest, largest and best preserved one among the thirteen tombs. The major part of the grave is the Chamber of Divine Favor constructed with precious wood called nanmu. Inside the chamber, delicate and invaluable jade, gold and silver articles, crowns and costumes for emperors and empresses account for 130 pieces. Zhaoling is the grave of Zhu Zaigou and his empress. Currently the Sacrifice Hall, the east and west rear palaces, and the Chamber of Divine Favor are opened for basic displays. The Divine Road is the main passage to the tombs, composed of the marble archway, the red gate, tablets, statues and gates carved with dragons and phoenixes. North to the tablet pavilion are 36 stone statues carved with only one stone. It is a stone carving art museum in real sense.

Visitors Guide

Address: The Ming Tombs in Changping District, Bejing

Bus Route: Take Bus No.345(branch) at Deshengmen to Changping, and then transfer to Bus No. 314 or Bus No.22 at Lishuiqiao to the destination.

Opening Hours: April–October 8:00–17:30;

November–Next March 8:00–17:00(The Devine Road Museum 16:00)。

Admission: RMB 20 Yuan from November to next March, 30 Yuan from April to October; the seniors over 60, the disabled, the students(postgraduates and student accepting adult education are excluded)are charged half of the price; the admission is free for active army men and the retired people with their proofs.

Tel: 86–10–60761424

老甲艺术馆

写意画家的杰作

老甲的画常用简练的笔墨,写出物象的形神。老甲艺术馆开馆以来,相继举办"老甲新作展"、"老甲艺术馆创作室八人展"、"老甲草原风情深圳北京两地展",主要展出画家近几年的作品,尤其是"老甲形式"的山水画作品,令同行和美术爱好者惊异非常,好评如潮。

老甲艺术馆的建筑呈长方形结构,方方正正的墙面无任何装饰,构造简洁明快,展厅正面矗立着四支毛石巨柱,柱后是近百平方米的浮雕作品《众志成城》,衬托出艺术馆建筑的分量与气势。主体建筑被草坪花圃、奇石雕塑、荷花池塘环绕,与馆内绘画艺术风格相辅相成,古朴、厚重、简洁、自然,使人站在艺术馆建筑的外面即能感受到生动与魅力。

画家老甲是草原之子,坝上凛冽的寒风锻炼了他强硬的筋骨,幽燕大地百姓的勤劳善良为老甲凝聚着人格力量,广阔的草原为老甲提供了取之不尽的创作源泉。他的画作以大写意的笔法,生动地描绘着草原,描绘着家乡。

老甲还选出不同时期,不同种类的作品在艺术馆进行日常陈列,使不同爱好、不同水平的观众都能从展品中找到自己可以理解的东西。

老甲艺术馆坐落在朝阳区霍营镇,远离市中心繁华地区,但是仍有众多专家、业内人士及国际友人来访。许多美术爱好者经常前来参观,感谢艺术馆展出的作品给他们带来好心情,让他们接近了艺术,认识了艺术。此时,老甲艺术馆的办馆宗旨又映现在人们心头:营造艺术氛围,传播艺术种子,展示艺术魅力,弘扬艺术精神。

参观指南

地　　址:北京市北郊霍营乡老甲艺术馆。

乘车路线:小 67、803、819、853、985 路公交车或城铁霍营站下。

自驾车线:京昌高速西三旗往东北 4000 米,霍营城铁站往东北 500 米。

开放时间:9:30-11:30,13:30-17:00。

票　　价:4 元;学生 2 元。

咨询电话:010-81702370

Laojia Art Gallery

This gallery was funded by Laojia (originally named Jia Haoyi), a first-class artist in Beijing Painting Academy. Covering 3,500 square meters, Laojia Art Gallery takes up a construction area of 1,000 square meters with 400-square-meter exhibition area. Inside the gallery, you will see a lotus pond, green lands, showrooms, corridors as well as a large-scale basso-relievo entitled "Unity is Strength". Laojia's works are represented by freehand wash paintings. You will find his works energetic and powerful instead of graceful and delicate, which exerts strong impacts on the visitors' vision. Laojia once remarked, "I paint what I want to paint, I use the means I might use, and I want to obtain the effects I want to achieve-follow up my own feelings." Laojia's works have been displayed on many art exhibitions at home and abroad and treasured up by many art galleries in foreign countries.

Visitors Guide

Address: Huoying Township, Changping District, Beijing

Bus Route: Bus No.67、803、819、853、98 or urban railway to the station of Huoying

Self−drive Route: 4,000 meters northeast of Xisanqi, Jiangchang Express−way; 500 meters northeast of the station of Huoying Opening Hours: 9: 30−11: 30, 13: 30−17: 00 including on Saturday, Monday and holidays.

Admission Fee: RMB 4 Yuan

Tel: 86−10−81702370

坦克博物馆
坦克在创造和平

　　亚洲唯一的一座坦克博物馆坐落于风景秀丽的颐和园和八达岭长城之间。博物馆大楼门前停放着一辆坦克，神圣的"八一"字样让它显得雄赳赳气昂昂。步入宽敞明亮的展厅，1400余份文献资料和图片、照片向你详细叙述中国人民装甲事业的发展史和世界军事大国构建坦克堡垒的战火硝烟。

　　这里的11个展厅，分别陈列展示人民装甲发展史、坦克装甲车辆、坦克训练模拟器以及兵器仿真模型四大部分。从1916年英国在第一次世界大战中使用的第一辆坦克"小游民"到今天新型的主战坦克，从59式中型坦克到目前造价最为昂贵的日本90型坦克，从世界服役时间最长的前苏联T34型坦克到中国人民解放军在解放战争战场缴获国民党军队的美制坦克，整个就是一部人类创造使用坦克的历史。

　　人类追求和平的愿望让硝烟滚滚的战场远离了人们的视线，坦克也就走进博物馆，走进了庆典阅兵的广场，走进了拍摄电影的镜头。但是，坦克作为战争武器的使命依然承担在肩，"战斗兵神"、"陆战之子"的称谓让人们感到坦克的庄严责任。此处的件件展品是历史的见证人，又是和平的守护神，这里弥漫着的和平气息，谁能说不是坦克阵营威风凛凛的正气所创造呢？

　　展厅里整齐排列的一个个庞然大物，好像是即将出征的战士，为准备执行命令而冲锋陷阵；在每一个雄姿的后面，都有着十分动人而主题相同的故事，那就是为了国家的强盛和民族的复兴，它曾经是坚强的盾牌与锋利的剑戟。

参观指南

地　　址：北京市昌平县阳坊镇88372部队。

乘车路线：沙河乘914路到坦克博物馆，或颐和园乘330路到西小营换911路于阳坊下。

自驾车线：北京—八达岭高速公路，经沙河出口可达。

开放时间：8：30-17：00。周一休息。

周边景观：白虎涧自然风景区。

票　　价：18元；学生9元。

咨询电话：010-66759901、69767910

The Tank Museum

The sole tank museum in Asia is situated between the beautiful Summer Palace and Badaling Section of the Great Wall. In front of the museum, there is a tank with Chinese characters " 八一 " (August 1, the foundation date of the PLA), which makes the tank look majestic. Entering the spacious and bright exhibition rooms, you will find nearly 1,400 materials, photos, pictures which tell you the development of China's armor cause and the efforts world military powers have made to build strong tank forts.

11 exhibitions rooms inside the museum respectively display the development history of China's armors, tank armored cars, tank training simulators, and weapon imitated models. From the first tank named little vagabond used by England in 1916 during the first world war to the brand-new battle tanks nowadays, from 59-style mid-sized tank to Japanese 90-style tank, the most costly tank in the current world, and from the Soviet T34 tank which has the longest service in the army to the tank captured by the PLA from the Kuomintang army in the liberation war, all kinds of tank will tell you the story of human's creation and employment of tanks.

Visitors Guide
Address：No.88372 Army Unit ,Yangfang Town, Changping County, Beijing
Bus Route：Take Bus No.914 at Shahe to the Tank Museum, or take Bus No.330 at the Summer Palace to Xixiaoying, and then transfer to Bus No.911
Self-drive Route：Beijing--Badaling Expressway via Shahe Exit
Opening Hours：8,30-17,00 close on Monday
Nearby Sight：Baihujian Scenic Spot
Admission Fee：RMB 18 Yuan；9 Yuan for students
Tel：86-10-66759901、69767910

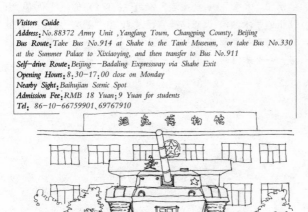

中国航空博物馆

感叹飞行之梦

自古以来，人们渴望"胁下生双翼，捕逐出八荒"。三国时就有人在胳膊上绑上羽毛，从高山跃下，虽然结果肯定是悲哀的，但那种梦想着实让人感慨一番。所以，当你来到中国航空博物馆的时候，该是多么自豪吧。100多种型号的近300架飞机，其中符合国家一级文物标准的有30架，符合国家二、三级文物标准的有50架，这些世界航空珍品，极富收藏和研究价值。同时，还收藏有地空导弹、雷达、航空炸弹、航空照相机、飞行服装、航空伞具、航空轮胎等2468件武器装备样品，中外航空图书资料2万余册，重要友好往来礼品1000余件。这些藏品虽然仅有小部分是我国研发制造，但所有展品都是历史的真实见证，或战争缴获，或友好馈赠，或外贸购买，或协作调配，几乎每件藏品后面都有一段鲜为人知的史实故事。你在这里的感受会时而惊心动魄，时而荡气回肠，时而抑郁沉闷，时而心花怒放，因为新中国的航空史和人民空军发展壮大的历程伴随你参观的脚步，激动你的心。

这里是航空珍品荟萃的宝地，但是在这里你的另一种体验也许会更加弥足珍贵：你坐在高射炮炮手的座位上，遥望瞄准器后面的血色和硝烟；你登上毛泽东主席最后一次乘坐的伊尔-18型飞机，抚摸老人曾用过的座椅；你站在DC-8型飞机的手术台前，遥想这座飞行过70多个国家，为近2万名白内障患者免费施行手术的空中眼科医院穿行在蓝天白云中……不由自主，你的眼眶已经湿润了。

参观指南

地　　址：北京市昌平区小汤山镇。

乘车路线：安定门乘912路、二环路乘820路公交车直达；西客站乘845路、得胜门乘345、345支路在沙河北大桥转乘945或820路至中国航空博物馆。

自驾车线：京昌八达岭高速路第11出口即小汤山出口右转向东9公里处路北。

开馆时间：8：00-17：00。

咨询电话：010-61784882、66916901

China Aviation Museum

Aircraft is the theme of the Aviation Museum which boasts Asia's largest and one of the world's rare collections of aviation relics. Currently, it houses more than 200 aircrafts of over 100 models. It also has surface-to-air missiles, anti-aircraft artilleries, anti-aircraft radars, air-to-surface bombs, aircraft cameras and more than 700 exhibits of weaponry and equipment, among which many are prized national relics and world aviation treasures. The China Aviation Museum displays the vigorous development of China's aviation cause and the glorious path of the growth and development of the Peoples' Air Force through its rich collections and accurate historical materials.

The China Aviation Museum is the venue for large-scale social activities for promoting national education on defense and comprehensive education on science. The summer and winter camps, military trainings and other activities with aviation features have attracted groups of youths with a passion for aviation and the People's Air Force. Parachuting, model aircraft exhibitions, remote-controlled aircrafts and ships, and other activities such as the movies and videos with aviation themes shown in the spherical movie theatre in the museum have also attracted the large audience.

Visitors guide
Address: *Xiaotangshan Township, Changping District, Beijing City*
Bus routes: *Take Bus 912 at Andingmen and Bus 820 at Second Ring Road directly to the museum; alternatively, take Bus 845 from Xike Train Station or Bus 345, Bus 345—branch at Shahebei Bridge and transfer to Bus 945 or Bus 820 to reach the China Aviation Museum.*
Self–drive routes: *Take Exit 11 (Xiaotangshan Exit) of Jingchang—Badaling Expressway. Turn right and travel 9 km eastwards. Museum is at the north of the road.*
Opening hours: *0800—1700 hrs*
Tel: *86-10—61784882, 66916901,*

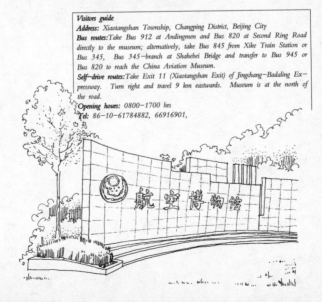

第十四章　大兴区

北京麋鹿苑博物馆

麋鹿朋友

"角似鹿非鹿,头似马非马,身似驴非驴,蹄似牛非牛",这是什么动物?干脆,叫它"四不像"吧。我们的古人这样形象地描述麋鹿,他们向世界贡献这种珍稀动物的同时,还叫响了这个名称。

北京南海子麋鹿苑博物馆是一座以繁养国家一级保护动物麋鹿为主,集生物多样性保护教育为一体的户外博物馆。也许南海子是元、明、清皇家猎苑的遗址的关系,1865年,中国特有麋鹿在这里被科学地命名。沉痛的是几十年后,由于水灾和战乱,珍稀的麋鹿在本土上消失了。也算是一种幸运吧,南海子的科学家们于1985年从英国乌邦寺引进还家,使这里恢复了麋鹿家园的风貌。不知是人为的巧合还是历史的相契,麋鹿的命运与民族国力的兴衰竟是如此相像。

麋鹿苑博物馆并没有将这种沉重的话题抛开,而是在室外展区内设立了世界灭绝动物墓区,以极具震撼力的造型展示了几百年来人类行为给动物世界带来的灾难,警示人们在珍爱人类生命的同时,也珍爱动物的生命,切不可以涂炭动物生灵以炫耀自己的智商和能力。把中国传统的护生理念与建立一座珍稀动物博物馆融为一体去展示一种新的人文思想,让更多的人接受这种崇高的洗礼。

博物馆里澳洲的鸸鹋、印度的孔雀、欧洲的駝鹿,还有在野外灭绝近半个世纪,如今又重新引进回国内的唯一的野生马——普氏野马,与200余头麋鹿生活在一起,使前来参观的人不由得动情起来,人类不也是这种和谐生活的一个成员吗?

参观指南

地　　址:北京大兴南海子麋鹿苑。

乘车路线:乘324、341、343、353、377、729、736、742、854、859、926等路公交车到东高地站换乘736路公交车于麋鹿苑路口下车东行800米;乘352、377、729、736、750、854、859等路公交车于旧宫下,乘出租车往南3公里。

自驾车线:从旧宫往南3公里。

开放时间:8:00—18:00。

票　　价:20元;学生10元。

周边景观:航天博物馆、北普陀影视城、北京经济技术开发区等。

咨询电话:010-87962105、87918537

Beijing Nanhaizi David's Deer Park Museum

In the David's Deer Park located 10 km south of Beijing in Nanhaizi, there were more than 200 David's deer, commonly known as "nondescript", a State Class One Endangered Species. We could also see many deer species and several bird species, including the Australian emu, the Indian peacock, the European yellow deer and the only species of wild horse - Pushi wild horse originating from China but extinct for the past half a century and now being introduced back into China.

As an important component of the protection of biodiversity, "public education" has been implemented in various forms in the David's Deer Park. The main programs include outdoor display area, Extinct Animals Tomb education area, David's Deer Travails Display, Chinese Traditional Murals, nature games education area, wild David's deer herd observation, bird-watching, "Green" Seminars and Movie Theatre, evening barbeques, conference reception, meals and lodging, Green Training Projects and other items.

Visitors guide
Address: *Nanhaizi David's Deer Park, Beijing*
Bus Route: *Take Bus 736 and alight at David's Deer Park Road junction. Walk about 800 m.*
Self-drive Route: *From Jiugong, drive 3 km south.*
Opening Hours: *08:00−18:00*
Admission Fee: *RMB Yuan, 10 Yuan for students*
Surrounding Places of Interest: *Aviation Museum, Beibutuo Movie City, Beijing Economic and Technological Development Area and others*
Tel: *86−10−87962105,87918537*

第十五章　平谷区

上宅文化陈列馆
上宅故事

　　这里的故事发生在八九千年以前，这是一个生机勃勃的人群。他们以自己的聪明才智开始农业和畜牧业生产，为自己创造着前所未有的幸福生活。虽然没有青铜器具和铁器，但他们用双手制造了大量的石器，开垦土地，种植庄稼；还用灵巧的双手制作了五彩缤纷的陶制艺术品，美化生活，展示甜蜜。

　　告别了茹毛饮血的岁月，石磨盘旁边，他们碾米；告别了空手与野兽格斗的日子，高举双刃石斧，他们狩猎。石铲、石磨棒、柳叶型石刀、复合刃器使人类前进的脚步更加铿锵，于是这个古老的氏族部落演绎了许许多多喜怒哀乐的故事。

　　望着这么多的陶器，你会想到妇女们用深腹罐存水贮粮，用圈足钵洗菜淘米。一碗饭，一盆汤都映着一个个笑脸。那些石雕的小动物、陶制的猪头、羊头饰品、空心陶球、海马形饰、耳铛形器，形象逼真有之，抽象写意有之，具体细腻有之，概括造型有之。人们用敏锐的观察力与惊人的艺术创造力去精雕细刻自己生命的质量。用这些栩栩如生的小动物寄托图腾崇拜的虔诚心灵，怪不得这里的故事曾是那么惊天动地。

　　20世纪80年代初，平谷上宅发现新石器时代遗址，2000余件石器、1000余件陶器让国内外考古界十分震惊。于是，这里有了我国第一座以考古学文化命名的上宅文化陈列馆；于是，中华先人曾经演绎的故事在来这里参观的人们心中传颂。

参观指南
地　　址：北京市平谷区金海湖旅游区内。
乘车路线：东直门乘918支线到金海湖。
开放时间：夏季8:00-17:00；冬季8:30-16:30。
休闲方式：每年4月下旬大型国际桃花烟花节；每年5月-11月大桃、鲜枣等水果采摘活动。
周边景区：金海湖旅游区、京东大峡谷旅游区、老象峰旅游区、飞龙谷旅游区、京东石林峡旅游区、丫髻山旅游区。
票　　价：5元；学生票3元。
咨询电话：010-69991268

Shangzhai Culture Exhibition Hall

In the early 1980s, a major event that took place in Pinggu shocked the circle of archaeology at home and abroad. That is the discovery of the Shangzhai Ruins. More than 1000 items of earthenware and over 2000 items of stoneware were excavated. The discovery of millstone plates, clubs and double-blade axes indicated the existence of prehistoric tribal clans with fixed residences. The discovery of artifacts like earthenware of hollow spheres, replicas of seahorses, heads of goats, bears and pig heads, as well as stoneware of goats, miniature tortoises and monkeys show the increasingly sophisticated division of labor in the society. Some fields have already produced specialists. The lifelike earthenware pig's head has a thin long shape, ears facing back, mouth sticking forward and a pair of fangs engraved at the sides. The head of the miniature monkey is detailed with eyes, eyelashes, ears, a nose and a mouth sculpted. Unlike the head, the torso of the monkey adopted an abstract style with bold generalizations to form a cicada shape. The rare specimens with the shape of a bird's head - earthenware support, earthenware pillars and hollowed-out instruments showed that several thousand years ago, our Pinggu ancestors already had "totem worship" activities.

Visitors guide
Address: *Inside Jinhaihu Tourist District, Beijing City*
Bus Route: *Take Bus 918-branch at Dongzhimen to Jinhai Lake*
Opening Hours: *8:00-17:00 in the summer; 8:30-16:30 in the winter*
Recreation activities: *In late April, there will be a major International Peach Blossom Fireworks Festival. From May - November, there will be harvesting activities for peaches, dates and other fruits.*
Scenic spots in vicinity: *Jinhaihu Tourist District, Jingdong Daxia Valley Tourist District, Laoxiang Peak Tourist District, Feilong Valley Tourist District, Jingdong Shilinxia Tourist District, Yahuan Mountain Tourist District.*
Admission Fee: *RMB 5 Yuan, 3 Yuan (Student)*
Tel: *86-10-69991268*

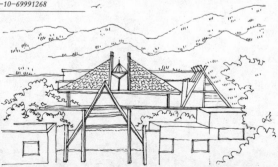

第十六章　密云县

密云博物馆

潮白河向南流去

潮河从北向南流淌。白河从西向东流淌，两条河流汇合在密云境内，合流后的潮白河又蜿蜒向南流去。在潮河和白河汇流的地方，密云水库大坝拔地而起，将近50亿立方米的洪流拦蓄起来，造福人类。三条河流给密云大地带来无限的滋润和生机。

走进密云博物馆，众多的展品像一颗颗璀璨的珍珠，在你眼前亮亮晶晶地闪烁。"今日密云展"把今日密云的城市新貌、保水富民、经济腾飞、文体旅游等崭新面貌展示出来，写就了新世纪密云地区社会大发展的篇章。"密云历史文化陈列"展示自原始社会至明清各时期的文物共200余件，史前的原始野牛角化石及新、旧石器，商周的陶乳鬲、高足罐，战国的青铜剑、红陶炉，唐三彩注子、三彩炉，宋代绿釉水瓶、辽三彩盘、三彩马蹬壶，元代内府梅瓶、龙泉窑、钧窑、彭城窑瓷器，明代的大铁炮、大铁钟等告诉人们密云物华天宝，人杰地灵的悠长历史和灿烂文化。"杵臼文化陈列"展出各式杵臼66件，一则弘扬华夏杵臼文化，二则使爱好者一饱眼福，引起参观者极大兴趣。"刘祯祥捐献文物陈列"是密云著名民营企业家，县第六、七、八、九届政协委员刘祯祥先生近年来悉心征集收藏民间文物捐献给密云博物馆的文物展览。

密云博物馆坐落在密虹公园北侧。外观为圆柱形的新馆大楼同周围建筑展姿媲美，同时也向世人宣告，这里还将把密云生态精品卫星城建设的辉煌成就展示给中国和世界。还将把密云的明天告诉中国和世界。

参观指南

地　　址：北京密云县西外大街2号。

乘车路线：东直门乘980路公交车，密云果园站下车，超市发商场对面100米处。

开放时间：夏季　8:00-11:30，14:30-18:00；
　　　　　冬季　8:00-11:30，13:30-17:00。
　　　　　周六、周日闭馆。

咨询电话：010-69088441

Miyun Museum

Miyun Museum is located in the north of Mihong Park. At present, there are 4 parts of display in this museum. "Today's Miyun" is composed of 6 parts: New Look of the City, Protecting Water and Enriching the People, Rapid Economic Growth, Recreation and Sports Activities, Traveling and Building Civilization. More than 280 photos and over 30 recent publications fully show the great changes in Miyun. "Liu Zhenxiang Cultural Relics" show people 37 pieces of cultural relics, mainly chinaware of the Qing Dynasty, donated by the entrepreneur and collector Liu Zhenxiang. "Mortar and Pestle Cultural Display" presents 66 mortars and pestles both home and abroad.

"Miyun Historical and Cultural Display" is divided into 7 parts in accordance with the time sequence and they are prehistoric culture; Xia, Shang, Zhou Dynasties and Warring States Period; Qin and Han Dynasties; Sui and Tang Dynasties; Song, Jin and Liao Dynasties, Yuan Dynasty, Ming and Qing Dynasties. It displays more than 30 photos, among which important ones are Liao Dynasty cone-shaped tower, Yanglinggong Temple, Dragon Spring Temple of Yuan Dynasty, stone-carved characters of ethnic minorities, Yanshan Mountain Ligong Stele of Ming Dynasty and Simatai Great Wall.

Visitors Guide:

Address: 2, Xiwai Street, Miyun

Bus Route: Take Bus 980 from Dongzhimen to Miyun orchard, to the opposite of Chaoshifa Mall

Opening Hours: Summer 8:00———11:30, 14:30———18:00

Winter 8:00———11:30, 13:30———17:00 (except Saturday and Sunday)

Tel: 010-69088441

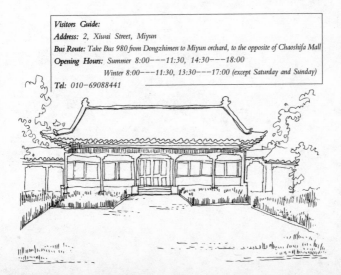

第十七章　延庆县

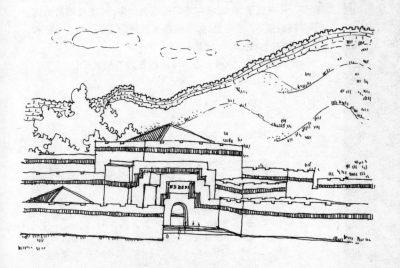

中国长城博物馆

长城注解的地方

　　人们都把长城比作民族的脊梁。挺立在云山之间,那种雄伟,那种壮观,那种独具的体魄和气势,都让人的心胸有一种浩荡之感,当你漫步在中国长城博物馆的展厅内,这种感觉会达到极致。不要把馆内高低逶迤的通道疑作你已经置身于长城的烽燧垛口之间,也不要被声光电模拟出的长城征战的千军万马而惊碎你的遐想,因为你确实用炽热的目光飞驰在山海关到嘉峪关的万里城墙上,有青山绿水,有大漠孤烟……

　　中国长城博物馆建立在北京八达岭景区内,其连体烽火台状的外观造型与长城浑然一体,交相辉映。在这里,你会有无尽的激动去探究长城的布局与结构,去发掘长城古老的历史和从初建到两千多年的发展变化脉络,去感受历史上发生长城内外的重大战役的金鸣旌摇,去领略沿线的名胜景观的水光山色。也许长城的概念发生了反差极大的变化,你会对长城内外兄弟民族相互交融共同发展和全国各民族、世界各国人民对长城的关心与爱护发出什么样的思索与解释呢?

　　当你看看世界各国元首、政府首脑在八达岭长城上的照片,那一脸灿烂的笑容里隐约飞扬着“不到长城非好汉”的自豪。长城变了,由城墙内外刀枪剑戟的厮杀,变成雄关山门下道路通衢、车水马龙;由烽火台上狼烟滚滚,变成被山花和丹林簇拥的金色长龙,逶迤在群山之中。

　　走出博物馆,你再去骄傲地眺望那万里长城吧!

参观指南

地　　址:北京市延庆县八达岭景区内。
乘车路线:919路公交车八达岭站下。
自驾车线:八达岭高速公路八达岭出口。
开放时间:夏季8:45-17:00;冬季8:45-16:30。
周边景观:八达岭长城、长城全境影院、詹天佑纪念馆、野生
　　　　　动物世界、熊乐园、八达岭滑雪场、阳光马术俱乐部等。
周边餐饮:八达岭饭店、金源隆饭店。
票　　价:凭景区门票免费参观。
咨询电话:010-69121890

The Great Wall Museum of China

The grand and spectacular wall body, the exquisite and beautiful brick inscription, the strict and perfect defense system, and the countless poems and essays on the Great Wall, are connotations of China's profound cultures. The Great Wall Museum of China is a special museum centered on the theme of the Great Wall to demonstrate its history and current status. The museum is unique in design. The zigzag passages inside the building are winding like the Great Wall. Mountain passes and beacon towers are found everywhere, and you will find yourself on the Great Wall section of Jiayuguang Pass or Shanhaiguan Pass. The exhibition is composed of seven parts: the Great Wall of past dynasties, the Great Wall of Ming Dynasty, the construction equipment, the battles on the Great Wall, the economic and cultural exchange, the treasury of national art, love China and repair the Great Wall, which demonstrate the creation and development of the Great Wall, its structures and patterns, major battles inside and outside the Great Wall and the historical sites and cultural relics along the Great Wall.

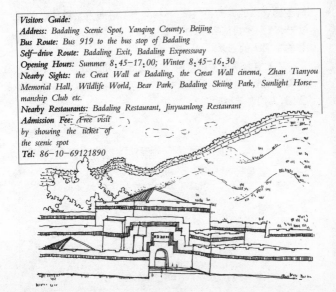

Visitors Guide:
Address: *Badaling Scenic Spot, Yanqing County, Beijing*
Bus Route: *Bus 919 to the bus stop of Badaling*
Self-drive Route: *Badaling Exit, Badaling Expressway*
Opening Hours: *Summer 8:45-17:00; Winter 8:45-16:30*
Nearby Sights: *the Great Wall at Badaling, the Great Wall cinema, Zhan Tianyou Memorial Hall, Wildlife World, Bear Park, Badaling Skiing Park, Sunlight Horsemanship Club etc.*
Nearby Restaurants: *Badaling Restaurant, Jinyuanlong Restaurant*
Admission Fee: *Free visit by showing the ticket of the scenic spot*
Tel: *86-10-69121890*

詹天佑纪念馆

百年重读詹天佑

当行进在京张铁路上的旅客列车驶过青龙桥车站时，车厢内的人们都不约而同地把目光投向窗外，向那尊铜像行注目礼。

100年前，詹天佑主持修我国自建的第一条铁路京张铁路。崇山峻岭中，钢轨逶迤爬行，"人"字形线路是世界铁路史上由中国人首次创造的。挖掘隧道的"竖井施工法"，在中华民族深受帝国主义侵略的年代大长了国人的志气。

站在詹天佑纪念馆的平台上眺望群山，长城在山脊起伏，铁路在山腰向远方延伸，伟人的风采与大自然的风光协调揉合，令人心旷神怡，荡气回肠。京张铁路建设付诸詹天佑的精力，而培养中国第一代铁路工程师更是倾注了他的莫大心血，他把开展学术研究，发扬国人技术，开创中国近代工程技术事业作为毕生的目标。从走出美国耶鲁大学校门，投身铁路建设，到抚清护路，拥护辛亥革命所走过的历程，纪念馆通过大量的展品把詹天佑的精神世界刻画得丰满伟大，他曾经使用过的测绘仪器、用具、印章、勋章以及铁路施工器具仍在放射着熠熠光辉。

京张铁路以后，詹天佑又主持修建了川汉、粤汉、汉粤川等早期铁路的建设。那种自强不息、勇于革新的创造精神，那种不媚洋人的大无畏气概，那种努力引进西方工程技术的求实态度，那种拼搏实干、艰苦奋斗的坚强性格，塑造了一个大写的中国人的形象。

"工学之前途发达可期，实业之振兴翘足以俟，将不在让欧美以前驱，岂仅皆扶桑而并骑"。百年之后，重读詹天佑这些话，人们能不感动吗？

参观指南

地　　址：北京市八达岭旅游景区。

乘车路线：德胜门乘919路公交车八达岭站下车。

开放时间：8：30-16：30（周一休息）。

参与项目：模拟火车站、沙盘。

票　　价：12元；学生6元。

周边景观：中国长城博物馆、八达岭长城、长城全景影院、野生动物世界。

咨询电话：010-69121506、69121561

Zhang Tianyou Memorial Hall

Go up the stone stairs of Zhang Tianyou Memorial Hall, you could see a gigantic relievo recording the bitter and struggling history of the Chinese People. It is an immortal epic, also a manuscript of Chinese modern history. A century ago, it was Zhang Tianyou who took charge of China's first self-built railway project, the Jiangzhang Railway. Looking into distance from here, we could see the Great Wall winding across the mountains. The railway passes through the memorial hall and extends faraway. The hall is divided into Paying Homage Room, Prelude Room and Exhibition Room where Zhang Tianyou's life journey is retraced from schooling, participating in the railway construction, protecting the railway to supporting the Revolution of 1911. Meantime, the mapping instruments, seals and medals of Zhang Tianyou and the tools for the construction of Jingzhang Railway are also on display. Inside the memorial hall, there are some participate-in programs for the audience such as the simulated railway station and the sand table. You could know not only more stories about Zhang Tianyou and but also the earlier situations, technologies and achievements of China's earlier railway construction from another perspective.

Visitors Guide

Address: Badaling Scenic Spot, Beijing

Bus Route: Take Bus 919 at Deshengmen to the stop of Badaling

Opening Hours: 8:30−16:30 *(Close on Monday)*

Participate−in Programs: Simulated railway station, and sand table

Admission Fee: RMB 12 Yuan; 6 Yuan *(Students)*

Tel: 86−10−69121506、69121561

山戎文化陈列馆

山戎祭

也许人们对匈奴、鲜卑等中国古代少数民族的名称再熟悉不过了,但如果问你"山戎"这个中国古代少数民族,你知道多少呢?

1984年,山戎墓葬群惊现于天下。一年后,考古人员对其进行科学的勘探发掘,584座山戎墓葬连同金、鎏金、青铜、陶、玉、玛瑙等23000余件文物为中华民族辉煌历史增添了丰厚的篇章。1990年,在墓葬的原发地建立山戎文化馆,大型的酋长墓、小型的部族成员墓,及中型的女性墓等10座墓葬分布其间,于是这块林深野僻的山脚土石成了游人如织的胜地。历史学家在这里看到三千年前的文明,考古学家在这里与上古时期的人物交谈,那些众多的普通游客来这里触摸胜地的灵气,让山戎古人作证,生命的意义永无休止。

山戎人如同中国古代少数民族一样,"以射猎禽兽为生","随畜牧而转移","逐水草而迁徙","毋城廓常处","人习战以侵伐","无文书,以语言为约束","常为燕、齐之边患"。撷取这古籍记载,使我们看到三千年前一个民族的生息与强盛,而山戎文化陈列馆里的墓葬规模与缤纷的殉葬饰物,那些马、牛、狗等的头骨和肱骨,那些酋长佩戴的金耳环、金项圈及腰间青铜短剑,那些青铜车马、械具、兵器、刮刀及各种饰物,将山戎人的民风与文化浸入参观者的脑海。

正当许多的历史学家和考古学家为山戎人过早地消失而惋惜的时候,山戎墓葬群的发掘和山戎文化陈列馆的建立,使人们不由自主地庆幸和激动。

参观指南

地　　址:北京延庆县张山营镇玉皇庙村东。

自驾车线:北京八达岭北麓玉皇庙村东400米

乘车路线:德胜门乘919路公交车至延庆站,换乘920等去山戎馆的汽车。

开馆时间:夏季8:00—18:00,冬季9:00—16:00

票　　价:5元

咨询电话:010-69199534